10/23

D I A N A

DEATH OF A GODDESS

Also by the same author:

DIANA
DEATH OF A GODDESS

DAVID COHEN

arrow books

Published by Arrow in 2005

3 5 7 9 10 8 6 4 2

First published in the United Kingdom in 2004 by Century
The Random House Group Limited
20 Vauxhall Bridge Road, London SW1V 2SA

Random House Australia (Pty) Limited
20 Alfred Street, Milsons Point, Sydney,
New South Wales 2061, Australia

Random House New Zealand Limited
18 Poland Road, Glenfield
Auckland 10, New Zealand

Random House South Africa (Pty) Limited
Endulini, 5a Jubilee Road, Parktown 2193, South Africa

The Random House Group Limited Reg. No. 954009

www.randomhouse.co.uk

A CIP catalogue record for this book is available
from the British Library

Papers used by Random House are
natural, recyclable products made from wood grown in
sustainable forests. The manufacturing processes conform to
the environmental regulations of the country of origin

ISBN 0 0994 7134 5

Typeset by Palimpsest Book Production Limited,
Polmont, Stirlingshire
Printed and bound in Great Britain by
Bookmarque Ltd, Croydon, Surrey

Contents

Acknowledgements

This book would not exist if David Carr Brown and I had not made two films together, *Autopsie d'un Massacre* and *Death of the Solar Temple*. I am also very grateful to Francis Gillèry who directed *Lady Died* for France's La Cinquième.

David Lloyd at Channel 4 was very supportive when I first had information about a conspiracy. Later Chris Shaw at Channel 5 commissioned a film on the French inquiry. I thank them both. I would also like to thank a number of people who read and commented on the manuscript at various stages or who provided me with interesting information and insights – Aileen La Tourette, and Samantha Boyce. I also want to thank Paul Chinnery, head of legal at Channel 5, Jonathon Carr Brown, Ludi Boeken, Eric Dussart, Bobby Buechler, Paul Chauvel, Pierre François Olivier, Renaud Marhic, Julia Ross, Murielle La Coche. Danielle Hall, Michelle Ross Stanton and Joe Holden worked on the Channel 5 films with great enthusiasm.

Sophie Clausen drew maps at a moment's notice and Marc Collins of the Yard organised a video grab at lightning speed.

My agent Sonia Land gave me wonderful encouragement and support. Mark Booth and Kate Watkins at Random House could not have been more thorough in dealing with a complicated MS. Many thanks to them and to a very precise but, in the ways of publishing, anonymous copy editor who forced me to check and re-check facts.

Prologue

Most people remember where they were on August 31st 1997. I woke up in Camden Town, exhausted. I had been shooting a film for six days a week. It wasn't going well. The cast were tense and tired, and the money was running out.

I switched on the radio just before six o'clock, expecting soothing Classic FM. Instead I got hushed voices. They told me that, at 5am doctors at the Salpêtrière Hospital in Paris held a press conference. Professor Bruce Riou told some 20 journalists the tragic news. Princess Diana had died in a high-speed car crash.

I had seen Princess Diana in person only once. I was sent to cover the opening of the Ballet Rambert ballet school to comment on her body language. It was the day of her divorce. As a psychologist, I was supposed to offer major insights on breakfast television. Did the way Diana walk reveal her true feelings about Camilla?

Diana's body language didn't reveal much, except that she wanted to get into the building as fast as possible.

I never imagined that a year later, I would be investigating her death.

On September 18th 1997, 19 days after Diana died, Guy contacted me. 'You have to come and see me, Cohen,' Guy said. 'As soon as you can.' It wasn't like him to sound anxious.

Short and burly, Guy looks like the bouncer he once was. He usually wears *film noir* uniform: black polo neck, and black leather jacket. His fingers are nicotine brown. His own body language is intense. He stands very close to you and stares unflinchingly into your eyes.

Guy was 50 years old in 1997. He comes from the South of France and speaks with a heavy Marseilles accent; the English equivalent would be a West Country burr. I have criss-crossed hundreds of miles of France with him and he often insisted on detours to show me places of criminal interest, sites where he had pulled a fast one and, sometimes, a violent one. 'Some car,' he often said with pride, patting the steering wheel of his big red Mercedes.

Love of cars made him a criminal. As a teenager Guy passed the exam to become a customs officer. He graduated third in his year, something of which he's still proud. But by his twenties, he was sick of the battered old car which was all he could afford on his salary. He wanted flash chrome, leather trim and the latest gadgets to impress the girls.

Eventually, Guy became the driver, personal assistant and enforcer for the leader of a French cult, the Order of the Solar Temple. The Order was an exotic muddle of Catholic and old Egyptian rituals and, most certainly, a scam. Its leader, Jo di Mambro, promised profound insights and salvation to those who followed him and claimed to be a master of the Rosicrucian tradition sometimes known as the Rose and the Cross. He played classic guru sex games. He decided who his followers slept with, who they married, sometimes even where they worked. He also had a hygiene fetish: fruit and vegetables had to be washed in disinfectant to guard against pollution. Naturally, if you joined the elect, you had to hand over much of your money to him. Di Mambro could get through £10,000 a day with no difficulty.

Di Mambro managed to attract many rich and powerful people into the Order of the Solar Temple. Camille Pilet, who ran Piaget watches in Geneva, Guy Berenger, one of the chief physicists at the nuclear research facility CERN, Robert Falardeau, a senior Canadian civil servant, and Michael Tabachnik, who had been conductor Pierre Boulez's assistant, were all devotees. Di Mambro flattered their vanity. If they followed him, they would become part of an elect group who understood how both the material and the spiritual worlds worked. He also preached the wonders of alternative medicine.

Few people outside the Order knew much about it till October 5th 1994. Then, 48 members were found burned to death in chalets at Salvan and Chiery in Switzerland and five others in a fire in a house near Montreal, Canada. I was commissioned by Channel 4 and France 2 to make a documentary, *The Death of the Solar Temple*. I traced one of the only survivors, Thierry Huguenin; he had run away from Salvan an hour before the fire started.

I did not know Guy when I made the documentary. He first contacted me two days after the film had been broadcast on France 2. He said it had revealed much of the truth about the Order but not all of it. He wanted to meet. He promised interesting new information. He would draw up outside the famous Parisian restaurant Maxim's in a red Mercedes and we would go for a drive. I was nervous about going alone but I waited outside Maxim's. When his red Mercedes drew up, I suggested he park it and that we go somewhere rather more public, a café. I was relieved he agreed to go and have some coffee.

Guy offered me new information about links between the Order of the Solar Temple and a sister organisation called the Sovereign Order of the Solar Temple. The Order had a temple in Monaco. Guy said that one of Prince Rainier's closest advisers, Jean Louis Marsan, ran the temple for 20 years until he died in 1998. It had grown out of another esoteric group that had been run by a Nazi collaborator called Julien Origas. Origas served four years in prison after being arrested in 1947 and then re-invented himself as a mystic. With backing from right-wing extremists, he brought together a group of Templar organisations. There are well over 200 such Templar orders in France, most claiming deep spiritual insights. In 1984, Origas knew he did not have long to live and handed over his organisation to Guy's boss, di Mambro. The handover ceremony took place at a small village in southern France called Le Barroux.

After about an hour in the Paris coffee bar, almost casually, Guy let slip the fact that Grace Kelly had joined the Order of the Solar Temple in 1982. I was astonished but, at that time, I knew very little about her. I found out that by the 1980s, she was unhappy in her marriage and had grown quite fat. According to Pierre Galante of *Paris-Match*, Grace used to slip away to Menton near Monaco and eat large portions of pasta.

I was able to confirm much of Guy's information and it formed the basis of a film, *Secret Lives: Grace Kelly*, which I made with David Carr Brown for Channel 4. We showed Grace had joined the Order and paid an initial subscription fee of $8 million. Guy had been a witness at her initiation ceremony at a country house near Morgon. He created some of the dramatic *son et lumière* effects. The princess lay on an improvised altar in the basement as religious music played. The spooky, sexual ritual didn't end there. Luc Jouret, the gifted psychic healer who was the Order's second in command, lay down on her. It was a spiritual union, the princess and the healer. Guy arranged for gold dust to shower down on the couple. Angelic harps twanged. Then, di Mambro announced Grace was the Supreme Priestess of the Order.

A few weeks later di Mambro demanded that Princess Grace pay more money, a further $12 million. Guy claimed that she was killed because she threatened to leave the Order and might have exposed the way it worked. Her death was made to look like a car crash, he alleged. This was not unusual; there had been two other deaths in car crashes in the Order, including one of an American millionaire called Severino.

As well as working for the Solar Temple, Guy also worked for the Rothschilds and for the World Health

Organisation. These experiences make him, he reckons, an expert on human behaviour. Three passions rule life, according to guru Guy: money, drink and *cu*. *Cu* is French for arse: 'Some hormone-happy bloke has a hard one for a girl who couldn't care pig for him. Never mind what her heart says, she'll close her eyes, open her legs for diamonds and furs.'

Guy did not panic easily, so when he rang me a few days after the death of Diana and said it was urgent I see him, I took it seriously. I explained to him I was finishing a film and I could only come to Switzerland when we had finished shooting.

So on September 20th 1997, Guy met me at Geneva airport with one of his minders, Bobo. Bobo is a giant with a bad blackhead problem. He was wearing a magnificently lurid red shirt. Bobo is, Guy assures me, a peaceable chap, except when he is paid not to be.

I gave Guy a bottle of Scotch. He teased me saying he would have preferred a cigar. He said we were going to a place he loved, and then Bobo drove us to Divonne les Bains. The town is famous for its casino which does more business than Monte Carlo. Guy had once owned a nightclub there. He had seen there the human spirit in search of sex, drink and dosh 24/7. 'One evening di Mambro walked in, asked for a soft drink and that was the start of our relationship,' Guy said.

In Divonne les Bains, Guy took me for a tour. It could have been a jolly Sunday stroll as he walked me round all the town's significant spots. Then, he re-enacted the moment when he was handed $500,000 by the fountain outside the casino. He did not know at the time that the payment was part of a plot to murder Diana.

After that we went to eat at Guy's flat. He then lived with Nicole, a plump woman who produced amazing meals. She and Bobo helped him run his legitimate business, a small wholesale florist.

By the end of that day, Guy had finished telling me a sensational story. If what he said were true, there were parallels between the death of Diana and that of Grace Kelly. There is one photograph of Princess Diana and Princess Grace together – two of the great beauties of the 20th century. Diana is glowing but still a little awkward, Grace motherly but sad. The picture was taken early in 1982 and I find it rather haunting.

Conspiracy theories bloomed after Diana died. Saddam Hussein and Colonel Gaddafi said they were outraged at what British Intelligence had done. Some of the Arab press claimed the House of Windsor could never tolerate Diana marrying a Muslim – especially not the son of Mohamed Al Fayed the owner of Harrods. (Dash it all, you couldn't have a dago like Dodi as stepfather to the future King of England.) Mohamed Al Fayed later accused British Intelligence services of causing the deaths. Ironically, his bitter accusations are among the factors that have made it easier to bury legitimate questions about just what happened in the Alma Tunnel.

As a trained psychologist, I'm sceptical about conspiracy theories. Humankind cannot bear too little gossip. As an undergraduate I studied the theory of cognitive dissonance, a term I will explain. Professor Leon Festinger, who developed cognitive dissonance theory, argued that when people feel disturbed or afraid, they seek to justify those uncomfortable feelings. We don't like to shake with fear and then admit it was due to something trivial. If we feel very scared, we want to justify our terror and so, Festinger argues, we often spread alarming rumours. Conspiracy theories are a kind of rumour. They attract the devil in us that wants to think the worst but they are also a way of dealing with the anxieties which major traumas provoke. And the death of Diana was a major trauma in the UK.

This book is the story of my attempt to confirm or deny – I stress both alternatives – what I was told three and a half weeks after Princess Diana died: that there had been a plot to murder Diana. With my friend David Carr Brown I have followed this story to Tunisia, Geneva, Quebec, Los Angeles, Paris and, even, Preston.

I did not become a conspiracy freak. I dropped the story after two British TV programmes were broadcast in June 1998. Channel 4's *Dispatches* claimed it was an accident; ITV in a counter programme fronted by royal correspondent Nicholas Owen, suggested it was a sinister security-service conspiracy. They had a witness, François Levistre, who claimed that bright lights of the sort commandos use were flashed in the tunnel at Henri Paul and that caused the crash. Unfortunately for ITV, their main witness turned out to have a criminal record and a past as what the French call *un mythomane*, a myth maniac.

A number of books spun conspiracy tales. My favourite is *Secrets of Diana*, which suggests the Spencer family had managed to lay their hands on the Holy Grail. Diana was killed, of course, in the quest. (This is the second time I have learned where the Grail is in the last few years. It is also apparently in the Barclays Bank branch in Aberystwyth where it was deposited by monks from Caldey Island!)

I became interested in the story again in 2000 for three reasons. First, there seemed to be an unwarranted delay in holding inquests into the deaths of either Dodi or Diana. Secondly, I was still in touch with Guy, who gave me more information. Third, I was asked to co-produce *Lady Died*, for French TV channel La Cinquième; the film was supposed to examine how the French press reported Princess Diana's death. The commission from La Cinquième was interesting in itself. The channel is state owned and commissions nothing the French government does not want aired. It was almost as if the French state wanted questions raised anew.

With few exceptions, the French press had reported uncritically what the police told them about August 31st. I lived in Paris and Geneva as a child and I spoke the language before I spoke English, as I was ten when my family came to live in London. It's easier to probe when you speak the language.

After *Lady Died* was broadcast on September 1st 2002, we gathered more evidence, enough to persuade Channel 5 to commission a new film that investigated the French investigation. Francis Gillery, who had directed the French film, became one of my tenacious co-producers. *Diana – The Night She Died* analysed the all-too-fallible French inquiry. As Christian Curtil, a French lawyer who represented bodyguard Trevor Rees-Jones, told me, 'There was too much pressure and there was a feeling the truth would never be known so the inquiry had to be stopped and it was stopped. So there were many things that were not investigated upon.' Curtil was in a good position to have some sense of the pressures on the *juge*, as we shall see.

The *Observer* called *Diana – The Night She Died* – broadcast on June 4th 2003, and updated on November 2nd 2003 – an 'important documentary'; the *Independent* said it was 'methodical in raising key questions'. The *Guardian* précised the main arguments of the film and added that 'Woodward and Bernstein would have been proud'. Since at various points I comment on the vanity of investigators I should add the film didn't get universal praise: The *Daily Mail* and the *Evening Standard* both attacked it for being too conspiracist.

A television documentary can only say so much. You can cram about 5,000 words into a 50-minute film. This book takes this investigation a lot further in a number of ways and answers some of the questions raised in the film. Among much else, I examine all the things that, as Curtil said, 'were not investigated upon'.

A major problem in getting at the truth of what happened is that France has no equivalent of inquests. In Britain, a coroner usually hears all the evidence in public. He or she decides, sometimes with the help of a jury, whether a death is murder, suicide, accident or due to natural causes. An inquest can also return an open verdict, which means no one can really be sure but there are suspicious circumstances. Coroners can summon witnesses who can be cross-examined. Often bereaved families use the inquest to get the beginnings of justice.

Suspicious deaths in France, however, are investigated in secret by the *juge d'instruction*. That's usually translated as the investigating magistrate but the literal translation is 'the judge of the instruction'. Instruction is the key word. The judge instructs the police, telling them what to investigate and what to ignore. Nothing is done in public. Witnesses aren't cross-examined. No jury decides if it was an accident, suicide or murder. Only the magistrate and the lawyers of the parties involved see the relevant files, and French lawyers are very discreet. Though everyone wanted to know whether or not Diana was pregnant, no lawyer, for example, asked to see the medical file on Diana. Virginie Bardet, who represented one of the photographers accused of causing the crash, told us that she had not asked for the medical dossier 'to be taken out of its seals' because 'it really had no bearing on my client's defence'.

I have talked with most of the lawyers involved – the cream of the Paris bar, including Christian Curtil who represented Rees-Jones in France and who has been especially helpful. David Crawford, a wry country solicitor from Oswestry, who represented Rees-Jones in the UK, has also been helpful. Crawford has become something of an expert on France's long history of scandals where the authorities have suppressed the truth. I love France but please note that the motto of the French is *liberté, fraternité, egalité*; *verité*, or truth, is not part of the slogan.

Three different French lawyers were so unhappy at the French inquiry's refusal to examine certain issues that they allowed us to film the 27 volumes of evidence the inquiry gathered. No other journalists have seen this material.

Inquests into the deaths of Dodi and Diana were promised on September 3rd 1997 by the then Royal Coroner, Dr John Burton. At the end of August 2003, Dr Burton's successor, Michael Burgess announced there would be an inquest. It finally opened on January 6th, 2004. The coroner surprised everyone by announcing first that he had to read the 6,000 pages of the French inquiry report, the dossier that I have had access to. It is extraordinary that he did not ask for this earlier. This document is, of course, in French and so the coroner could not begin to read until it had been translated. He estimated he would resume the inquest in 12 to 15 months.

The day before the inquest opened, the *Daily Mirror* revealed that the name which they had blacked out when they first published, in late October 2003, a letter from Diana which her butler Paul Burrell had kept was in fact 'my husband'.

Dr Burgess also confronted openly the many conspiracy theories that have been mooted in the press and on the web. He asked Scotland Yard to help him by investigating the events surrounding Diana's death so that he could sift out fact and fiction. A day later, *The Times* carried a headline saying it was likely that officers of MI5 and MI6 would be questioned by Scotland Yard. In the *Evening Standard,* Tim Lott pointed out that if a Mrs Windsor residing in Chelsea Towers had been killed in a car crash and Mr Windsor turned out to have a mistress he wanted to marry, the police would question him because husbands and ex-husbands are always under suspicion in such cases. But there were different rules for princes. On Saturday January 9th 2004, *The Times* reported that it was very likely Scotland Yard would interview Prince Charles.

I

The Fairy Tale That Never Had a Chance

In the summer of 1997 Princess Diana was a free woman for the first time in her life. Before she had become engaged to Prince Charles, Diana had lived a sheltered life and was perhaps surprisingly innocent for someone brought up in the 1970s. She had been a touching but rather gawky teenager and was often described as a perfect English rose, but roses project something she did not: self-confidence.

When the press started to leak the romance between Charles and Diana, Buckingham Palace told them: 'She hasn't blotted her copybook'. Freud would have picked up the sentence and analysed the word 'blot' under his psycho-probe.

But Diana walked up the aisle a virgin bride. There was one stop-breathing moment during the wedding ceremony. Prince Charles made an error when he had to say 'with all my worldly goods I thee endow'. What he actually said was 'with all *thy* worldly goods I thee endow'. Again you don't really need Freud to work it out. A man who can't offer what he has when he is getting hitched up, feels he's being stitched up.

Since Queen Victoria, the Royal Family has presented itself as Britain's model family, the best of the bourgeoisie. The late Queen Elizabeth the Queen Mother and George VI were the stable, happy couple that every Mr and Mrs Middle England wanted to be. The Queen and Prince Philip tried to follow in that tradition, so Diana had every reason to believe she was marrying into a wholesome well-adjusted family. We have discovered their flaws only since the Royal Family has become fair game for pundits – and, of course, psychologists. The Windsors have turned out to be the very model of a modern family with divorces, infidelities and as many scandals as one might find in the suburbs.

If Diana had hoped to find a perfect family, she ended up in yet another dysfunctional one. Diana had dreamed of marrying Charles since her early teens. Such a fantasy was not odd given the very difficult childhood she lived through. Though she loved her father, he was violent; her mother, Frances Shand Kydd, left Johnnie Spencer and her children in a very public divorce. Sometimes, Diana told friends that she had to look after her father.

It took very little time for Diana to realise she was marrying into a family with its share of secrets and lies. Her first disappointment was the most bitter. Even before her wedding, Diana found out her husband was still involved with his long-time 'amour', Camilla Parker Bowles.

We know rather more about the conversations Prince Charles had with his favourite uncle, Louis Mountbatten. Lord Mountbatten died tragically when his boat

Shadow V was blown up by the IRA and his murder makes it difficult to be critical of him. Nevertheless, his advice to his nephew suggests he was a very old-fashioned man. Mountbatten advised Charles to sow his wild oats and then pick a bride who would do what was expected – look decorative, produce heirs, do a bit of charity work and give no trouble. Mountbatten was, of course, hardly an expert on happy marriages. He almost certainly had homosexual relationships and his wife, Edwina, apparently had a long affair with Nehru, the Prime Minister of India.

Diana had second thoughts about her marriage, but she would have had to be heroically self-confident to dare cancel the wedding of the century. The tea towels had been printed. The souvenirs were on sale.

Young as she was, Princess Diana acted very reasonably in this crisis. She asked Charles to break off all contact with his old lover. But he refused. She was particularly upset when she discovered Charles was giving Camilla a bracelet inscribed with their pet names for each other – from Fred to Gladys. It was all perfectly innocent now, he insisted. Camilla was just a pal he went riding with. You'd have to be paranoid to think anything else.

I have already mentioned some strange parallels between Diana and Grace Kelly. One of Diana's first solo engagements was to represent the Royal Family at the funeral of Princess Grace in September 1982. Diana felt a bond with the Princess. Grace had given her advice on how to cope with the pressures of being an ordinary mortal turned royal. Diana handled herself well and hoped Charles would greet her on her return to England. He was not there, however. His absence was typical.

Over the next few years it became all too clear that Diana's reactions were not paranoid. Camilla was the woman Charles really loved. Diana had dreamed of marrying Prince Charles – the fairy-tale prince of every fantasy from *Sleeping Beauty* to *Pretty Woman*. Now, she felt betrayed to the core of her fragile being.

One of the most successful films of the 1980s was *The War of the Roses* in which Michael Douglas and Kathleen Turner played a couple whose marriage turned hellish and magnificently melodramatic. He pissed over the dining table during one party she had organised. Charles and Diana were too toff ever to behave in such a way but 'the war of the Waleses' had turned vicious by the late 1980s. It climaxed in a particularly unpleasant whispering campaign. Hell hath no fury like a woman scorned, the palace muttered. Consult the shrinks' textbooks.

It didn't help her cause with the macho culture of Prince Charles's entourage at St James's Palace that some feminist writers took Diana's side. In her 1988 book *Diana, Princess of Wales: How Sexual Politics Shook the Monarchy*, Beatrix Campbell suggested Diana was the virgin on a slab. In her crinoline wedding dress, Diana was frilled-up sex on display. Lucky Charles would have the honour. There's a rude cockney rhyme: 'She offered her honour, he honoured her offer, and he spent the night on her and off her.'

From 1960 to 1985, one of the great human-rights scandals was the treatment of dissidents by the Kremlin. Many of those who criticised the Communist regime were diagnosed as mad and locked up in asylums like the notorious Serbsky Institute in Moscow. They invented a wonderful new diagnosis there. The dissidents were said to suffer from 'sluggish schizophrenia'. People who suffer from schizophrenia usually hear voices, act in a paranoid manner and behave in an obviously disturbed way. Soviet dissidents had 'sluggish schizophrenia' because they didn't show any such symptoms. It's probably a bit harsh to compare St James's Palace with the Kremlin under Brezhnev, but the parallel works surprisingly well. Diana came to be seen as a dissident by the Royal Family and she was treated in some very important ways much like the Soviet Union treated its dissidents.

In their book, *Diana: Story of a Princess*, Phil Craig and Tim Clayton provide convincing evidence that a campaign which would not have disgraced the commissars was orchestrated by St James's Palace. When Jonathan Dimbleby was planning Prince Charles's official biography, he was told Diana's mental state was . . . well . . . mental. Penny Junor who wrote *Charles: Victim or Villain?* told Craig and Clayton: 'Dimbleby helped me to come to the syndrome – there were several people who had mentioned Borderline Personality Disorder.' Psychiatrists provided learned opinions that, sadly, the Princess had suffered from borderline personality disorder as well as eating disorders. Personality disorder is a state of anxiety and fluctuating moods. Some borderline personalities even develop so-called *alter egos*. They report they have two, three, eight or, in some cases, hundreds of different personalities, many minds in one body. There is a link between child abuse and multiple and borderline personality. Some evidence suggests abused children can escape from the horrors they face by inventing other selves so when the abuse happens, it happens to a part of the self that is split off. The argument is controversial but many psychiatrists, like the Canadian Charles Ross, believe a dynamic of that sort takes place. It was tragic, sighed the whisperers. Diana's father – conveniently dead so he couldn't sue for libel – had been a monster. No wonder the lady was a flake.

It's also useful to look at the position in which Diana found herself in terms of the work of the psychiatrist R.D. Laing. He argued individuals were often labelled mad because they were in an impossible 'family nexus'. You didn't have to be a genius shrink to understand Princess Diana's 'nexus'. She had to act as if she loved, and was loved, by her husband. But she knew from night one that the great love was a great sham.

A Hollywood film couldn't have done it more dramatically than when the newly engaged couple were interviewed. When they were asked if they loved each other, Diana said, 'I love him'. Prince Charles replied, 'Whatever that means'.

The body language was also revealing. Charles appears diffident and grins with what seems to be embarrassment; Diana smiles a radiant 'my wish has come true' smile. In the press comment that followed, no one seems to have wondered just what was going on, let alone asked how Charles's refusal, or inability, to speak the L-word might affect his bride.

In a well-ordered family, the grown-ups – the Queen and Prince Philip in this case – would have realised

something was wrong. However, they belong to the
generation that lived through the war and didn't really
talk very much about feelings or problems. Diana, I
suspect, seemed to them to come from a different
planet, and they were certainly reluctant to intervene.
By the time the press were told that the Queen was
deeply concerned about Charles and Diana's marriage,
it was far too late to save it.

When, in 1992, Andrew Morton's book *Diana, Her
True Story* revealed Diana's version of events, the world
was amazed. Her suffering was a shock.

Many women – and men – would have cracked up
totally under the kind of pressure Diana lived with.
She was said to have made one suicide attempt but she
showed surprising resilience. Being a mother rooted
her and, unlike many anxious people, she became an
excellent parent.

Diana had not gone to university or even achieved
one solitary A level. Before she went into treatment
with Susie Orbach of the Women's Therapy Centre in
1991, she had almost certainly not read Germaine Greer
or other feminist authors. But she belonged to a generation of women who had been changed by feminism.
As she went into therapy, Diana began to understand
she was not to blame for all her problems. Unlike
women in the 1950s, even 1960s, who might have put
up with a loveless marriage, Diana felt she had a right
to happiness. When it became clear she would never
get it from Charles, she turned to other men.

At first she chose her lovers badly. Her first affair
was with James Hewitt, a polo player who loved horses
and had an army career. He was in many ways rather

similar to Prince Charles. But the affair did not survive when Hewitt was posted abroad.

Diana's relationship with the upper-class art dealer Oliver Hoare was murkier. She became obsessed with him. She rang him constantly and Hoare's wife became upset. When some of these calls were traced back to Kensington Palace, it was an embarrassing revelation. Nothing pleased 'friends of Charles' more than to be able to feed the press the scoop that Diana was a telephone stalker.

But there are other aspects to the relationship with Oliver Hoare. His mother-in-law, the Baroness de Waldner, was a good friend of Prince Charles and he often spent time at her chateau in a small French village called Le Barroux near the old Roman city of Orange. Le Barroux has a population of around 350. It also has some connections with the history of the Knights Hospitallers of Jerusalem, a branch of the Knights Templar. It was here in 1984 that the Nazi collaborator Julien Origas handed the Templar flame to Jo di Mambro. Soon after, di Mambro bought a property there and ordered some of the Order's members to live there and refurbish it. Doing menial work would enhance their spiritual condition. One of these 'workers', Thierry Huguenin complained bitterly to me that re-building this property and another close by cost him years of his life and left him with a bad back. Prince Charles's visits to Le Barroux are a topic I will return to later in the book.

Given her bad choices and bad luck, it is perhaps not that strange Diana did not quite give up on Charles. After all, he was her first love – and her first lover.

Despite all the betrayals, she seemed to think she could win her prince back and, finally, make the fairy tale work. The press gave her hope. It was Diana, not Camilla, who was written up as the most beautiful woman in the world. With a chuckle of sheer amazement, Mohamed Al Fayed once asked me what man with blood in his veins could prefer Camilla to Diana. One looked like a star, a princess, radiant, while Camilla looked . . . The mogul of Harrods then compared Mrs Parker Bowles to a donkey, a crocodile and other less-than-seductive animals.

By 1992, however, it was clear that they had no future as a couple and Charles and Diana separated. It is perhaps ironic that the then Prime Minister John Major announced the separation with such gravitas, given his history with Edwina Currie. When, finally, the negotiations for the royal divorce started, they were bitter.

Anthony Holden's 1979 biography of Prince Charles was his second book. His first was the life of Graham Young, a teenage poisoner who was released from Broadmoor, the high-security hospital, only to murder again. I had met Holden when we were both at Oxford and I contacted him again in 2002 when I was making a film about Broadmoor. He gave a gripping account of how Graham Young fooled the shrinks into thinking he was cured. In Holden's three books about Prince Charles, portraying the heir at 30, 40, and 50, the tone changes radically from that of a supporter to that of a critic.

'Diana was terrified of losing her children. She felt she had good reason to be,' Holden told me. 'She was frightened of the family power and what they could do to her.' Holden pointed out that, even after she was divorced, Diana required the Queen's permission to leave the country.

An ordinary woman would have expected to get a large share of her husband's wealth and custody of the children, especially given Charles's imperfect record as a father. He had not turned up, for example, when his son was being operated on for what might have been a serious head injury. Diana, on the other hand, had shown she was a devoted mother. She loved, hugged, talked to her boys. Even her rather eccentric request that her butler Paul Burrell buy Prince William 'top shelf' magazines made some sense. She didn't want her sons to know nothing about girls, when there were so many rumours of gay sex in St James's Palace. Nevertheless, Diana had to share custody with Prince Charles. The future king had to groom his sons for *their* future.

Financially, Diana hardly did brilliantly either. The final settlement of £17 million was large but not so generous, given that a recent estimate issued by St James's Palace tots up Prince Charles's private fortune at £352 million. At least, though, with £17 million in the kitty, Diana would never again have to send Paul Burrell out to sell her dresses so she could have some readies for herself and pocket money for William and Harry, as he claimed in his recent book she had to after the separation.

But the Royal Family extracted a price for the £17 million. Perhaps the most unpleasant aspect of the divorce was that Diana was stripped of her title as Her

Royal Highness by the express order of the Queen. Holden told me that Diana felt they had destroyed her in the process of the divorce. 'They had battered her,' he said and he believed it was partly because they hated her success with the press.

There has always been some muddle as to why Diana no longer had royal protection after the divorce. Did she refuse it so that she could finally be free? Or did the Palace withdraw it and leak gossip that the flaky Princess often got too close to those who guarded her?

For a long time, Buckingham Palace had been wary of the relationships between Diana and some of the police who protected her. In her biography of Prince Charles, Penny Junor claims Diana had her first affair in 1985 not with Hewitt, but with one of her bodyguards, Sergeant Barry Mannakee who was one of the royal protection squad. 'She said to a mutual friend that Mannakee was the love of her life,' Holden told me.

Diana's friend Rosa Monckton pointed out that it was extremely convenient for Junor (and others who made this claim) that both individuals involved were dead. Diana and Mannakee were close, Monckton admits, and Diana did give him a teddy bear as a keepsake. But she insists it was a platonic relationship. The Palace disapproved of the friendship, however, and Mannakee was withdrawn from royal duties in 1985.

A year later, Mannakee died in a road accident in East London. He was the first of a surprising number of those involved in this story who died suddenly and, very often, on the roads. Holden added that the death of Barry Mannakee 'remains to many a rather mysterious event. She [Diana] herself was very suspicious about it. She could be a conspiracy theorist herself.'

But it wasn't just the collapse of her marriage that changed Diana. Early in the 1980s, she had decided to change herself. Sloane Rangers are supposed be pretty and rather dim. Diana would break that mould.

The charity worker

Diana had had one job as a nanny before she got engaged. Her employer was astonished by the immediate rapport she had with the children. She was brilliant at playing with them; she was very tactile. Diana sometimes told friends this was partly because she had had to cope with her parents' divorce. A child in the middle of such battles learns a lot. Diana had a gift for making real contact with all kinds of people and she started to use that gift from the mid-1980s.

Prince Charles had, at first, encouraged his new wife but the first difficulty in the marriage was when the junior partner started to get too many glowing headlines. The Prince was human, he started to become jealous. The press adored her while they mocked him as the polo-playing aristo who communed with his fruit and veg. (No one then knew that flunkeys also had to squeeze his toothpaste and hold his specimen bottle.) He also just seemed aloof, which is perhaps not surprising given his own upbringing.

Diana was moody but not aloof. She could use her own distress to reach out to others. From the moment

Diana touched people who suffered from Aids, she turned into a star in the charity field. She could communicate very sensitively with people in distress. She had been there, lived it, was still living it. And it did not embarrass her as it would most upper-class Brits.

'Diana, with her innate sense of public relationship, championed urgent contemporary issues like cancer and battered women,' Holden said. She was well aware, Holden suggests, that fighting for organic carrots and Ye Olde Architecture 'would make Charles look out of touch'.

Those who worked with Diana respected not just her human but her political skills. David Edwards was for many years the executive director of Social Services in the North for the charity Turning Point. I first met him at the Smithfield Project in Manchester. It's base is a red brick building in a grim industrial suburb. Inside, the atmosphere is jovial but a little forced. Everyone here doesn't really want to be here but they're trying to fix themselves. There's a busy café, consulting rooms, therapy seven days a week. The most remarkable facility is a ward where addicts can come for fourteen days to detox.

David Edwards told me he had been hugely impressed by the way Diana handled her charity work. He saw that she worked at understanding the policy issues, which made her effective in meetings. He remembered a number of occasions when she went for the jugular in committee meetings or receptions. 'She said to me before meetings "who is the person I go for?" and she would be very direct and say we need this to happen and we need so much money. And Diana would smile and say I will come back next year and I expect to find the project running.'

Edwards is only one of many fans of Diana in the charity world. Ann Moriarty said to me 'I am really not someone who was likely to be impressed by royalty but I was quite astonished by the way she was on top of her brief.'

And Lord Deedes, who started to work for the *Daily Telegraph* in the 1930s, became a Tory Minister and, later, editor of the *Daily Telegraph* was impressed by the way Princess Diana worked when they travelled together to Angola to campaign for the ban on land-mines.

'She wandered off alone amid the graves and encountered a woman mourning her lost son. Total strangers to each other, they embraced spontaneously. Was she doing it to impress me? No, she was in fact out of my sight, but caught by a photographer. This empathy she conveyed to the distressed seemed to pass like an electric current, but much of its effect, I came to see, was achieved by total and unremitting concentration. During three fairly tiring days, Diana never flagged.'

Princess of Broadmoor

Broadmoor was opened in 1863 as an asylum for the criminally insane, in the middle of beautiful Berkshire countryside. After 1841 the law no longer allowed criminals who were insane to be executed, so there had to be a place to put them. Victorian psychiatry was a strange mix of the cruel and the inspired. If Broadmoor was in the calm countryside, it would help soothe the sick minds. One of the most famous early inmates was the painter Richard Dadd, who invited his father for a walk in the Kent countryside and then slit the old man's throat. Dadd was found not guilty of murder by reason of insanity. He lived out his life in Broadmoor. The asylum gave him a studio where he painted some of his greatest works. A number of his paintings are in the Tate.

By the 1950s Broadmoor, however, had lost its idealism. Inmates were often beaten up; some were strangled with wet towels; there were experiments with chemical castration (Cohen 1981, Murphy 1995). It had become notorious – the institute for the most dangerous and depraved men and women in Britain. The tabloids carried many stories about the maniacs and mad axemen behind the walls. The Yorkshire Ripper was moved there in the early 1980s to cap its grisly reputation. Broadmoor was an even less popular cause than Aids. And yet Diana took it up, both officially and unofficially.

In 1994, Diana opened the Richard Dadd Centre, which specialises in research and treatment for the dangerously mentally ill. She became its patron and she took her duties very seriously. Alan Franey, who was Broadmoor's chief executive from 1988 to 1996, told me Diana often visited the hospital privately. She liked talking to inmates and often insisted on spending time with them without any nurses in the room. In Broadmoor, the nurses are usually members of the

Prison Officers' Association so they are a strange mix of carers and warders. Patients are often inhibited in their presence.

The inmates did not frighten Diana, and she did not inhibit them either. Franey was astonished by her ease when she talked with them. She sometimes even sat in on group therapy sessions.

I suspect Diana's ease may have something to do with the psychiatrists and psychologists she chose for herself. Neither are traditional Establishment figures. In the 1980s, Diana saw the psychiatrist, Dr Maurice Lipsedge who made his name studying the mental health of West Indians and other immigrants. Later, Diana saw Susie Orbach who wrote the groundbreaking *Fat Is a Feminist Issue* and was one of the founders of the radical Women's Therapy Centre.

In her dealings with Broadmoor, Diana was astute. In the brief speech she made on opening the Dadd centre, she lavished praise on the staff. They had a tough job but she also stressed that society doesn't understand serious and violent mental illness. Franey told me Diana was planning to make a film about the hospital. He thought it a brilliant idea.

The love of her life – the Queen of Hearts and the heart surgeon

Anthony Holden described to me how funny and charming Diana could be. 'In early 1993, I wrote a cover story for *Vanity Fair* magazine. I had tried to get an interview with Diana,' Holden told me. Diana had refused but he had still written a piece which was largely on her side. The first thing that turned Holden against Charles was the fact that the Prince used his position to criticise modern architecture. 'I then got a slightly mysterious phone call saying meet me at 12.40 at San Lorenzo's in Beauchamp Place, her favourite restaurant,' Holden said.

Holden turned up and noticed the only table with flowers was the one next to his. At one o'clock Diana arrived with the nanny, the princes and the wife of the Brazilian ambassador. 'It was very charming; the boys ran around the restaurant. She said "What are you boys doing here?"' Holden was invited to her table. 'She couldn't invite people like critics of the monarchy to Kensington Palace. She said in the end it was just to say thank you for the piece in *Vanity Fair*.' Holden was touched because he felt that from 1979 to 1988 he had been an unofficial PR man for Prince Charles. His 1979 book had praised the Prince as a potential moderniser of the monarchy. 'And did I ever have a word of thanks from him? No.'

From then on, Holden lunched with Diana every few months. 'She was very gossipy, very funny. There was never a particular agenda for these lunches. A thing that amused me was that we talked once about the Pope and the Queen Mother whom she described as the chief leper in the leper colony. And then we talked about Hillary Clinton. I was suggesting that Diana start a Foundation and she said, "If I may drop a name" . . . and I thought well whose name might this be? God . . . we'd been dropping every name in the universe and she said "I talked to Colin Powell, and he advised me against it."'

Diana was able to focus better on her work after 1995 because she had finally met a man who was very different from Prince Charles. Hasnat Khan has resolutely refused to talk about his relationship with Diana. Faris Kermani, a Pakistani filmmaker friend of mine, who talked to friends of Hasnat's, believes the reason is simple: the Islamic concept of *izzat* or honour. An honourable man does not talk about a woman. It's not an idea so foreign to British culture. P.G. Wodehouse's *The Code of the Woosters*, for example, is very similar: a gentleman does not bandy a woman's name about. As a result, everything we know about the relationship between Hasnat and Diana comes from hearsay and second-hand sources.

It's not obvious why Hasnat Khan became, as Holden puts it, 'the love of her life after the death of Barry Mannakee'. Hasnat Khan and Princess Diana were introduced on September 1st 1995 at the Royal Brompton Hospital in London. Diana was visiting Joseph Toffolo, the husband of her acupuncturist.

Hasnat Khan had been in Britain for only three years. He was born in Lahore in north-east Pakistan and his family has Pashtun links. After going to one of Lahore's smartest schools, Hasnat studied medicine in Australia. He had family there: his uncle Javed Khan, was a heart surgeon in Sydney. Hasnat clearly impressed his seniors because within two years he was working for a man who has been called the greatest heart surgeon ever – Victor Chang.

Chang was responsible for developing a number of revolutionary techniques in heart surgery and was a household name in Australia. When the Australian

Prime Minister John Howard presided over a poll to name the greatest Aussie of the 20th century, Chang beat the three rivals including the great cricketer, Donald Bradman.

On July 4th 1991, Dr Chang was driving to work when his Mercedes Benz was forced off the road by two Malaysian crooks. They attempted to extort $3 million from him. Chang argued with them and they shot him. The first bullet went through his cheek. The second bullet went through his brain.

Hasnat Khan was devastated by the murder of his mentor and left Australia to come to London. He had good enough credentials to be hired by another great pioneer of heart transplants, Magdi Yacoub.

The relationship between Diana and Hasnat developed fast. At first she went to visit him at the Royal Brompton Hospital late at night. When a *News of the World* photographer caught her leaving the hospital, Diana phoned the paper's royal reporter and insisted she had been visiting some very ill patients. 'I try to be there for them. I seem to draw strength from them.' The press believed her and no hint of the relationship with Hasnat appeared.

Hasnat Khan wanted to keep their affair secret but the couple didn't just meet in private. Hasnat is a jazz fan and Ronnie Scott's jazz club in Soho was one of his favourite nightspots. Diana went there with him. In many ways, they had a very normal love affair. Diana invited Hasnat Khan to Kensington Palace. She got a microwave and cooked pasta for him. She also visited Khan at his flat in Chelsea. She complained he lived just like a man, in a total mess. She spent week-ends with him and his relatives in Stratford-upon-Avon.

Diana bought a copy of *Gray's Anatomy* so she could understand what her lover was talking about. She watched a number of heart operations Hasnat performed, a story that did get into the press, but no one spotted that her presence might be linked to the identity of the surgeon. In love, she had a nice sense of humour. When Hasnat was practising heart operations on sheep, eleven animals died. She sent him an inflatable sheep so he could be guaranteed one animal would not give up the ghost.

But there were also extraordinary aspects to their relationship. Sometimes Diana wore disguises when she and Hasnat went to Ronnie Scott's. If you are the quarry for the press, fooling the hacks is, of course, fun. To avoid the journos and the Kensington Palace police, butler Paul Burrell often had to smuggle Khan into Diana's apartments in the back of his car. Dishing up the lover was, it seems, part of the silver service.

In 1996, Diana went to Pakistan to open a cancer hospital, the funds for which had been raised by Imran and Jemima Khan, the daughter of Sir James Goldsmith. Diana and Jemima were friends and a number of writers suggest that Diana took their marriage as a 'model for herself – chic Western woman settles with sophisticated Muslim man. Result – happiness.' Diana liked the extended family, the warmth, the lack of stuffiness she found in Pakistan.

Given the evenings at Ronnie Scott's and the visits to Stratford-upon-Avon, Holden is certain the security services who watched Diana were well aware of the affair with Hasnat. But Holden insisted to me he was sure Buckingham Palace had no idea that Diana was having an affair. She was certainly very determined to keep the secret, partly, at least, because Hasnat Khan did not want it to leak out.

No one has asked whether Prince Charles became interested in Islam because he felt Diana was becoming so drawn to Muslim men. They had something he didn't – and something he aspired to – a kind of spiritual wholeness. As a young man, Prince Charles was much taken with Sir Laurens van der Post and his ideas of the noble but spiritual savage. Van der Post introduced him to the poet Kathleen Raine. She says she saw him as a rather lost young man even though he was forty. Raine founded a review in 1980 which was devoted to exploring the esoteric tradition. She was an authority on Blake and on Yeats, who filled his poems with references to the cabbala and other esoteric knowledge. She was also interested in the tarot, the Rosicrucians and the work of Henri Corbin, who used to run seminars in France that he called the University of St John of Jerusalem. In 1991, Prince Charles wrote an article for her journal and that proved to be the start of a long association which continued until her death in 2003.

Ronni L. Gordon and David Stillman of the Middle East Forum have pointed out Charles showed some interest in Islam in 1993. He then made a number of speeches, from 1996 onwards, in which he criticised Western attitudes to Islam. He suggested:

Islam can teach us today a way of understanding and living in the world which Christianity itself is poorer for having lost. At the heart of Islam is its preservation of an integral view of the Universe. Islam – like Buddhism and Hinduism – refuses to separate man and nature, religion and science, mind and matter, and has preserved a metaphysical and unified view of ourselves and the world around us. . . . But the West gradually lost this integrated vision of the world with Copernicus and Descartes and the coming of the scientific revolution. A comprehensive philosophy of nature is no longer part of our everyday beliefs.

Charles added that 'there are things for us to learn in this system of belief which I suggest we ignore at our peril'. Young Britons, he said, 'need to be taught by Islamic teachers how to learn with our hearts, as well as our heads'.

Learning with your heart is also, of course, a philosophy Diana believed in.

If how much you risk is a sign of how much you love, Diana was in love. Visiting Hasnat Khan's family in Pakistan was a risk; going with him to Ronnie Scott's was a risk; the comedy of smuggling him into Kensington Palace in the car boot was a risk. It seems hard to avoid the conclusion that the shy girl of the 1980s had become someone who loved, maybe even needed, to sail close to the wind. High gloss, high class and high risk, you might say.

Diana visited Pakistan twice; first 1996 then again in 1997, and she was careful to have an official reason. The press were told she was going to visit Imran Khan's hospital and she did so. But she had every intention of paying a far more private visit. On the first Saturday she was there, Diana went to visit Model Town, the town where Hasnat Khan's family lives. She spent the afternoon with eleven members of his family, including his mother. They talked and, bizarrely, watched cartoons. The Princess left looking pensive. There has been much speculation about what happened that afternoon. Had Diana come to ask her for Hasnat's hand in marriage? Did she try to see if she would be acceptable as a wife?

In November 1996, the *Sunday Mirror* finally realised the Queen of Hearts and the Heart Surgeon were having a serious love affair. *Mirror* reporters had spotted Diana's many visits to the Royal Brompton Hospital and the paper had picked up some gossip about Hasnat Khan. Now she was visiting the Victor Chang Cardiac Research Institute in Australia. Someone checked who had worked there and discovered the link with Hasnat Khan. But, by then, Diana was one of the smartest operators of the press in the world. Again, she cleverly squashed the rumours of romance, insisting that it was well known she was curious about heart surgery. She was interested in medical charities. After all one of her friends was Magdi Yacoub, the great heart-transplant surgeon.

Diana's relationship with Hasnat Khan still seemed intense during the first part of 1997, and in May she flew to Lahore again and spent two days there. She also saw his family again but this visit seems to have been a turning point. After Diana returned from Lahore, all Hasnat's doubts about whether it could work seem to have returned. He sometimes wouldn't speak to her on the phone. Diana even asked Martin Bashir, the reporter who did the famous *Panorama* TV interview with her, to ring Hasnat on her behalf. As a Cupid, Bashir failed, it seems. Holden believes the threat of publicity put Hasnat off. 'He didn't want to be part of all that, and who can blame him?' Holden says.

But if Diana wanted to win Hasnat back, her own behaviour was strange. Soon after she returned to London in May, Diana was photographed dancing with entrepreneur and socialite Gulu Lalvani at Annabel's night club at 2am. Hasnat was apparently furious.

And then, very suddenly, Hasnat Khan was yesterday's love. On July 6th 1997, Diana left England with her sons to fly to the south of France. She was going on holiday with the Al Fayed family. Diana told friends she wanted to make sure her boys had a good holiday. Mohamed Al Fayed assured her the press would not pester her because he had excellent security. Diana liked the idea that her boys would have Al Fayed's four young children to play with.

Freud talks of repetition compulsion and, in a crude sense, Diana was about to repeat the experience of having a relationship with a Muslim man. Psychologists claim that mixed relationships are inherently difficult because people from different cultures often don't share assumptions. Yet, you could hardly find two men less alike than Hasnat Khan, a relatively poor boy made good as an eminently respectable, dedicated doctor and Dodi Al Fayed. Respectable and serious were not part of Dodi's CV. Even his father despaired of him ever working consistently at anything.

It clearly wasn't a question of love at first sight. Diana first met Dodi at a polo game in the 1980s. In 1992 she had met him again at a film premiere of *Hook* to which she had taken her children. She knew he had a reputation as a playboy; he had tried to date Julia Roberts and Sharon Stone among many others.

Kisses on the Riviera

St Tropez was a sleepy little fishing village on the Côte d'Azur till Brigitte Bardot and the film director Roger Vadim made it famous in 1953. Even today it's low key compared to high-gloss resorts like Cannes and Monaco. High up the hill is the villa which Mohamed Al Fayed bought.

Diana and her children spent two weeks in St Tropez as guests of the Al Fayeds, who had just bought a new yacht, the *Jonikal*, for $20 million. Trevor Rees-Jones, the ex-army man from Oswestry who worked as a bodyguard for Mohamed Al Fayed, recalled everyone had a lovely time. There is an engaging photograph of Trevor and Diana waving at each other, mates on the beach. Al Fayed's wife and their children were there and got on well with the princes. 'The boys loved the family,' Mohamed Al Fayed told me.

As a journalist, I am sceptical of Al Fayed but I have a good sense of the prejudice about which he often complains. My father also came to England from the Middle East. He believed the British were gentlemen. He was a modestly successful company doctor and was hired by Lloyd's, for example, to sort out one insurance scandal. I was present a number of times when my father was treated with real prejudice in the City.

He was not 'one of us'; his English was too flowery; his manners too mountebank.

One sign of that very British prejudice is the way the press mock Mohamed Al Fayed although he gave them one of the great political scoops of the 1990s – the Cash for Questions scandal. Al Fayed exposed politicians like Neil Hamilton, who took a wedge (or should it be wage) in return for asking questions in the Commons. Those revelations fixed the image of John Major's government as sleazy. Major led a party where too many leading figures were only too willing to be bought.

One might have expected Tony Blair's new government to be more sympathetic to Al Fayed because he had damaged the Tories so much. Yet Jack Straw, the new Home Secretary, carried on the tradition of refusing Mohamed Al Fayed a British passport.

One woman who is in an excellent position to reflect on the scoops of the summer of 1997 is Elisabeth Andanson, the elegant wife of the paparazzo, James Andanson. Her husband spent a good deal of July and August 1997 following Diana. Andanson told his wife the press were obsessed by Diana. She was on the covers of all the glossies. But it was more than just professional interest. Everyone wondered what she would do now that she was free. Everyone was puzzled that Diana was spending time with the Al Fayeds, a family that the British Establishment sneered at. It could be argued that just as being with Aids victims and Broadmoor inmates did not embarrass Diana, being with the Al Fayeds also did not.

For a while, in July in the South of France, there

was supreme gossip, according to Elisabeth Andanson. Could it be that Diana was doing a Jackie Kennedy and that Mohamed Al Fayed was about to reveal himself as her Onassis? There is one shot of Diana and Mohamed Al Fayed together, his arm around her waist. *Paris-Match* actually posed the question. Diana, showing her savvy, had been careful to insist she was on the Riviera as the guest of Mrs Al Fayed.

The 17th-century French mathematician and philosopher Pascal noted 'le coeur a ses raisons que la raison ne connaît pas'. No one knows why people fall in love. Dodi's main occupation had been as a film producer. He had invested in *Breaking Glass* and, then, in the Oscar-winning *Chariots of Fire* in 1981. A year later, he co-produced *The World According to Garp*. But between 1983 and 1997 Dodi hadn't been much involved in films, though he was still on the fringes of the film world. It was reported he gave a party where American actor Jack Nicholson was presented with a birthday cake stuffed with cocaine.

But women liked Dodi because he was good company and a good listener, as many of his old flames told the press when he suddenly became the lover of the most beautiful woman in the world. He had also lost his mother when he was in his twenties and that, apparently, gave him an air of vulnerability.

Dodi had been married once and girlfriends included actresses Brooke Shields and Winona Ryder among many others. In July 1996, Dodi met the American fashion model Kelly Fisher. In March 1997, Dodi asked her to become his wife and promised to pay her a $500,000 allowance before they got married. Dodi was attentive and gave Kelly two engagement rings and other expensive jewellery. According to Fisher's attorney, however, Dodi did have one strange trait. He obsessively telephoned Fisher's mother.

Kelly Fisher arrived in St Tropez on July 16th. Kelly and Dodi had decided on a date for the wedding – August 9th. There was only one hitch. Dodi was becoming very interested in Diana. What followed was a Feydeau-style comedy. Diana was either in St Tropez or on the *Jonikal* while Kelly Fisher was on a second Fayed boat, the *Cujo*. The bodyguards were sure Dodi bed-hopped from one woman to the other. Gloria Allred, Kelly Fisher's attorney in Los Angeles, told us her client believed Dodi was already having an affair with Diana while he was still sleeping with his fiancée. Dodi often told Kelly he had to go see his father. She accepted his frequent absences because she knew Dodi had to obey his father who held the purse-strings.

We will never be sure how much Diana knew at first about Kelly Fisher. But perhaps at some point, Diana realised that the situation was all too familiar. Yet again, she was one of three. The man she was falling in love with apparently was committed to some-one else.

On July 20th, Diana and her sons flew back to London. Dodi stayed on in St Tropez with Kelly Fisher. On July 22nd, Diana went to her friend designer Gianni Versace's funeral in Milan. The next day, Kelly Fisher and Dodi flew to Paris. From there, Kelly Fisher returned to Los Angeles, still thinking she was going to marry Dodi. Nothing about the Diana–Dodi romance had yet hit the press.

On July 25th Dodi whisked Diana to Paris for their first overnight stay at the Ritz. The visit was a great success. No one found out they were in the city. They could be the anonymous young lovers. It seems likely Dodi did not take her back to the Fayed flat at the rue Arsene-Houssaye because the wardrobes still contained some of Kelly Fisher's belongings.

In the next ten days the relationship between Dodi and Diana became more and more serious. Then, on the 4th of August, the photographer Mario Brenna took several pictures of Diana and Dodi nuzzling and kissing.

On August 7th Diana spent time with Dodi at his Park Lane apartment. Her visit made it into the papers. Nevertheless, she did not intend her new love to make her drop everything else. On August 8th she flew to Bosnia as part of her landmine campaign. In a series of interviews, Diana did not just draw attention to the plight of victims but argued it was a pity so much ingenuity was devoted to the killing and so little to improving the lives of the living.

By August 9th the press (who had been on the spot when Brenna took his photograph) had started to ask Kelly Fisher what she thought was going on between Dodi and Diana. Fisher had had enough. She called a press conference with her lawyer and cried as she denounced Dodi's faithless behaviour. She sued him for a catalogue of sins including breach of contract, equitable estoppel, fraud and money due on dishonour of cheque. The first cheque he had given her was returned by his bank. She stilettoed him nicely, telling journalists their physical relationship had lasted till August 7th.

It was just after this, on August 10th, that Brenna's photograph of 'The Kiss', as the *Sunday Mirror* head-lined it, was published. Other pictures showed Dodi and Diana holding hands in a powerboat. The image of the kiss might be blurred but the effect was elec-tric. Every tabloid scrambled frantically to get its own angle on the story that Dodi and Diana were an item.

On Tuesday August 12th, Diana and Dodi flew to consult her clairvoyant in Derbyshire. They took the Harrods chopper. The *Sun* had much fun imagining the seance, frilling its copy with naughty puns about Dodi's chopper and what a good ride it might give Diana. Interviews with readers were more mixed than one might have expected. Some advised Diana to dump Dodi; some were snide, saying that she was only going out with him for the money. If he came from a housing estate rather than Harrods, she wouldn't be interested in him. The *Sun* also did a round robin of Fleet Street's best astrologers; reading the entrails and planets most of them divined the relationship wouldn't last.

Despite headlines all over the world, Diana refused to let her new love deflect her from plans she had already made. Dodi was upset that Diana insisted she would take the holiday she had arranged to take with her friend, Rosa Monckton. But Diana did let the Fayeds provide transport and so, on August 15th, Diana flew with Rosa Monckton to Greece in the Al Fayed *Gulfstream* jet. Initially the women had planned to go on an ordinary flight. From Piraeus they sailed on a private yacht through the Aegean. Diana had fun planning ways to outwit the photographers. They had a lovely time, even though they were finally photographed on the island of Hydra.

It is hard not to marvel at how much Diana had changed, and at the contradictions in her personality. In fifteen years, the gawky star-struck bride had changed into a woman who was carrying on a very public affair with a Muslim playboy while campaigning against the arms trade. The arms trade is a ruthless business and one in which fortunes are made. (Ironically her new lover's uncle, Adnan Khashoggi, was a big player.) France has long been a major exporter of arms. It is a topic we will return to later in trying to understand the events surrounding Diana's death. She also made it plain that if the boys disliked Dodi, she would not hesitate to give him up.

The 'girls only' holiday led to one revelation, which Rosa Monckton wrote about much later. Diana had her period in Greece, which proved she could not have been pregnant then. After her return to London, Diana joined Dodi again. Diana spoke on her mobile to Rosa Monckton and told her being with Dodi was 'bliss'. The phrase the press loved was 'besotted with Dodi'.

If the reaction to the romance was a little cool in the press, it was icy at Buckingham Palace. It can't have been helped by sharp pieces like that in the *Sun* which imagined how the House of Windsor might change should Diana and Dodi marry. 'He was complete anathema to Buckingham Palace . . . The notion that there might be step-grandchildren of the Queen who were Muslim was anathema,' Holden said.

As we shall see, the Palace was already having a

dossier on the Al Fayeds prepared by MI6. After the battle for control of Harrods, the Department of Trade had questioned whether Mohamed Al Fayed was fit to be the director of a publicly quoted company. Like Robert Maxwell the bouncing Czech and Jew, Mohamed the 'How did he get his hands on Harrods' Muslim was beyond the pale.

When Diana was Prince Charles's wife, politicians, police and the security services had briefed her. Now that she had been cut out of the royal loop, she had far less information. No one has been able to work out how much Diana knew about Dodi. And there was much to know, little of which was flattering.

Despite his glamorous associations and his links with the film business, Dodi was a rich kid who had failed at everything he had touched. He had dropped out of Sandhurst. The only thing he had enjoyed about the military life was playing polo. He had never made a living, relying completely on the allowance his father provided. Mohamed often tried to get him to work at something useful but with no success. David Puttnam had even had to have Dodi removed from the set of *Chariots of Fire* because he was trying to hand out cocaine to the cast. Mohamed had also tried to get Dodi interested in working at Harrods. Dodi was supposed to put in two days a week but he often did not turn up. At one point father and son were not talking to each other and Mohamed got so fed up with his son's huge credit-card bills, he refused to settle them. By 1997, that row was over, however.

The tabloids, of course, had reported Dodi's ex-girlfriends and who he squired at jet-set resorts like St

Moritz and Monaco. But in 1998, CBS's prime current-affairs programme *Sixty Minutes* commissioned award-winning reporter Bobby Buechler to prepare a dossier on Dodi for a possible TV programme. I met Buechler in Tunis. He is a grizzly bear of a man and he also has a Californian private detective's licence. He had spent months talking to those who knew Dodi in Los Angeles. Dodi's reputation was not good. He was known to have left bills unpaid and he was the defendant in thirteen civil cases in Los Angeles. Buechler told me that 'all the cases have a similar ring. Breach of contract, fraud, loss of rent, failure to repay loan, breach of guarantee and bounced cheques.' In two of those cases, Dodi Al Fayed was named as a co-defendant with his film company Allied Stars. As late as spring 2003, two of the cases were still active; the others seemed to have been settled out of court.

Prince Charles had many faults as a husband but it's safe to suppose he never bounced a cheque or found himself being sued for not paying the rent. Dodi's world was not a world Diana was familiar with.

Dodi was also a difficult man to work for. Trevor Rees-Jones often complained Dodi always had to get his own way and wouldn't stand for any discussion.

A hunger to be serious

In the middle of this period of emotional turmoil, Diana gave an interview to the heavyweight French paper *Le Monde* that was due to be published on August 27th. The interview said nothing of her personal life.

It concentrated almost entirely on political issues and Diana's charity work.

Diana made a number of points in that interview. She spoke with real feeling about the power of photographs – and what they meant to her. She highlighted a picture of herself with a young blind boy who was dying. Something in him had spoken to her; she had asked his mother if she could pick him up. The boy did not understand what was going on, and said he didn't want people to make fun of him. Diana calmed him down and told *Le Monde* that photo was very precious to her.

In the interview, Diana didn't discuss battles between her and the paparazzi, nor did she say anything about Dodi. Diana was eloquent on the question of landmines and the suffering they caused. She discussed her future role, not as Queen of Hearts, but as an ambassador for good causes.

In *Le Monde*, Diana was also critical of the Tories. She said they had been ineffective. The new Labour government was much better. Robin Cook, then Tony Blair's new Foreign Secretary, praised the interview. The interview was translated to say she had said the Tories were 'hopeless'. Tory MPs were outraged: Diana had become party political. Diana denied that she had used words that meant hopeless but *Le Monde*'s reporter, Annick Cojean, stood by every quote.

Before the interview appeared on August 27th, Diana went back to the South of France with Dodi. The couple embarked on the *Jonikal* on August 23rd. They then spent a week cruising round the Mediterranean. The romance was now big news and the press harried them. On the 24th the couple went ashore at Monte Carlo. Dodi took Diana to the shop of the society jeweller Repossi to choose the ring that would trumpet this was true love, not yet another fling.

The press was excited as they tracked the couple. In his diary, the French photographer of celebrities James Andanson scrawled *Elle est revenue* – she has come back.

The next day, the *Jonikal* anchored at Portofino in Corsica. Then they headed for the island of Elba where Napoleon had been sent into exile. According to Trevor Rees-Jones, Dodi suggested they have a barbecue on the beach. The couple apparently cuddled at dusk behind the rocks. As he guarded his boss while Homer's wine-dark sea lapped around them on the beach, Trevor had a revelation. His job wasn't too bad even if he had to cope with Dodi's moods, whims and bullying. The press didn't spot the barbecue on the beach.

The *Jonikal* then sailed over to Sardinia and moored off the Costa Smeralda at the north-east of the island. The jet set jet-ski along the unspoilt beaches, the wildlife is magnificent, the resorts exclusive. However lovely the setting though, the tensions were familiar. David Crawford, the lawyer for Trevor Rees-Jones, told me his client was often surprised that the paparazzi seemed to know where the Al Fayeds and Diana were going almost as soon as it had been decided. Some have claimed Mohamed Al Fayed was using the romance between Dodi and Diana to buff up his own profile. According to publicist Max Clifford, Fayed spokesmen were telling him where the couple would be and . . . well, he was disposed to help certain journalists and tell them where the lovers were. That was the kind of thing Max was there for.

When the *Jonikal* reached Sardinia, the paparazzi were waiting – and some of them clubbed together to hire a boat, the *Iliad*. Wherever the *Jonikal* would go, the *Iliad* would follow. There is footage of the paparazzi lined up on the boat – their lenses black like long bird beaks. Long lenses wobbling on the waves don't give the clearest shots and they certainly don't make every frame a Rembrandt, but the shots were enough to show the affair between Dodi and Diana was passionate. In one shot, Diana leans into Dodi's shoulder and seems to be whispering to him.

The world's papers wanted as much of the love fest as they could get. On August 27th, James Andanson hired a helicopter. As the chopper hovered low over the *Jonikal,* Dodi told Trevor Rees-Jones he was completely fed up. Now they weren't safe from prying eyes even on their own yacht.

The holiday was planned to end in time for Diana to get back to England to see her boys off to school at the start of the term. On Saturday, August 30th however, Dodi and Diana changed their plans and decided to have a last day in Paris. Diana would be back in Britain on Monday morning rather than on Sunday.

Mohamed Al Fayed had no doubt what would happen as soon as Diana told her sons and made sure they approved of Dodi. Dodi would slip Repossi's finest engagement ring on Diana's hand and the couple would walk off into the sunset holding hands. Cue '*The Wedding March*' – and apoplexy at Buckingham Palace.

In his surprisingly modest Harrods office, Mohamed Al Fayed still has a picture of the Queen. He explained to me why Dodi and Diana were made for each other. Al Fayed doesn't usually speak calmly and he was a little dramatic in his gestures but I think he was perfectly sincere. Diana had had a troubled childhood. She had been starved of love, which was why she had so many problems with food. But the Al Fayeds, Mohamed told me, weren't cold fish like the Windsors. They had heart and warmth. You got hugs with the *hummus*, passion with the *pitta*. It wasn't surprising she fell in love with Dodi, especially as Dodi didn't come alone. The lad was part of a package of Middle Eastern magic.

Holden does not believe her relationship with Dodi would have lasted and is no fan of Al Fayed. 'I think it was just a summer romance that would have fizzled out. But, say what you like about Fayed, they come from a culture where the family is everything and it's big and warm.' I'm not sure if Mohamed Al Fayed will be flattered or appalled by the comparison Holden went on to draw. 'It's a little like *The Godfather* . . . the Mafia is about family values as well as much else . . . She'd been received into a large warm family, as much for who she was as a human being.' Al Fayed has never been on trial for any offence, of course, except that of upsetting the British Establishment and, as he puts it, 'all their boloney.'

When Diana and Dodi's affair started, Al Fayed had an experienced press spokesman, Michael Cole, who had been the BBC's royal correspondent. Nevertheless, Cole doesn't seem to have had much influence with Dodi because Dodi got tense when the press were hovering. It was partly his personality, partly anxiety the papers would dig up more dirt about his past and his business interests. Dodi's nervousness would influence the events of the next 24 hours.

Around 2pm on Saturday August 30th, Dodi and Diana flew by private plane from Sardinia to Paris. There's jerky footage of the couple, their bodyguards and entourage getting into the plane at Olbia airport. Diana is wearing beige. She and Dodi had less than twelve hours to live.

At Le Bourget airport in Paris, a few photographers met the couple. One of the photographers was twenty-eight-year-old Fabrice Chassery. His job was to follow Dodi and Diana. 'I wanted to get a romantic shot of them holding hands,' he said.

At the airport, Chassery also photographed two French policemen who were waiting for the plane. The fact that they were there is the first small oddity about these events. After a number of murders in the early 1990s, the French government decreed that they had to be told about any VIPs landing in Paris. Le Bourget certainly knew Dodi and Diana were landing. Yet, later on, the French authorities claimed they had no idea that Diana was arriving. In fact, motorcycle outriders escorted her car until they crossed the Boulevard Périphérique which encircles the city.

Those who greeted the little party at Le Bourget airport included forty-one-year-old Henri Paul. He was a short, nearly bald man who wore glasses. He was deputy head of security at the Paris Ritz. His boss had just retired and Henri Paul hoped to take over his job. He had come to the airport after playing tennis with his best friend, Claude Garrec. 'He said he was very excited by the prospect of meeting the Princess of Wales,' Garrec told me.

After Le Bourget, Dodi and Diana were driven to the Villa Windsor, the grand house in which the Duke and Duchess of Windsor had lived, near the Bois de Boulogne. Henri Paul drove the Range Rover which was the back-up vehicle and ferried all their luggage.

The Villa Windsor was now owned by Al Fayed. Jacques Chirac, then the Mayor of Paris, was pleased with the way Mohamed Al Fayed had revived the Ritz Hotel and he offered him the Windsor mansion on a fifty-year lease as long as he restored the house to its old glories. Al Fayed did that and, when he was still trying to please the Establishment, he offered Prince Charles anything he wanted from the Villa Windsor. Charles took a cushion with the embroidered tag 'Ich dien', I serve, the motto of the Prince of Wales.

Dodi and Diana spent about half an hour at the villa. Later it would be hinted that the visit suggested they would make this their home. Diana and Dodi then drove from the villa to the Ritz. From the Imperial Suite, Diana rang one of the journalists she was closest to, Richard Kay of the *Daily Mail*. She told him she would soon be making a startling announcement.

Then, the couple went to Dodi's flat at No. 1 rue Arsene-Houssaye in the centre of Paris. The flat has a plush living room with a huge sofa and a state-of-the-art marble bathroom. There was trouble with the photographers outside in the street. A security man jostled one of them. Diana had the sense to deal with this at once and sent out one of the staff to apologise.

For one of the paparazzi outside, Fabrice Chassery, the incident was significant. It showed there was no deep aggro between the photographers and Diana.

At around 8 o'clock, the couple went shopping. Mohamed Al Fayed dwells on the fact that they went to Repossi's to look at the ring Dodi was buying for the Princess. Then they drove to the Champs-Élysées. Tourists surrounded them when they tried to get out. There was no proper protection and so they stayed in their car. Then they went back to Dodi's flat.

Dodi had booked a table for dinner at a smart Parisian restaurant, Chez Benoit for 9.30. There is some evidence, as we shall see, that three other guests were at one point supposed to meet the couple there. But Dodi seems to have been unnerved by the thought of having to walk past a crowd to get inside. So he asked Claude Roulet, assistant director of the Ritz, to see if the restaurant was besieged. When Roulet reported there were many photographers outside Chez Benoit, Dodi cancelled their reservation.

So Diana and Dodi returned to the Ritz, the great hotel owned by Dodi's father. The French government would claim later that there had been *une bousculade*, a scuffle, as the couple entered the Ritz. Nothing of the sort appears on the video and when the couple entered the Ritz through the swing doors, they seemed quite composed. They ate in the private Espadon restaurant of the Ritz. She had sole; he had turbot. After dinner, they went upstairs to the £6,000-a-night Imperial Suite. There is video of Trevor Rees-Jones watching as they go up the stairs. It was late in the evening, but not yet time to go to bed.

Around 11pm Dodi took a call on his mobile phone. He seemed worried after the call, according to staff at the Ritz.

The Ritz has security cameras all over the hotel. I have watched all the video footage taken that night after 10pm including the footage from camera C 46 outside the Imperial Suite. It shows the bodyguards waiting outside. At 11 o'clock champagne was wheeled in.

An hour earlier Henri Paul returned to the hotel. There is footage of him parking his car at 9.53pm and then entering the hotel through the front door at 10.09. There is some dispute about whether Henri Paul came back because Dodi asked him to, or whether Henri Paul did so of his own free will, because he wanted to be part of the action. But no one disputes Dodi trusted Henri Paul and there is no argument about what happened next. Dodi asked Henri Paul to drive them back to the flat and elude the paparazzi. The two normal drivers, Jean François Musa and Philippe Dourneau, would not be used for that.

Henri Paul was well qualified to drive. He had been on a course for chauffeurs run by Mercedes. He was also a man who had security connections – and they probably dated from when he had started work at the Ritz in 1985.

Midnight at the Ritz

Just before midnight, Dodi rang his father in Britain. Mohamed Al Fayed told me Dodi said he wanted to

go back to his apartment at the rue Arsene-Houssaye.
'He said "I am going now to the apartment. I have a
bottle of champagne there, I have the ring. The Place
Vendôme is full of people."' Mohamed Al Fayed stressed
he counselled his son against leaving the hotel. 'It is so
dangerous. Please just stay there,' he implored. They
had the best suite. The Ritz had everything a romantic couple needed including the very best champagne.
'"I will think it over. I will discuss it with Diana."'
Those were the last words he and his son spoke, Al
Fayed told me.

In one of the interviews for our French film, Francis
Gillery talked to Maître Jean Marc Coblence who represented Serge Arnal, one of the paparazzi. Coblence was
mocking. Dodi, the famous playboy, was phoning his
father to ask for advice. Should he take Diana to the
Al Fayed flat or should they stay in the Ritz? You are
about to go to bed with one of the most beautiful
women in the world, Coblence smiled, and you run
to Papa.

Dodi did not take his father's advice, however. Al
Fayed's explanation is simple. He claimed to me Henri
Paul had been briefed a few hours earlier by the security
forces he freelanced for. His handlers told him the safest
way to elude the photographers and get Dodi and Diana
back to the flat was to go through the Alma Tunnel.
Al Fayed does not suggest Henri Paul plotted his own
death. Rather, the driver was a poor sap conned by the
intelligence services into taking the route that suited
them, the route along which they had prepared a death
trap. Al Fayed claims with real conviction that British
and French secret services collaborated on 'the

execution', as he calls it; but, it has to be said, he has little evidence to back up such a serious charge.

Before the conversation between Dodi and his father, there were discussions at the Ritz about how to elude the paparazzi. Trevor Rees-Jones is not very precise about them in his book. With the help of Henri Paul, Dodi devised a plan that seemed simple and clever.

The Ritz is the major shareholder in a car-hire company, Étoile Limousine, which nearly always provides cars for the hotel guests. Around 11.30, the Ritz asked Étoile Limousine to provide a second Mercedes. It would act as a decoy car. This second Mercedes car was delivered by Frederic Lucard. He would later claim Henri Paul seemed rather excited and that was used as evidence that the driver was drunk.

After 11.30 Henri Paul walked out of the Ritz a number of times to tell the hacks on the Place Vendôme to get their cameras ready. Soon, the glamour couple would be coming out and getting into this Mercedes just outside on the Place Vendôme. They'd be twenty minutes, ten minutes, five minutes. He was teasing them. It worked nicely as a ploy because some of the photographers wondered what he was up to. While all eyes were on the Mercedes at the front, Diana and Dodi would slip out by the back entrance of the Ritz into the second Mercedes.

But the plan broke one key rule of personal security. You do not send a person who might be a target out in a car on their own. John Macnamara, the director of security for Harrods, had insisted there should always be a back-up vehicle as a buffer between the couple and anyone who tried to follow. When Diana and Dodi had been picked up at Le Bourget, Henri Paul had driven the back-up Range Rover behind their car. Now, to fool the photographers, the Ritz was planning to send out the back-up vehicle first and, then, the decoy car on a different route. The Mercedes carrying Dodi and Diana would be travelling solo.

In his *Diana: Closely Guarded Secret*, Inspector Ken Wharfe bitterly attacks the bodyguards, Kez Wingfield and Trevor Rees-Jones, for not insisting on a back-up vehicle to protect the Mercedes. When he was in charge of Diana's security, Wharfe argues, he did not answer to her but to his superiors at Scotland Yard. This did lead to tension but his job was to make sure the Princess was safe. She might not like the restrictions he imposed but, Royal Highness or not, Diana did not pay his wages.

In Paris, however, the bodyguards were employees of the Ritz. Trevor Rees-Jones said both he and Kez Wingfield protested about the risks of the decoy car plan. They could do nothing, however, because it was said the scheme had been cleared with London. That meant Mohamed Al Fayed had approved it. Neither Rees-Jones nor Wingfield dared confront Dodi. Neither dared ring London and ask Harrods' grandly named Ops Room whether the boss had really accepted the decoy car plan. Mohamed Al Fayed has always denied that he approved anything of the sort.

Dodi did not just insist Henri Paul drive, he also insisted that only Trevor should accompany him and the Princess in the second Mercedes. There was one strange feature about the car. The Mercedes the couple were initially going to use had tinted windows to make it impossible for the paparazzi to get pictures of those inside. The second Mercedes, however, had clear windows.

Many of those who have studied what happened that night find it strange Dodi should have specifically asked for Henri Paul to act as the chauffeur. His normal driver was available. But in the course of our investigation, we stumbled on one lead which could explain this. It seems Dodi wanted to go somewhere badly and that perhaps he preferred his father not to know where they were going. As we have seen, father and son did have their problems. Dodi could trust Henri Paul not to blab to London. The decoy car plan ensured something else. Of the bodyguards, only Trevor Rees-Jones would know where they went after leaving the Ritz. The more senior man, Kez Wingfield, would be driving back to the flat near the Étoile. Trevor was more junior and, perhaps, the least likely to raise questions. This is something explored in greater detail later.

Dodi's nervousness would have made more sense if the crowd outside the Ritz had been large or restive. It was not, however, as video taken by two Australian tourists, Chloe Papazahariakis and Vlad Borovac shows. They filmed a small group of maybe twenty photographers and some thirty celeb-watchers. The footage shows a polite crowd, not a frightening mass of fans behaving in an aggressive way.

At ten minutes past midnight, the Ritz cameras show Dodi and Diana leaving the Imperial Suite and walking down a corridor in the hotel. The bodyguards follow. The next images come from inside a small lobby at the back entrance of the Ritz at 12.18. These pictures show the couple talking to Henri Paul. One can see Dodi with his arm lightly touching Diana's back. Henri Paul disappears from the lobby for about a minute and, then, comes back to the couple and confers with them. Then all three leave.

At 12.19 the couple walk out of the back door of the hotel. The video images from the Ritz cameras then show Henri Paul leading them and Trevor Rees-Jones down the rue Cambon at the back of the hotel. The second Mercedes is waiting.

Diana and Dodi got into the back of the Mercedes. They did not put their seat belts on. Nor did Henri Paul as he took the wheel. At some point after leaving the Ritz, Trevor Rees-Jones put his seat belt on.

It was just past 12.20 when the Mercedes started down the rue Cambon. It's a narrow street with one traffic light about 100 metres from the back entrance of the Ritz. There is another set of lights at the bottom of the street. There, the car turned right into the rue de Rivoli. From that turning, it is some 200 metres to the grand Place de la Concorde.

One witness saw the Mercedes drive through the Place de la Concorde. Mohammed Rehabouille said the Mercedes did not seem to be going particularly fast. He also said nothing about the car being surrounded by motorbikes.

The shortest route to Dodi's flat was up the Champs-Élysées but, at the Place de la Concorde, the car turned left instead of right. It then sped along the riverbank of the Seine. It was now going away from Dodi's flat.

A few moments after the Mercedes drove away, the Ritz cameras trained on the rue Cambon revealed something else. It's a few frames of a white Fiat Uno disappearing – down the street, in the direction of the Mercedes.

At 12.23 Henri Paul reached the dip that curves right and leads to the Alma Tunnel. The map on page 61 shows the geography. If the Mercedes had turned right at the top of the dip, it would have driven into the Avenue Montaigne, one of Paris's grand avenues. If one were trying to avoid the Champs-Élysées, which are often crowded on Saturday nights, the Avenue Montaigne would be a sensible detour to take back to the Étoile and Dodi's flat.

But the Mercedes did not turn towards the Avenue Montaigne. Instead, it carried on down into the tunnel. No one has ever explained why they were taking this route – and the French inquiry did not try. Trevor Rees-Jones's lawyer, David Crawford told me: 'It is a mystery why they were where they were, because there are many different ways of getting to the apartment that they were going to, it was at the top of the Champs-Élysées, without going via the Champs-Élysées. Where they were is inexplicable.'

There are only three possible explanations of the inexplicable. The first, which some conspiracy theorists have put forward, is that motorcycle riders blocked the road at the turning into the Avenue Montaigne. On the internet there is a reference to a woman called Brenda Wells who made precisely such a claim. No one has ever been able to trace Brenda Wells, however, since twenty-four hours after the crash. If you stand at the Place de l'Alma, where there were many witnesses, you can see this turn-off. But no witness, other than the missing Brenda, ever suggested there was some obstacle there which forced the Mercedes down into the tunnel.

The second explanation is that Henri Paul was taking this route to confuse the paparazzi. But the photographers saw where the Mercedes was going, first at the back of the Ritz and then at the Place de La Concorde, where Henri Paul turned to drive alongside the Seine. If they were headed to Dodi's flat, it would have made more sense for him to take the turn off at the Avenue Montaigne when he got there. I also find it odd that if the aim was to confuse the paparazzi, Henri Paul did not get Rees-Jones to ring the bodyguards in the decoy car to explain what they were doing.

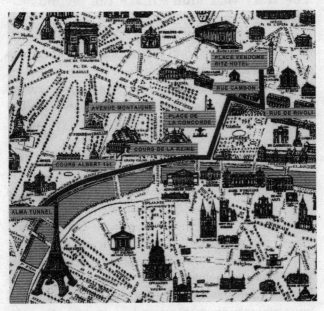

© Egon Clausen 2004.

The third explanation is that the Mercedes was going to call somewhere else before Dodi and Diana returned to the comforts of the rue Arsene-Houssaye.

When we were making the French film, we got some information which offers a credible explanation of why Dodi was keen to leave the Ritz that evening. He had fixed to go to a meeting at the Passy Kennedy building. This is an office block about a mile on from the Alma Tunnel. The route through the tunnel would make perfect sense if Dodi had to meet someone there.

The story that didn't make the second edition

As Henri Paul drove into the tunnel, the first editions of the Sunday papers were already for sale in Britain. At King's Cross Station, you can buy them from around 11 o'clock, midnight Paris time. That night, the first edition of the *Sunday Mirror* carried a story headline: 'Queen to Strip Harrods of its Royal Crest.'

Andrew Golden reported that senior palace courtiers were 'ready to advise' the Queen she should refuse to renew the Royal warrants for Harrods. Golden reported that the Royal Family 'is furious about the frolics of Di and Dodi which they believe have further undermined the monarchy'. Golden went on to say that Prince Philip was especially critical, referring to Dodi as an 'oily bed hopper'. Prince Philip, according to a friend of the Royals Golden quoted, 'has let rip several times recently about the Fayeds – at a dinner party, during a country shoot and while on a visit to close friends in Germany'. The story added Prince Philip had been 'banging on about his contempt for Dodi', thundering that he was 'undesirable' as a future step-father for Prince William and Prince Harry.

Golden added a quote from a source 'close to Buckingham Palace' to the effect that Diana had been told 'in no uncertain terms about the consequences should she continue her relationship with the Fayed boy'. Golden had been told that Diana might be forced into exile or that she might be 'socially ostracised'. MI6 had prepared a special report on the Fayeds, which would be presented to the Queen the following week at a meeting of the Way Ahead Group. The group was discussing future tactics for the monarchy. Diana would be put under great pressure to dump Dodi. As soon as news of the crash came out, the *Sunday Mirror* dropped the story.

At around 12.23, the Mercedes entered the Alma Tunnel. A second or so later, it crashed against the thirteenth pillar in the middle. The pillar is 64 metres inside the tunnel. Dodi Al Fayed and Henri Paul both died soon after the crash. Paul was especially unlucky. A recent study in the American Journal of Emergency Medicine has found that in cars where airbags are released only 2.7% of drivers die, whether or not they are wearing seat belts.

Half an hour after he had talked to Dodi, Mohamed Al Fayed told me 'my security people ring to say there was an accident'. He had to stop talking a moment because he was starting to cry. Then, he collected himself in his anger. The *Sunday Mirror* article was very significant, he insisted. 'The bastards', as he called them, had announced their intentions. 'All the things Diana told me during her holiday – that she had to toe the line, that Dodi was not the right person for her, she had to respect the tradition of the family.' It was too much of a coincidence for him that 'this article come out on the same day where they talk about getting rid of her?' For Al Fayed this proved an execution – and he often uses that word – had been planned.

Jean Durieux, one of *Paris-Match* magazine's most experienced investigators, said he was not sure what Dodi's meeting in the Passy Kennedy building might have concerned. But it was a business meeting. There was a deal to be done. When Dodi did not turn up for the appointment, those who were expecting him became very disturbed.

2

Police and Paparazzi

Towards the tunnel;
12.23am August 31st 1997

Dodi's decoy car plan had not worked perfectly. It's basic catch-the-celeb technique to watch the back as well as the front; six to seven photographers, including Fabrice Chassery, were waiting in the rue Cambon at the back of the Ritz.

Chassery saw Dodi and Diana get into their Mercedes. Jacques Langevin took a picture of Dodi as he got into the back of the car. When the Mercedes drove off, Chassery decided he had had enough for the day. 'The photograph we wanted, the photograph that was worth something, was a photograph of the two of them holding hands,' he said. They were not going to get that now.

But other paparazzi still hoped for the ultimate romantic 'Paris-by-night' kiss. So two of them, Serge Arnal and Christian Martinez, set off in cars after the Mercedes; twenty-four-year-old Romauld Rat, a photographer who worked for the Gamma agency got on his two-man motorcycle with his driver, Stephan Darmon. It was a fairly staid procession with the paparazzi less than 300 metres behind the Mercedes till the red lights on the Place de la Concorde. When they turned green, Henri Paul put his foot down and sped towards the Alma Tunnel. In their slower cars, the photographers were left behind. Soon, the Mercedes streaked out of sight.

Between the Place de la Concorde and the Alma Tunnel, there is another tunnel.

As the Mercedes drove into the Alma Tunnel, the paparazzi were 800 to 1,200 metres – or ninety seconds to two minutes – behind, but it would be reported that very night they were 'in pursuit' and 'buzzing around it like flies'. The latter is certainly untrue. Some of the photographers, like Chassery, even claimed they weren't following Diana and Dodi at all. They were just going home and, for them, that meant driving through the Alma Tunnel. They got their cameras out again only when the Mercedes crashed. Then, they had a job to do. These photographers also included Lazlo Veres and Nikola Arsov.

Fabrice Chassery was on the Champs-Élysées when another photographer, David Oderkerken, sometimes known as David Ker, rang him. 'He said there had been an accident in the Alma Tunnel and I made straight for there.' Another of the photographers, Serge Benhamou, also cannot have been following the Mercedes because he drove into the tunnel from the far side, from the Trocadero end.

We can, at least, establish the moment of the crash to within twenty seconds with real confidence. At 12.23 and forty-three seconds, Paul Carrill, who was standing on the Place de l'Alma above the entrance to the tunnel, telephoned the emergency services; at the same time one of the photographers, Serge Arnal, phoned 12 – France has more than one equivalent of 999. After Carrill and Arnal, many others phoned. Central Control at 12 did not, however, alert the traffic police, but they did immediately send in the *sapeurs-pompiers,* the firefighters who are also trained to provide paramedic services.

August 31st 1997; 'Paparazzi scum' – what witnesses saw and didn't see immediately

Fabrice Chassery was not the only person to arrive soon after the crash. No one has ever been able to confirm how many people walked into the tunnel when they realised something interesting had happened. James Huth, a dentist, for example, walked down from his nearby apartment. Others rushed down from the cafés at the Place de l'Alma. Some people who were driving through the tunnel, like Abidjan A – the French inquiry dossier only gives Christian names and the first initial of the surname – stopped and got out of their cars. Both police and the emergency services found a crash site buzzing with life. Some cars were still driving through the other side of the tunnel towards the Place de la Concorde.

The Mercedes had careered off the thirteenth pillar and back into the middle of the road. Despite the fact that the S280 is built so strongly, the front of the car

had concertinaed. Drawings made by the French investigators highlight six different places at the front of the
car where there was damage. The roof had not been
badly affected, however. Some of the most used images
of the Mercedes were taken after the roof had been
cut off so that the emergency services could get Trevor
Rees-Jones out, making the wreck look even worse
than it was.

The crash had triggered the horn of the Mercedes.
Everyone there remembers how loud, intense and eerie
its blare was. The noise did not make it easier for
witnesses to remember what had happened or to focus
on what they were seeing.

At around 12.26 Romuald Rat got off his motorbike in the tunnel and left his driver to park it. Running
towards the Mercedes, he took three pictures. Smoke
was still puffing out but that didn't worry him. He
looked into the car. He looked inside and 'I recognised
Mr Al Fayed. At that point I was shocked, because it
wasn't a pretty sight. I drew back for a few seconds.'

By a remarkable coincidence one of the first people
on the scene, Dr Frederic Mailliez, was a specialist in
emergency medicine, working for SOS Médecins. He
was returning from a dinner party with an American
friend, Mark Budt, when he saw the traffic slowing
down and that there was smoke. 'As we got close, I
realised that the incident had just happened. I stopped
my car at once.' Mailliez was in his SOS Médecins car
and had his emergency light. He clamped it on the
roof of his car. 'There were already people there and
a sense of panic.'

A pedestrian, Belkacem B, felt that panic. 'At once

I saw the driver had been squashed to a pulp, with his
hand through the windscreen. I saw the passenger had
his jaw cut. His body was held upright by his seat belt
and leaning against the airbag. He was trapped in the
vehicle and there was no way to open the door. I
thought it better not to touch him. In the back seat
was a man of about forty, stretched out, his feet in an
awkward position, his eyes turned back in his head. I
saw right away he was dead. Beside him, between the
right-hand front seat and the back seat, a blonde woman
was doubled up on herself with a gash on her forehead and her watch-strap undone. She moaned, and
said a few words in English. "My God, My God," I
think. She still had her shoes on her feet.'

Belkacem asked one of the photographers what they
should do. She thinks it was Rat who replied, 'Don't
touch anything. It's Princess Diana. She's with Dodi!'

Romuald Rat was clearly shocked but composed
himself, it seems, and started to observe. Dodi's eyes
were half open. 'I could see nothing more could be
done for him. The Princess was on the floor, between
the two seats, her back to me. I said to her in English:
"Be cool, the doctor is coming."' Rat had no idea,
of course, if that was true. Just then, Trevor Rees-
Jones started to move around violently in his seat. Rat
went to look at him and touched him 'to let him
know I was there'. Rat also promised him the doctor
was coming, he said. He then went to the front of
the car. Henri Paul was completely trapped. The horn
was still blaring. 'I wanted to see if I could disconnect the battery, but with the state the car was in, it
wasn't even worth thinking about.' And then, Rat

recalled, 'someone showed up carrying a small white oxygen mask'.

That person was Dr Mailliez. He was giving first aid around 12.28 and has always insisted that the photographers did not hamper him. 'People did swear at me. People said "someone had been injured we mustn't touch her". I said firmly that I was a doctor and that I knew what had to be done.' Mailliez realised Dodi and Henri Paul were beyond help. 'I saw that the first emergency was the passenger in the right-hand rear seat. She seemed to be alive. She was jammed in between the front and back seats.' The paparazzi knew, of course, that Diana was in the car but Mailliez did not. He was more concerned with her injuries than with her identity. 'I did not recognise who she was. I only found out the next morning,' he said.

The photographers knew that the crash could be a gold mine. The story that Diana and Dodi had crashed would be front-page news from Tokyo to Texas. Pictures of the shattered Mercedes – especially pictures of Diana and Dodi Al Fayed – would be worth a fortune.

Christian Martinez who had been following in his car took sixteen pictures in the tunnel. Eight were just of the car. One of these pictures was probably the first taken of the Mercedes. It shows the airbag in front of Henri Paul was still inflated; the headlights were on and there was smoke around the vehicle. Martinez then walked around the car and took seven other photos going from the front to the rear.

Rat claims he started to take more pictures only after the police arrived. If that is correct, he did not take any shots for about six minutes between 12.26 and

12.32. Rat took a total of nineteen pictures. They were all taken from less than five metres away. One showed a man by the car, a man whom the police did not identify.

Seven minutes after the crash, the police still do not seem to have known there had been an incident. It was not until 12.30 that the law found out – and it did so in a curious way. Pedestrians stopped two police officers, Lino Gagliardone and Sebastien Dorzee, on the nearby Cours Albert-1er and told them there had been a terrible accident. The two officers then hurried over to the tunnel.

Just after 12.30, Gagliardone and Dorzee found a distressing and chaotic scene. Ambulances had not yet arrived. Dodi Al Fayed was dying and Henri Paul was dead. Princess Diana was dazed and badly hurt. Trevor Rees-Jones was bleeding profusely. Diana and Trevor were both moaning in pain.

People do not behave logically at the site of accidents. Rat was a badly shaken young man. He had a row with Christian Martinez. Rat says he tried to stop Martinez taking more pictures inside the car and that Martinez would not do so. They exchanged insults. Rat told Martinez to get back, and take no pictures of the interior of the car. Martinez told Rat '*de se baiser*' – to 'fuck off'.

'We were all distressed at one moment or another,' Martinez said. 'We left, we came back: our only reaction was the desire to remain close to the scene. The only one who moved in on the car was Rat.' Rat's driver Stephan Darmon claims he was upset photos were being taken and he sat down some distance away.

The accusation would be, of course, that the

photographers were so cynical the only thing on their minds was getting pictures.

Serge Arnal, who had been the second person to ring the emergency services, was on the scene about ninety seconds after the crash. He did not make for the car at once, he explained, because he hates the sight of blood. His blood phobia did not deter him too much in the end, however. Arnal took thirty-one pictures, according to the French files, twenty-seven of them showing Diana receiving the first medical attention she got, as Dr Mailliez gave her oxygen. In theory, Arnal's pictures of Mailliez attending to Diana should provide good evidence of the condition she was in. Most of Arnal's pictures had been taken from close up, at no more than 1.5 metres from the car. But these pictures have never been seen.

The first fire engine from the station at the rue Malar got to the Alma by 12.32. They were specialists in disincarceration – removing people from inside crashed vehicles. By now, the two survivors were being treated by two well-qualified professionals, Mailliez and an off-duty firefighter, Dominique Dalby, whose training included paramedic skills. It is perhaps a sign of the heightened emotions at the time that Dorzee's account bristles with hostility to the photographers. He estimated there were far more than seven on the scene. He reckoned it was ten to fifteen. 'The flashes were going off like machine guns, and each of them must have shot off a whole film.'

Dorzee made for the partly opened right-hand rear door. 'I had to open the door a bit more to gain access, and immediately recognised Princess Diana. I tried to push back the photographers, who were enraged. In the struggle, I was pushed several times. At no time did a photographer come to lend a hand. They just went on taking pictures. It was clear I was getting in their way. When I opened the back door further, I saw the passenger on the left of the back seat was dead.'

What is odd is that, according to Mailliez, he was treating the Princess at this very moment. Yet, Dorzee never mentions him. Dorzee found Diana as Rat had done. 'Her head was between the two front seats, facing sideways. She could see her companion in front of her. She moved, with her eyes open, and spoke to me in English. I think she said "My God" as she saw her friend was dead. At the same time, she stroked her stomach. She must have been in pain. I tried to lean into the car, with my feet still on the ground outside, to try and prevent the photographers from taking more pictures. She turned her head towards the front and saw the driver, and took in more of what had happened, I think. She started to get upset. A few seconds later, she looked at me. Then she laid down her head and closed her eyes.'

Dorzee was also very determined that no one should steal anything. 'I noticed that there were jewels scattered on the floor.' He made sure no one picked them up.

Between 12.32 and something like 12.45, the two beat officers Dorzee and Gagliardone tried to handle a difficult scene. Nothing had prepared these two men to deal with the situation they found themselves in and there is some evidence they lost their cool. The next day, they complained to the press and took the moral high ground. They claimed Martinez told them: 'You are really pissing me off. I'm going back to Sarajevo. There the cops don't mess around with us and let us work. You've only got to go to Bosnia and you will see.'

'We are in Paris now,' Gagliardone replied, apparently.

'I'm only doing my job,' the police claimed Martinez said.

The policeman replied that he too was only doing his job.

By 12.45 more than 100 shots had been taken of the car and of those inside.

The picture trade

On their mobiles, the photographers told the agencies they worked for about the material they were getting. At picture agencies like Gamma and Laurent Sola Diffusion, it was suddenly frantic. Within an hour of the crash, faxes and e-mails, offers and counter-offers poured in. 'It was crazy that night,' Chassery said, with agencies offering sums in excess of £100,000 for a picture.

There was a real irony here. Editors were in the midst of frenzied bidding to get images and at the same time planning pious editorials about the evil paparazzi. Buckingham Palace, the French authorities and Mohamed Al Fayed were united in their condemnation. Al Fayed's spokesman, Michael Cole, rose poetically to the crisis. He compared the paparazzi to Red Indians surrounding a stagecoach. In a graphic image, Cole sniped that these modern day 'braves', 'instead of firing arrows, were firing lights at the people inside the car'.

The photographers were able to carry on working because the first two police officers on the scene did not impose control. In all the twenty-seven volumes of evidence gathered by the French inquiry, I have been unable to find any precise time for when the Paris traffic police or other officers reached the scene.

By 12.45 there were four ambulances from SAMU at the scene – and many policemen were arriving.

The first priority at the scene of a crash is to assess the state of the victims and to get help for those who are injured. If it is a major incident, officers are supposed to isolate the site so that scene of crime officers can gather forensic evidence, which may be needed to establish what happened and for possible use in any prosecution.

Unlike the police, no one from the emergency services complained of how the photographers behaved.

Even once they had got control, the police faced a daunting job. There were potential witnesses at four different places over a distance of 600 metres. Some had seen the Mercedes enter the tunnel; some outside at the other end of the tunnel had seen vehicles exit. There were witnesses in cars driving in the opposite direction to the Mercedes and there were witnesses in vehicles behind the Mercedes.

One additional problem was that Paris had then, as now, a large number of *sans papiers*, people without papers or illegal immigrants. At least four potential witnesses disappeared because the last thing they wanted was for the police to interview them.

In the end, the police took statements from seventeen witnesses at the tunnel as well as ten photographers, but none of these had seen the moment of impact. Most witnesses were at either end of the tunnel and what often seemed to have made the greatest impression on them were sounds. Eight of the ten witnesses who were closest said they had heard two crashes.

Around 12.40, Paris police chief, Philippe Massoni was woken up with the news of the crash. Curiously, he did not wake his boss the Minister of the Interior, Jean-Pierre Chevenement immediately. My information is that it was another thirty-two minutes before Chevenement was told of the crash. Both men had a high profile. Chevenement had started to consider standing for the Presidency of France. Massoni had been appointed by the President of the French Republic. Once it was known Diana was injured, there was a flurry of political activity. At 12.40 the Paris police rang the British Embassy to inform them Princess Diana was hurt. Sir Michael Jay, the British Ambassador, took some time to locate. Only he could inform the Royal Family.

Soon after 1am, President Clinton and his wife were informed by a military aide while they were on holiday at Martha's Vineyard.

The Paris police chief made for the tunnel and got there around 1.15. Massoni was joined there by Patrick Riou, head of the Paris police judiciaire. Riou's brother is a surgeon at the Salpêtrière Hospital and, four hours later, would play a central role as events unfolded. There is always a prosecutor on call and that night it was Maud Coujard. She had considerable experience of road traffic accidents.

The arrest of the paparazzi

At 12.50 Mohamed Al Fayed was being woken up at his home in Oxted. He ordered his helicopter to come and pick him up at once.

Soon after 1am it was no longer possible to walk through the tunnel. The head of France's CID, Madame Martine Monteil arrived as well as Massoni. She conferred with Coujard. Their first reaction was to treat the incident as suspicious, and so they set up a murder investigation.

The presence of the most senior police officers in France led to dramatic action. Under French law there is a provision, called the Good Samaritan law. If you see someone who is injured, the law requires you to assist him or her. If you walk on by, you are likely to be prosecuted. But the photographers did not expect what happened next. Just outside the Alma Tunnel, seven of them were told they were under arrest. The seven were Jacques Langevin, Christian Martinez, Romuald Rat, Stephane Darmon – a driver for one of the photographers, Serge Arnal, Lazlo Veres and Nikola Arsov. By the end of the night, they would be charged with manslaughter and with breaking France's Good Samaritan law. They would remain accused of the latter offence for over two years.

Blaming the photographers for doing nothing to help would have been a difficult charge to sustain. Arnal rang the emergency services the moment he saw the crash. Rat claimed to have made some effort to comfort the victims. Dr Frederic Mailliez who was helping the victims four minutes after the crash repeatedly said that the photographers did not hinder him or the emergency services.

Sensing trouble, three photographers left the scene before they could be arrested – Fabrice Chassery, Serge Benhamou and David Oderkerken or Ker. But this would not be the end of the affair for them.

The fate of the paparazzi

Around 1.30, the arrested paparazzi were driven away in a police van to Paris police headquarters. News teams filmed them leaving. 'Those images of the photographers when they were driven away in the police van,' said Jean-Marc Coblence, the pugnacious lawyer who represented Serge Arnal, 'those images were flashed round the world and those pictures immediately made everyone feel that the guilty party had been found.'

The paparazzi were taken to the police station in the rue des Courcelles. They were all tested for alcohol and all of them were below the legal limit. They were then taken to the police headquarters at the Quai des Orfèvres. Many of the photographers had been inside the police HQ as journalists. They were treated very differently now. Their cameras were confiscated, all their negatives seized.

Each of the seven was interrogated individually. All told the same story. The paparazzi had not been close to the Mercedes when it drove into the Alma Tunnel. But the police did not believe them. The photographers assumed they would be allowed to go home that night but, instead, they were put in *garde à vue*, police custody.

Langevin said he felt he had become ensnared in some kind of net.

Coujard's boss, the Procurator General, was especially adamant. He wanted to charge the paparazzi with manslaughter. She persuaded him to wait before doing anything so drastic. The paparazzi were, after all, already in the cells.

William Bourdon, who represented Langevin, believes the decision to arrest the photographers was made at a high political level. Bourdon argues it was not hard to work out what the authorities were likely to be thinking: 'There were discussions of this sort – "The British press will be very emotional. They will go wild. We have to show that we know who the guilty parties are."' And so the paparazzi got the blame.

David Ker made straight for the office of the Sygma agency and became involved in selling pictures. At 3am Laurent Sola, the head of LSDiffusion, which sells pictures all over the world, called in Dominique Petit who was skilled in scanning pictures into computers. The technology was not as well developed in 1997 as it is now so specialist skills were needed. Petit did his job fast and some pictures were sold in principle that night. The *National Enquirer* in New York offered $250,000 for Arnal's. British papers were offering sums in the region of £1 million. Ker claimed however that at 5.45am, when they knew Diana was dead, these contracts were all cancelled. Sola says he then removed the pictures from the internet so that no one could pirate them.

For their part, the French authorities wanted to make sure none of the pictures would be seen. When they realised that some of the paparazzi had left the tunnel fast and that others may have managed to send rolls of films by messengers to their agencies, the police took drastic action. They raided all the photo agencies the photographers worked for and confiscated every single negative. When Sola removed his pictures from the internet in the middle of the night, he imagined he would always have the negatives. By dawn, however, he had nothing left in his possession.

Before the end of the night, the Minister of the Interior, Jean-Pierre Chevenement promised that the French government would investigate fully the crash.

Inconsistencies in the official accounts appeared from the start. The first is petty. In Paris all calls to emergency services are logged and recorded. It would be reasonable to expect the final summary the French authorities produced to be precise about such calls. But they are not. On page 18 it says that Serge Arnal called 12 and on page 20 it is noted that he called 112. No one seems to have spotted the difference, cared to get it right or explained whether it was a typographical error.

E is for 'eyewitness' and E is for 'error'

Psychologists have researched the foibles of eyewitness evidence for more than thirty years. Dr Elizabeth Loftus of Northwestern University has shown how fragile eyewitness memory is. Cornell University's Dr Stephen Ceci, working with children, has shown how easy it is for the context and the kinds of questions that are asked to influence not just the answers that are given, but what subjects sincerely believe. One of the first experiments I did as a student was a lesson in all this. I was one of a group of Oxford arrogants who believed we were in class to hear a lecture on animal behaviour. A few minutes into a talk of how great apes groomed each other, a middle-aged woman burst into the lecture room. When she left, we were asked to write down what she wore, what she had said, how she had behaved. We were bright, the alleged crème de la mental crème, and we were amazed we remembered so little of what we had seen. It was humiliating to get so many details wrong.

The sieve memory is affected and distorted by many stimuli – stress, wakefulness, and personal history, what you were doing in the nanosecond before you noticed. The crash scene was horrific. High levels of stress tend to impair recall. It is not surprising, then, that the accounts of witnesses were so muddled.

The first example of this confusion is simple. Four witnesses spoke of a large motorcycle behind the Mercedes; two witnesses described a motorcycle with two riders on it. One of the paparazzi, Romuald Rat was, indeed, on a motorbike being driven by Stephane Darmon. Two riders on one bike is quite a rare sight; yet only two people out of the seventeen eyewitnesses interviewed spotted the existence of this two-person vehicle.

Much of the evidence was contradictory and so I think it is useful to focus on what we can find that is consistent in the accounts witnesses gave.

When the Mercedes was at the Place de la Concorde,

it does seem clear it was not going particularly fast. Rehabouille and another witness at the Concorde, Jean Louis Bonnin said that the car was not going especially fast. It picked up speed on the way to the Alma. Of the witnesses who saw the car enter the tunnel, most said it was travelling very quickly but only one, a chauffeur called Olivier P, felt confident enough to estimate the speed of the car. He suggested two weeks later that the car had been going at 150 kilometres per hour.

The witnesses were more muddled about what bikes and cars were behind the Mercedes. Some witnesses did speak of many motorbikes around the car. But one of the first and best-placed witnesses was Dr Mailliez. He and his friend, Mark Budt, spoke of just one motorbike. Mailliez said that a motorbike stopped, made a U-turn and then drove out of the tunnel. The rider of that motorcycle was not a photographer at all, it seems. Certainly, Dr Mailliez did not see the man take any pictures. This bike rider was the person best placed to discuss what had happened just before the crash. He was also, I believe, caught by Romuald Rat on one of his thirty-one photographs. We identify in the next chapter who that person was.

The eyewitness evidence about the presence of other cars was much more confused. The dossier cites at least five people – Olivier P, Georges and Sabine D, Souad and Mohammed M – who described another vehicle moving slowly in front of the Mercedes as it entered the tunnel. This vehicle was on the right-hand side in what is the fast lane. According to Olivier P, 'the smaller car was driving in such a way as to slow down the Mercedes. It was a dark coloured car like a Ford Mondeo.' Later on, however, Olivier P said this car was doing nothing dangerous to stop the Mercedes overtaking it.

No driver of a Ford Mondeo ever came forward. Olivier P also had to admit later that he had his attention distracted by the clients he was driving. He then heard a 'small crash'.

A grey Citroën BX was almost certainly in the tunnel and going in the same direction as the Mercedes, but the account given by its occupants Souad and Mohammed M is odd. Both said they were driving home to a suburb, St-Denis, after a dinner out. They claimed to be going at about 80 kilometres an hour – the speed limit in the tunnel is 50 kilometres. In his tail mirror, Mohammed saw the Mercedes skidding towards his car and he accelerated to get out of the way. The most remarkable claim Mohammed made was that there was also a motor bicycle in front of the Mercedes. This bike, he said, was zigzagging to slow down the Mercedes.

The couple claimed to have seen the Mercedes crash. They both noticed Henri Paul slam into the steering wheel of the car. Yet, they did nothing to summon emergency services. They just carried on home. It was not till the next day, well after the news was in the headlines, that they reported to the police HQ at the Quai des Orfèvres. The police took a statement and inspected their Citroën. 'They even searched the car,' said Souad, who explained that she had started to cry when she saw the crash.

On September 12th, Mohammed and Souad were seen by *Juge* Stephan the investigating magistrate. *Le Monde*, however, dismissed their evidence as very poor and suggested that they had been influenced by all the press blaming the paparazzi. It's interesting the police never charged this couple under the French Good Samaritan law, even though they had witnessed an accident, seen people hurt and ignored it all.

Other witnesses at the Trocadero end of the tunnel spoke of a car leaving the tunnel 'in a hurry' just after the sound of the crash. The witnesses could not agree on the make of this exiting car. Some spoke of a Citroën; some like Olivier P claimed a small black car left the tunnel quickly; others like the Souads spoke of a Fiat Uno and, later, of a white Fiat Uno. A couple, Georges and Sabine D, claimed to have seen a Fiat Uno zigzag out of the tunnel and that the driver of the car was behaving strangely. Gary Hunter, a lawyer, said he saw two cars disappear fast out of the tunnel and that one was a white Fiat Uno. But he was never interviewed by the French police even though he offered to speak to them. The Fiat Uno was to become, as Michael Cole put it, 'the grassy knoll' of the affair.

The French police were faced with contradictory claims – and some of these were made to them on the site within an hour of the crash. This made it vital to gather all the forensic evidence possible so they would have something concrete to help them confirm what people said they saw.

There is more agreement on the sounds before and during the crash. Many witnesses spoke of hearing a loud noise as the car was going into the tunnel and then, two crashes – the first a minor crash and the second the fatal one that followed. Before the real impact Benoit said he heard 'the squeal of tyres and then a minor crash'. This leaves open two questions – did the car brake and, then, what was this minor crash?

An hour after the Mercedes crashed, the scene in the Alma Tunnel was eerie. The lights of the emergency vehicles kept on rotating. Red and amber lights going round and round. One ambulance's oxygen supply made a strange noise. One man was talking frantically on his mobile. Fragments of the Mercedes were strewn all over the place. Dodi was lying on the road; he was pronounced dead at 1.20. Firemen were lifting the roof off the car to allow Trevor Rees-Jones to be cut out of the car. His injuries were horrific.

Within thirty minutes, news of the crash was being reported. We talked to one of the first journalists who was summoned to the scene. Radio France Internationale always has a journalist on call. That night it was a small, rather attractive woman called Anne Corpet. 'I was a little drunk as I was coming back from a dinner party with my husband. I was not that pleased when my editor rang me to say there had been an accident at the Alma Tunnel.' It was not her kind of story at all. 'I wanted to go home to sleep.' She wouldn't get to bed for another twelve hours.

Anne got to the Alma Tunnel by 1.45am. 'The tunnel was already closed by the police and the dead had been taken away. We were not allowed inside. But we waited as we wanted to see the car.'

There were fewer journalists than one might expect. She reckoned there were about ten French journalists present. 'I saw a colleague from France Inter with a great green shirt. He had also come from a dinner, I think. There were foreign journalists too.' She was not the only member of the press to arrive unprepared. 'Many of them had forgotten their notebooks.' A few were also a little the worse for drink.

The press on the spot did not want to blame the paparazzi, she said. 'We didn't believe that they stuck so close to the car as to cause the accident. So later we were very willing to think it was Henri Paul's fault,' she admitted, 'for reasons of professional solidarity.' The event felt 'utterly irrational', Anne added. A star like Diana couldn't just die in a road crash. 'We knew there had to be guilty parties.'

The press had to wait behind the barriers the police had set up by 1.15. 'We couldn't interview anyone on the spot and no one had actually seen the accident. We saw the police working. There was someone very high up in the tunnel. But the police would not speak to us. We could not get any information from them. They were tense, they were annoyed, the death of someone so famous in the tunnel bothered them. It was obviously something that was going to be hard for them to handle.'

Anne searched for eyewitnesses and, eventually, 'I found the owner of a restaurant who had heard something and so we did a little bit with him.'

As none of the press managed to talk to the police, they did not notice one curious fact. It is routine to get forensic specialists to carry out an initial examination of the car at the scene. But the three Paris detectives who specialised in car crashes were not available that night. Someone then made the decision to remove the Mercedes from the scene of the accident very quickly.

There is no doubt both the beat officers and the senior police were very tense. While in detention, the photographers were told they would be prosecuted if they said anything about what happened that night. Two of their lawyers – William Bourdon and Virginie Bardet – later confirmed that and both were outraged their clients had been treated like common criminals. Jean Ker, a *Paris-Match* investigator, whose son David had fled the scene and was one of those arrested later, explained to me how distressing the experience had been. One of France's most distinguished war photographers, Patrick Chauvel, who knows many of the paparazzi well, said that one of them had never really recovered his composure after these events but refused to name him. Radio reporter Anne Corbet said that many of the photographers still feel 'traumatised' by what happened that night.

Eyewitness testimony and the log

One of the routines of road-accident investigations is to search the vehicles involved and keep a record of the property found on the dead and injured. During the making of our two films, we had access to the twenty-seven volumes of evidence which the French inquiry under Herve Stephan gathered. These documents include the detailed report of what was found on the bodies and at the site of the crash.

The most startling find on Henri Paul's body was a relatively large sum of money – 12,560 French francs, about £1,400. It is worth looking at this relatively large cash sum in the context of Henri Paul's secret-service connections. For ex-MI6 man Richard Tomlinson the money suggested Henri Paul had just come from a meeting with one of his security handlers. 'The amount is quite typical of what would be paid to someone who is providing information,' Tomlinson told me. Al Fayed asked me, rather rhetorically, where would someone like Henri Paul get that kind of money.

On Princess Diana they found a bracelet with six rows of white pearls, a gold watch with white stones and a gold ring. When she was taken out of the car, Diana was wearing only one of her gold earrings. It shows how poorly the car was searched at the scene that it would be weeks before the other earring was found. It wasn't somewhere odd; it was just under the car's dashboard.

What the documents reveal about Dodi is more surprising, especially given that he had been seen taking a call on his mobile phone ninety minutes before he died. Dodi was sometimes described as being 'permanently glued to his mobile phone'. Dodi had 1,000 French francs on his body (about £105) but absolutely nothing else. No papers. No wallet, not even a cigarette lighter, and certainly no mobile phone, was found on him.

When I put the matter of the missing mobile to Mohamed Al Fayed, he dismissed it as not remotely significant. He waved his arms dramatically. One of the photographers must have stolen it, he insisted. He named Romuald Rat as probably the guilty person. It is a very serious allegation. Rat would have had to steal the mobile phone from a dying man between 12.26

and 12.28 at the latest. By then, Dr Mailliez and
Dominique Dalby were attending to the injured in the
car. Rat has always denied this allegation. Bizarrely,
when I repeated the story of the missing mobile in the
revised version of my film, Al Fayed's spokesman,
Chester Stern, said they now had the mobile phone.
He told me it had been recovered between 2002 and
2003. But he would not explain how, or what messages
were on it.

Removing the car

The bodies of Henri Paul and Dodi Al Fayed were
quickly moved to a morgue at around 1.20. Princess
Diana was in the ambulance before 1.15 though it has
proved very hard to pin down the time when she was
finally extricated from the Mercedes. At around 2.10
Trevor Rees-Jones was finally freed and rushed to
hospital.

Very soon after, mechanics arrived and started to fix
grappling irons on to the Mercedes. Then, the car was
lifted on to the kind of truck that is used to remove
vehicles which have been clamped. 'It was removed at
about three in the morning,' Anne Corpet of Radio
France Internationale said. 'We were very struck when
we finally saw it being taken away. The Mercedes was
crushed at the front. We said to each other it was in
such a state we realised there were likely to be deaths.'
She saw the car with the roof off, of course.

Hundreds of tourists came into the square at the top
of the Alma Tunnel. The cafés stayed open later than

usual. The truck sped away from the searchlights but the crowds still hung around.

Many investigations

It is impossible to understand what happened over the next few months without having a sense of the complexities of the French police and judicial systems. Two national police organisations report to different ministers. In Britain it is simpler, as all police forces report to the Home Secretary, as does MI5, which is responsible for internal security.

The most visible police in France are the gendarmes. But these men and women are not local bobbies with *kepis* instead of helmets. The *kepis* are military caps. The gendarmes are, essentially, police officers who belong to the military and who report to the Ministry of Defence.

The traffic police in Paris are part of the gendarmerie but they are a group with a special sense of their own identity and their own discontents. According to the war photographer Patrick Chauvel, who made a film about them in 2000, they often feel isolated. Many complain of the stress as, day in day out, they see, handle and photograph corpses. Chauvel told me he was struck by how ghoulish the pictures they took were. For him, it showed how the job had hardened them.

The elite squads of the French police are supervised, however, not by the Ministry of Defence but by the Ministry of the Interior. One squad is the police judiciaire, whose priorities include the rather charming 'central offices for the repression of banditry'. Georges Simenon's great fictional detective Maigret was one of the chief inspectors of the police judiciaire. The adjective *judiciaire* reflects the fact that these officers are part of the judicial process.

There are some 7,400 officers of the police judiciaire outside Paris and around 3,400 in Paris. The police judiciaire also run some of the support services a modern police force needs including the management of the five forensic laboratories in Paris, Lille, Lyon, Marseilles and Toulouse. All the forensic work done after the crash came under the police judiciaire.

Within the police judiciaire, the *brigade criminelle* is the squad responsible for investigating serious crime. Martine Monteil was head of the *brigade*, the first woman to be appointed to such a high-profile police job.

The French internal security agencies are the *Directoire de la Securité du Territoire* and the *Direction Centrale de la Police Judiciaire*. In French history, the Directoire was the name given at the time of the French Revolution to those who controlled Paris, often by using informers. Like MI5, which was set up by the Metropolitan Police to deal with Irish terrorism in the 19th century, the DST focuses on internal security.

But there is another force which does not report either to the Minister of the Interior or to the Minister of Defence. The *Renseignements-Généraux* is perhaps the most curious agency of the French security services. Set up by de Gaulle after the war because he wanted to make sure he knew what the French people were thinking, the agency is a mix of the French equivalent of Oxbridge elite and MI5 types and it employs about 1,500 officers. Most of them have excellent academic records. They carry out investigations and write what are in effect position papers – they are called *papiers blancs* – which do not just report investigations but offer speculations. These are seen by the Prime Minister. No one ever admitted that the Renseignements mounted its own investigation into the crash. As we shall see, when I interviewed one of their officers later, I discovered it did investigate and had its own suspicions.

With so many different institutions involved in one of the most high-profile investigations ever in France, there were bound to be turf wars. One person was supposed to prevent these by controlling all aspects of the inquiry.

The investigating magistrate

The Minister of the Interior Jean-Pierre Chevenement appointed investigating magistrate Herve Stephan to head the investigation. He is called the *juge d'instruction*. Herve Stephan was not summoned to the tunnel that night, however, as he was not the 'emergency' investigating magistrate on duty. That was Marie-Christine Devidal. But the French government clearly felt that this event needed to be handled by someone who had more than judicial experience. Herve Stephan had dealt with at least one sensitive high-profile case earlier in his career. In 1997 he was sent to Syria by Jacques Chirac who was at the time Prime Minister while François Mitterand was President. Stephan's mission was to investigate whether a body was that of Georges Haddad, a well-known terrorist leader. Stephan went after Chirac agreed with President Assad of Syria that the French could have access to the police files and could search a particular address in Damascus. Stephan was not a typical *juge*, in other words, but a man who had been trusted to deal with highly confidential state business on the direct orders of the French Prime Minister. By August 1997, that Prime Minister was the President of France.

Although Marie-Christine Devidal remained involved in the inquiry, Herve Stephan became, in fact, the magistrate in charge of the investigation. In that role he directed what the police judiciaire should follow and what they should ignore. It has never been clear the extent to which Herve Stephan and Marie-Christine Devidal did control both the official and semi-official investigations. Four different investigations were set up that night. First, there was a perfectly routine traffic-police investigation into a fatal crash. This was part of the gendarmerie's job. Second, Madame Monteil, the head of the *brigade criminelle*, began an investigation. This treated the event as a possible assassination attempt. In theory the investigating magistrate directed both these inquiries. Third, there was an investigation by the *Directoire de la Securité du Territoire*, the French equivalent of MI5. Normally, the investigating magistrate would not be responsible for that or even know much about it. But, given Stephan's background, it is likely he had more than usual links with France's security services. Finally, there was the separate *Renseignements-Généraux* investigation.

Usually a *juge d'instruction* reports to the *procureur* or public prosecutor of the area in which he works. There is no doubt that Stephan did report to the French Attorney General. One of my police contacts said however that this was not the only supervision of Stephan. I was told that the Ministry of the Interior appointed someone to review his inquiry constantly.

But the French investigations were not the only ones. Princess Diana's mobile phone calls had been monitored at least since the Squidgygate affair when she complained to her friend James Gilbey about the royal firm and he offered Squidgy lots of hugs. A radio ham had 'happened' on that exchange which always seemed odd and a little too lucky. Anthony Holden said he was sure British security services eavesdropped on her.

After the crash, British and American security services seem to have started some form of inquiry of their own. The evidence for this is that one of the French forensic experts, François Nibodeau, claimed he had been hampered by what he called 'parallel inquiries'. Neither the British nor the American government has ever admitted there were such operations.

The mourning parties

At 1.10 Mohamed Al Fayed took a second call from a member of the British Embassy. He was told his son was very badly injured and that he might die soon. He was still waiting for his helicopter.

One of the key Harrods personnel who was alerted was John Macnamara. He had joined Harrods as head of security after twenty-six years at Scotland Yard where he reached the rank of Chief Superintendent. He had worked on many major murder and fraud investigations. Macnamara is not in awe of Mohamed who is often called 'The Chairman' at Harrods. On more than one occasion when I saw the two of them together, he interrupted Al Fayed to correct him or to provide additional information. Macnamara would inevitably compare how Scotland Yard would have investigated as opposed to the French.

'The first I knew of this was shortly after midnight when I learned that Dodi was dead,' Macnamara told me in the Harrods boardroom. 'Events took a life of their own overnight. The following morning I came to Harrods to arrange for the return of Dodi's body and we believed it was a tragic road accident.'

Macnamara was unhappy about one fact. The Mercedes should not have left the Ritz without a back-up vehicle. This went quite against the rules that he had set up, rules which were modelled on the procedures of the Royal Protection squad.

At 2am the British ambassador rang Sir Robin Janvrin, then Deputy Private Secretary to the Queen. Sir Robin rang Prince Charles at Balmoral. Charles told the Queen at once but he decided not to wake his children. At the time the news was only that Diana had been hurt.

At 3.45 Mohamed Al Fayed landed at Le Bourget airport. By then, he knew his son was dead and in the morgue. Diana was still alive so he made for the Salpêtrière Hospital. Everyone who saw Al Fayed at the hospital was struck by how dignified he was. 'He had the dignity of a great lord,' one witness said. Al Fayed talked to the British ambassador. There is much dispute about whether a nurse told him the last words Diana spoke, which were alleged to have been 'tell my sister to look after the children'. But Al Fayed certainly did not see Diana's body. He was not a member of her family and, of course, he was in the middle of dealing with one of the greatest calamities a man can have to bear, the death of his child.

Sweeping the tunnel

It would have been sensible and, indeed, normal procedure to close the tunnel until all the forensic evidence was gathered.

Roughly an hour after the Mercedes was removed from the Alma, however, Paris police allowed the Propreté de Paris, the green vehicles which sweep and spray the streets with industrial solvent, to go inside. As a result, the Mercedes was hardly studied at the crash scene. Two hours is not enough time to examine and swab in detail the wall of the tunnel to make sure all fragments, traces of paint and other clues have been accounted for. We shall see that this haste makes it impossible to be sure the police collected all the evidence that might help explain the crash, including traces that could reveal when the Mercedes started to brake. This was one reason it took so long to establish a coherent account of the sequence of events in the tunnel.

The sequence of events, it would eventually be established, was that the Mercedes had first hurtled into the right-hand wall of the tunnel and, then, had been swung into the pillar. Having hit the pillar, it bounced back into the middle of the tunnel. It took seventeen days, however, for the police to even raise the question of why the Mercedes had hurtled into the right-hand wall.

By around 4.30am the tunnel was re-opened to traffic. For John Macnamara that was shocking. 'The first thing you do in any major incident so that you can get the best possible evidence is to make sure that the evidence is not contaminated.' He compared the way the train crash at Potters Bar had been handled. 'There they were searching the wreckage and the whole area was closed for a week. Four hours is ridiculous. Tourists were walking all over it.' I asked how long it would be normal to close the scene of a major incident. Macnamara simply replied, 'There is no limit on time.'

I pressed him and asked him to suppose that this had happened at the Piccadilly underpass, how long would that be shut? Till all the possible evidence had been searched for and officers were sure there was nothing else to find, he said.

I asked Macnamara whether opening the tunnel so quickly would suggest the police had something to hide. 'I think one could be forgiven for coming to the conclusion that they wanted to destroy some evidence. It may be incompetence or it may be both. It was total confusion and disarray.'

Macnamara is not the only person who was amazed by the fact that the tunnel was re-opened. At 7 o'clock in the morning Christopher Dickey, chief of the Paris bureau of *Newsweek*, went down into the tunnel. 'I expected that it would be closed,' he said. But he wanted to catch the atmosphere. 'I was surprised to find the tunnel was open to traffic. This was Diana. She was dead. This was a huge thing.'

If you calculate the time devoted to searching for evidence in the tunnel, you come to a remarkable conclusion. Until 2.10 Trevor Rees-Jones was being cut out of the car and getting emergency medical attention on the spot. That made it very difficult for meticulous searching of the site to take place. News footage shows that it took some skill to fix the grappling irons on to the vehicle but this was completed by around 3am. The tunnel was re-opened between sixty and ninety minutes later. In other words, the French police spent under ninety minutes searching for forensic evidence. By 2.30 there were news teams filming anything that happened. They got excellent images of the mechanics at work but, while I have watched all the available news footage, I have come across no images of police doing an inch-by-inch search of the site, the kind of search one might have expected.

One final bizarre fact would later emerge. An off-duty policeman joined in the search just to help. He found fragments of a red tail-light. They had been piled up near one end of the tunnel. Nothing more would be heard of this potentially important lead for seventeen days.

When Macnamara told Mohamed Al Fayed of his concerns, they took a decision which would have unforeseen consequences. They decided to hire private detectives to carry out their own investigation. This was led by an ex-head of the *brigade criminelle*, Pierre

Ottavioli. At the age of seventy-six Ottavioli was not as energetic as he once had been but he had on his team Michel Kerbois. Kerbois is a big man in his fifties and proved to be an effective investigator. Both men had a good sense of the political pressure the police and the investigating magistrate would be under. They advised Al Fayed that he must not seem to be launching a parallel investigation because the French authorities would get very angry. The French had every reason to be defensive. Pieces of the Mercedes with the correct serial numbers are now being offered for sale as memorabilia. They had really not protected the 'integrity of the scene' properly.

3

The Saga of the Missing Witnesses

By 6am on August 31st only one of the four people who had been in the Mercedes was still alive: Trevor Rees-Jones. He was unconscious at the Salpêtrière. Rees-Jones did eventually recover but he said that he had lost all memory of what had happened after the car left the Ritz. It is not unusual for victims of trauma to develop post-traumatic amnesia. According to research, however, 70 per cent of victims regain some of these memories. Trevor Rees-Jones has always been adamant that he remembers nothing. His amnesia made it even more important for the police to gather every scrap of eye-witness testimony.

Just as the police failed to do some basic forensic work, they failed to interview everyone who was a potential witness at the scene. A number of witnesses left the scene without even giving their names and addresses. One was a cleaner for a photographic agency who did not have residence papers. Within twenty-four hours, more people would discover that the Paris police were neither as busy nor as keen as one might expect.

The experience of the people from Harrods

John Macnamara, had arranged the return of Dodi's body, and he was buried on Monday September 1st in Brookwood cemetery in Surrey. Macnamara was in Paris by the next day. 'First of all I imagined the police would come to the Ritz Hotel and retrace everything that had happened.' The police would also want, he supposed, to secure as much evidence as they could; but they did not come to the Ritz Hotel for over a week. 'We had done everything anticipating the French police would come. We secured the bar receipts,' he told me. These receipts would make it possible to prove what Henri Paul had had to drink. Macnamara said there were instructions given to the staff not to talk to anyone, other than the police, about the crash.

'Over a week went by and nothing happened. I contacted Madame Monteil. Head of bodyguards Paul Handley Greaves, Kez Wingfield and I were then invited to police HQ. They were very polite,' Macnamara admits. But 'I was left waiting two and half hours in a corridor. Paul Handley Greaves was left between prisoners shackled in chains. That was his experience of the Paris police.' The others did not fare any better. 'Kez Wingfield, who was one of the last people to be with Henri Paul, spent five hours in the police station and he did give a statement. But in the full report that the judge made that statement amounted to less than half a page. To this day I have not been seen by the French police,' Macnamara added.

Macnamara continues: 'It did not seem to me that

they had done the diligent enquiries one might have expected.' Over the course of an hour he listed to me a series of astonishing omissions. Many of them were simple. 'There were unidentified people outside the Ritz. We gave them pictures of these people but there was never an inquiry to discover who these people were.'

In the previous chapter, I outlined many inconsistencies in the eyewitness evidence gathered at the spot. But it has become clear many witnesses were not properly interviewed. Some did not want to be, like Ker and Chassery who left the scene before talking to the police. The police also did not interview Gary Hunter, a partner with Hepburns, a London firm of solicitors. Hunter heard the crash at 12.25 and raced to his hotel window. He said he saw a car turning from the tunnel exit and roaring down the rue Jean Goujon. He claimed it could have been a Fiat Uno or a Renault but that it was dark. Two other women were not tracked down by the police – Brenda Wells who claimed to have seen the exit before the Alma Tunnel was blocked and a woman who worked as a cleaner for the photo agency CAPA. She refused ever to say what she had seen because she felt it would only cause her trouble.

There were also a number of potential witnesses who were *sans papiers*, illegal residents in Paris like the cleaner from the photographic agency. The police did not manage to track many of them down.

When I first started to work with Francis Gillery, I didn't realise that he had a slight obsessive streak. I started to understand this properly when he explained to me how he spent hours trawling through French television coverage of fires in the Paris area. He had only one objective. On one of these news reports which went out between September and October 1997, Francis said he would find a senior police official who was being interviewed with the French Minister of the Interior, Jean-Pierre Chevenement. One of the key missing witnesses claimed that he had been threatened by a senior police officer.

The key missing witness is Erik Petel. He was twenty-six years old at the time of the crash. Petel had just finished working his shift in a restaurant near the Bastille. He was riding home on the new motorbike he had bought three weeks earlier.

Nothing caught his attention as he passed the Concorde. Though it was Saturday night there was not a lot of traffic. Petel drove towards the Alma Tunnel. As he did so, he was overtaken by the Mercedes. The car was going fast but there were no paparazzi around it. He is adamant he was not overtaken by any other car or motorbikes. What Petel did notice was that there were *appel de phares,* flashing headlights, from inside the tunnel. Usually French cars blink to warn other cars. There was known to be a speed camera at the entrance of the tunnel and, clearly, the Mercedes was doing more than the permitted 50 kilometres per hour.

'I started to go down the curve,' Petel said. There is a gentle incline, which bends to the left as you drive into the tunnel the way the Mercedes was going. 'And then I heard an implosion. I thought my exhaust was the trouble,' Petel explained.

Petel was distracted by the noise that, to this day, he still describes as an 'implosion'. Because his immediate reaction was that something had gone wrong with his new bike, he looked down at his instruments to see what that might be. I think this reaction is very interesting because it suggests a mechanical noise coming from within a vehicle. It's a point I will return to in the penultimate chapter. A few seconds later – and he can't be precise about how many seconds – there was a deafeningly loud noise. The Mercedes had crashed.

Even many of those outside the tunnel have commented on how loud the bang of the crash was. Even now Petel is almost awed by the sheer volume. 'The noise comes from in front, from behind, the noise is so loud so you didn't know where it was coming from.' Once the car hit the pillar, the horn of the Mercedes started to blare.

Petel braked and, as he neared the thirteenth pillar, he saw the Mercedes was still moving. The wreck was slowly turning into its final position. Its headlights faced him. Petel stopped, parked his bike by the wall of the tunnel and got off. He told us he could not be sure whether or not the wreck stopped other vehicles squeezing past it and continuing through the tunnel.

There was smoke coming out of the Mercedes. Petel insists he was first on the scene and made for the Mercedes and tried to open the front door. It would not budge. He saw some movement in the car. So, then, he tried the back door. He described clearly what he did next. 'I get hold of the person in the back. She had fallen against the back of the passenger seat in front and was bent over. I started to move her back. At that moment, her head flopped back.' When we interviewed him, Petel threw his head back to demonstrate how her head flopped back. 'I see blood coming out of her ear and blood coming out of her nose. And then,' he pauses and the French expression he uses is strange. He said '*c'est marrant*' . . . *marrant* means funny, weird. It is not a word you use around tragedies usually. 'I know this person I realised,' he said.

Though there are some differences in the way that eyewitnesses described the position Diana was in in the Mercedes, one piece of evidence backs up Petel's account. Romuald Rat said he went to the back door of the car after he had taken some pictures. He said that Diana's 'head was leaning slightly back'. This is exactly the position Petel himself demonstrated had happened. The police should have been able to compare these two statements on the night, statements which would suggest Petel was a very credible witness.

Petel's first reaction was simple. He had to summon help. He was unable to say how long he spent looking inside the car. The noise of the crash had been disorienting; the horn was still blaring. If Petel had been miraculously calm, he might have worked out it would be more logical to find someone who had a mobile and get them to ring the police. But he was very upset by what he was seeing. Petel insists he just did not think of that. He did not notice anyone near him.

Among the photographs taken at the scene, there is a picture of a man by the car. I have not managed to see that picture but it seems likely it was of Petel. The point is important because some conspiracy theories have made much of this picture – taken by Arnal as he neared the car thirty seconds later – and speculate that it was of some sinister secret agent.

In some shock, Petel got back on his motorbike. He manoeuvred it out of the tunnel going the wrong way, back on to the Place de l'Alma. He headed for a nearby phone box, got off and rang the emergency services. We shall see there was a comedy of errors around his call. 'I was very distraught,' Petel admits. But he did not expect the reaction he got from the emergency operator. His plan was to alert the police and, then, get home once he was sure an ambulance was on its way. But the operator, he felt, did not take him seriously, especially when he mentioned Diana had been injured.

So Petel decided to go in person to the nearest police station. He knew the area well as he had lived there and 'I made for the commissariat at Avenue Mozart.'

At the police station, Petel again did not get the response he anticipated. 'I explained what had happened to the duty officer but he did not react. I said you have to get the emergency services, people are injured, do something.' Instead, he was treated like an idiot. Perhaps the reason is simple. In Paris on Saturday night, like in other big cities all over the world, the police are used to drunks and crazies causing a nuisance. Claiming Diana, Princess of Wales was lying injured in a Paris tunnel seemed like a hoax. Not getting proper attention from the duty officer made Petel angry. He felt desperate because it was so urgent to get them to listen.

What Petel did next was not cool or sensible. 'So to get their attention I dropped a pile of folders. And his reflex is to get others to try to calm me. But the more they tried to calm me the more upset I got.'

The police eventually lost patience, overpowered Petel and put him in handcuffs. 'Then, they put me in an office to wait for other officers.' He admits it is hard for him to be accurate about how long he waited. Perhaps thirty minutes to forty-five minutes. Then, something very strange happened.

Policemen came to get Petel and told him he had to be questioned at Paris police headquarters. He got scared. He had been in trouble with the police once for fraud when he was a very young man. He insisted he did not want to leave his bike behind. If they were going to police HQ, he would ride there himself. Remarkably, Petel was allowed to do that. This was surely bizarre if he was in such a hysterical state he had to be handcuffed. But then the whole incident was not being handled all that logically.

So, around 2am, Erik Petel got back on his motor-bike and drove under escort through the streets. 'I had a police car in front, a police car behind and two motor-cycle riders. By now I was very worried because I thought they were going to make me carry the can for the crash.'

As he rode through the night under escort, Petel thought he was going to be framed – precisely because he had one offence against him. 'I would have escaped if I could have. The thought went through my head.'

'When we arrived, we were expected,' Petel said. They had come to the Quai de L'Horloge. It is a build-ing the public are rarely admitted into. The fact that Petel could describe the inside accurately would even-tually matter. 'They took me by the arms and we went to the first floor . . . it might be the second floor,' he added. He stresses no one was physically brutal to him.

Petel smokes heavily and he was upset to find he

was not allowed to smoke while he was waiting. Finally – and, again, he couldn't be sure if it was fifteen minutes or thirty minutes – an inspector came to talk to him. The officer took down his statement and then left. Then, a second inspector came to talk to Petel. The police seemed to be disturbed by his talk of an implosion.

'They insisted on the first noise. They said it couldn't have happened like that.' It was not that the police were trying to impose a theory of their own, but they rejected his talk of the first noise, the implosion, as impossible. 'They talked to me as if I just had not been there,' Petel said. Though he was shaken, Petel stuck to his story about the noise, the implosion, and stressed that no paparazzi were behind the car. What happened later suggests powerfully this was not a version the police wanted to hear.

Then, more inspectors arrived and Petel again gave a statement. Now something happened that still disturbs him.

'The door was open behind me,' he said, 'and a senior official came and he said it would be best if I did not make myself known. He only issued this threat. I didn't know then who he was.' But the officer's tone was such that Petel felt he had been warned off. Petel turned to see who the man was but he did not recognise him.

Petel had reason though to feel grateful to this senior officer because, almost immediately, 'he gave the order that I should be set free. I did not wait to quibble. I was out of there.' It was now close to 6am. Though Petel felt he had been threatened, 'I did not want to see this official ever again.'

After he left the police station, Petel went home. He was exhausted. But he rang his father. His father is a businessman who lives abroad and he was worried for his son. At once, Petel senior contacted his lawyer, Antoine Desguines. Desguines is a tall, rather sardonic man. He was on holiday and he did not want to hare back to Paris. But he realised this was an important business and he did so.

'I obeyed the officer,' Petel added. That would have been the end of the matter but some weeks later, Petel was watching the news and he saw a story about a policeman who was burned in a fire. Senior officials were explaining what had happened and paying tribute to the courage of the police. One of the men was the French Minister of the Interior but there was another man. 'I recognised the man, then,' Petel said. It was the senior official who had told him not to make himself known. Petel would only add that he now realised the official held a position to which he must have been appointed by the President of the Republic. It was the mystery of this man's identity that Francis was trying to solve by screening all the TV reports of fires towards the end of 1997. He found one report.

In November 1997 a Paris policeman was killed in a fire. The Minister of the Interior was interviewed, praising the courage of the police. By his side stood the Préfet of the Paris police, Philippe Massoni. We concluded from this that it was Massoni Petel had seen. We were not allowed to run this allegation in the French film but it was reported by a northern paper, *La Voix du Nord* when they previewed the film.

When we made *Diana – The Night She Died*, we

included the allegation in our final cut. Paul Chinnery, the lawyer for Channel 5, insisted I write to Massoni to ask for his comments. I did so having got his private fax number at the Élysées Palace, the office of the French President. Massoni did not respond to my fax. We had recorded a line of commentary which said Massoni 'refused' to respond. Paul Chinnery wanted to change the verb to 'decline' because he reckoned we then would have a good defence. Unfortunately the narration for the film had already been recorded by Charlie Stayt. Charlie had gone on holiday and we could not get hold of him to change that one word. So we cut this 10-second section from the film. But we repeated the film, having updated it, in November 2003. This time, we changed the commentary. Philippe Massoni declined to comment on the allegation I made.

On August 31st

That night French journalists were told by the police to ignore Petel and anything he might have to say. He was a junkie, he had a long criminal record. We filmed journalists at the Credo news agency, which supplies material to *Paris-Match*. They said police HQ kept repeating Petel was not to be believed.

After the French film went out, the journalists from Credo complained. They had no idea they were being filmed. They did not care, it seems, to publicise the fact that they were so dependent on police sources. The only problem they had was we had not been film-ing secretly. We were able to show footage in which they refer to the camera. When La Cinquième TV channel repeated the film in 2003, they kept this sequence.

Maître Antoine Desguines, the lawyer, was impressed by Petel. From the outset, 'I believed what Mr Petel told me and I saw no reason why his evidence should not be taken into account.'

By suppressing Petel's evidence, the French authorities were able to blame the photographers in the immediate aftermath of the crash. They were also able to muzzle them and seize their negatives. Everyone has assumed that this was all done on grounds of good taste. The paparazzi would try to sell gory pictures of the last minutes of Diana. Some did, but it's also now clear that the authorities were not prepared to let the photographers off the hook on the Sunday or Monday.

Desguines tried to get the inquiry to see Petel but the magistrate had no interest in doing so. Desguines was particularly concerned for his client because it is normal procedure to take a statement of what is said in a police station. The person who gives the statement is supposed to be given a copy of it but Petel had no copy.

Three days after the crash, Desguines felt he was getting nowhere and he feared for his client so he did something unusual for a lawyer. He decided to go on a media offensive. He contacted Jean Durieux at *Paris-Match*. Durieux is in his early sixties and has immense experience of the French justice system. Though he was given a very coherent account, Durieux did not ask to meet Petel because, he admitted to us, he was wary. 'I don't know . . . if something comes too easily it bothers me.' So Durieux did not run with the story.

Petel's experiences have convinced him that the crash was not an accident. He does not see any other explanation for the way he was treated. Like many of those who feel they were close to the case, Petel has a theory. He believes something happened to the car. For him, it is the noise before the crash and then the noise of the crash. It obsesses Petel.

'Chevenement said they would shed light on this business but no light was ever shed,' Petel pointed out.

Three months after the crash, Desguines was exasperated as he had failed to get either the inquiry or French press interested in what seemed to him a major story. Desguines has good contacts in Lille in northern France and he spoke to the country's main northern paper, *La Voix du Nord*. Finally, he found a journalist, Charles Duzwaski, who was willing to listen. Duzwaski noted that 'Here was a bizarre atmosphere around this saga. At first time I was wary but once I had verified I had no doubts about Petel. But I was writing in a northern paper. It was not my mission to investigate further.' Duzwaski added that he was at a disadvantage because he was working for a regional paper and there was a certain snide attitude in the Paris press. French radio attacked him for running the story. 'I am sure that if a big national paper had brought this out there would have been a different response.' He got the feeling that he was dismissed a little like a country cousin who was out of his depth.

Duzwaski met Petel and his father in Paris, and having talked to them and the lawyer, said 'I found no contradiction.' He also witnessed very personally the impact the story had on the press itself. 'Three days after the crash I was in Calais because we were doing a story on immigration and we were taking pictures. It had nothing to do with Diana and yet we were pilloried as paparazzi.'

Duzwaski understands 'why Petel was careful and afraid he could be hurt by the machine'.

By February 1998, Desguines persuaded Petel to talk to a large-circulation magazine, *Voici*. By now also Jean Durieux of *Paris-Match* had begun to worry that he had not followed up an important lead. 'I and my colleagues did not do our job as well as we might and me especially,' said Durieux. He has excellent contacts with the French police. He started to sniff around. Confirming at least part of the story didn't require that much work.

Durieux shifts in his seat. He is a man who likes to ask out loud the question that he will answer. 'What do I know of Petel? I now know that he did go to the police station. I know that he was interviewed by the *brigade criminelle*. And I know who interviewed him. I know exactly who.'

But Durieux would not tell us who that person was.

Meanwhile Antoine Desguines, Petel's lawyer, kept writing to *Juge* Stephan to insist his client should be seen formally. He was not exactly successful at first. Politely, the magistrate told him that Petel had no status in the affair. He was not accused of any crime. He was not related to any of the people who had died. Desguines was mystified. 'I don't know if there were some diplomatic games being played between Britain and France,' Desguines said. He checked to see if Petel had a criminal record but found only the minor fraud offence in his youth. But Petel was still being denied the right to tell his story.

The articles in *Voici* and *La Voix du Nord* were beginning to have some effect on the investigation. Finally, seven months after the crash, Petel was granted a meeting with *Juge* Stephan. He told his story yet again. According to Petel, his evidence was not challenged. In the final report of the inquiry there is no mention at all of him and of what he had to say. His evidence, if it had been dealt with properly on the night, would have made it very clear that the photographers were not to blame.

It is possible that the French inquiry did not want to drop all charges against the paparazzi because then they would have had no grounds on which to hold on to the photographs. France has a tough system of intellectual-property law under which a photographer has total control over how his material is used. By continuing to treat the photographers as suspects, the authorities could say that this was evidence.

In its final summary, the inquiry accepted that the paparazzi could not have been the cause of the accident because they were so far behind the Mercedes. The inquiry never explained on what evidence it had come to that conclusion. Since 1998 Petel has been less and less willing to talk. 'I had had enough of it by then. I now run a brasserie.' He appeared in *Lady Died* and in *Diana – The Night She Died* only because his lawyer was convinced it was a serious investigation.

Oswestry

David Crawford had worked all his life as a country solicitor in Oswestry. He had acted on a number of occasions for the Rees-Jones family and was a friend; so when Trevor was hurt, he went to see the family. They asked him to represent their son.

I wrote to Crawford when I started to make the British film. He felt free to talk to me because he was no longer instructed by Trevor. Apart from giving one interview when he was publicising his book, Trevor Rees-Jones has never spoken in public about the events of that night.

As soon as Crawford had been instructed by Trevor's parents, he went to Paris. He found that there was a great deal of pressure from Al Fayed for Trevor to appoint a French lawyer who would coordinate with the Al Fayeds' legal team. Al Fayed offered to pay all Trevor's fees but Crawford was worried that if the same legal team represented Trevor as the Al Fayeds, there could be a conflict of interest. Rees-Jones had been hurt in a vehicle rented from a company in which the Al Fayeds had an important stake. Trevor might need to sue that company, Étoile Limousine, for negligence – and that could cause all kinds of problems if his lawyer was part of the Al Fayeds.

Oswestry is on a branch line, a small country railway station. Crawford came to meet me and my cameraman. He drove us to his home where we spent the morning talking through the case. He had become fascinated by the French legal system, Crawford told me. He speaks excellent French and now that he is retired, he specialises in helping English people buy property in France.

Crawford drew up three criteria that the French lawyer would have to meet. He had to speak English, he had to have a reputation as a fighter and he had to have no ties to Al Fayed. He eventually settled on Christian Curtil. Curtil is elegant, amusing and fluent in English and German as well as French. The pressures on the lawyers were ridiculous. 'When the case started, I had journalists climbing on to my balcony at home. I would find myself sitting on a plane next to very attractive women who seemed fascinated by my work,' Curtil laughed. Anything to get the exclusive.

Long before he had appointed a French colleague, Crawford went to visit his client in hospital. Trevor was supposed to have a gendarme to protect him but Crawford told me he did get into Trevor's room. 'I found there was a real battleaxe there and she asked what I was doing there.' He was unceremoniously bundled out. He would soon find out why Trevor had such protection.

Crawford was shown the transcript of an interview *Juge* Stephan conducted with a member of the staff of the Étoile Limousine, the company that rented the Mercedes to the Ritz. This man claimed to have been party to a conversation which had taken place three or four days after the crash. He said that people in that room said that it was vital they 'get Trevor'. Crawford explained to me that he was very surprised to find that the dossier contained evidence of a serious threat to his client. Crawford was so worried he asked the magistrate for permission to interview the witness himself.

This was, Crawford said, 'very irregular'. Under the French system of the *secret d'instruction*, the lawyers of the parties are not allowed to meet witnesses, Crawford explained to me. But he managed to persuade *Juge* Stephan to give him permission to meet the man. Olivier confirmed to Crawford the story he had told the magistrate. Threats had been made against Trevor Rees-Jones. 'It's always possible that the man was a disgruntled employee,' Crawford told me, but he had no reason to suppose that was the case.

What is so extraordinary about Crawford's tale is that an Italian paper carried a brief report of an attempt on Trevor Rees-Jones' life. Two days after he had a successful operation, he was beginning to recover. At 3.15am on September 10th, while he was still very ill in hospital, he began to suffocate and went into a coma. Jacqueline Beaufort, a night nurse at the Salpêtrière, called for a doctor. They managed to revive Trevor Rees-Jones but he had been given three times his usual dose of sedative. The hospital added, according to the story, that Rees-Jones was getting back the use of his hand and could write again.

The Salpêtrière always denied this incident took place but, together with Crawford's other evidence, it is disturbing and it leads to one key question: what had Trevor Rees-Jones seen or heard – or what did people imagine he might have seen or heard – that was potentially so dangerous? As soon as he became conscious, however, Rees-Jones insisted he could remember nothing. He has never spoken of that threat against him. He does not mention it in his book. On October 30th 2003 the thriller writer Patricia Cornwell claimed on ABC Television after a six-month long investigation that Trevor Rees-Jones has been threatened with death if he recalls anything.

The questions remain why were so few witnesses properly interviewed and why was there such a concerted effort to discredit the man who had been the first witness to the crash?

Nearly everyone who has written about the deaths of Diana, Dodi and Henri Paul – and at one time there were 36,000 websites devoted to Diana – is either a passionate conspiracy theorist or a debunker, arguing only paranoids think it was anything other than an accident. There is little middle ground. No one has suggested, for example, that the simple, sober fact that the French authorities carried out an inadequate inquiry has made it harder to discover the truth. The question is why the French investigation had little of the guile and persistence of Maigret.

As we shall see, there were many reasons – and many parties – who preferred to make sure we would not get too much of the truth.

4

The Ambulance That Took
Too Long

At 1am, the director of the Paris hospitals Allan Durveillieux arrived at the Alma Tunnel. He wanted to make sure the injured got the very best medical care. Princess Diana was still in the Mercedes but she had been put on a drip; Henri Paul's body had been laid out on the roadway and covered with a blue plastic sheet. The ambulance crew were giving Dodi frantic heart massage.

Trevor Rees-Jones was still trapped in the front seat of the car. His condition looked far worse than Diana's. His face had been so squashed that his nose did not protrude beyond his lips. He was bleeding badly and, as the ambulance team feared he might have suffered spinal damage, they placed him in a cervical collar. The tunnel was a distressing, bloody scene but not especially gruesome in terms of road accidents. It had finally been cleared of paparazzi and onlookers so the medical teams could perform their jobs and try to save lives.

Dodi was declared dead just before 1.20. All the medical personnel agreed Diana seemed to have the least traumatic injuries. Dr Derossi who was supervising all the crews said her condition was 'severe but not critical'.

From the tunnel, Philippe Massoni, the Prèfet of Police, rang Chevenement, the Minister of the Interior and said there was no need for him to come to the Alma. It would make more sense for him to go straight to the hospital where Diana would be taken, as soon as she was released from the wreck. The Minister took the advice.

Three hours later, Philippe Massoni and Jean-Pierre Chevenement were in the Salpêtrière Hospital, waiting for news of Diana. Suddenly, they were told the surgeons wanted to see them. Chevenement had to apologise to the British ambassador, Sir Michael Jay, because he was clearly not invited. Nurses took the two Frenchmen to a room just by the operating theatre. The surgeons came out of theatre to meet them. Professor Bruce Riou and Professor Alan Pavie were still wearing bloodstained gowns. They looked forlorn. They had done everything possible to save Diana, they said, but they had failed.

Many commentators have tried to piece together the details of the medical treatment Diana received from the moment Dr Mailliez got to the Mercedes and gave her oxygen. It has proved extremely difficult. The French have consistently refused to give information and that, of course, fed conspiracy theories. One was wonderfully wild. According to this scenario, secret-service agents replaced the Paris paramedics and once the spooks got close to Diana, she had no chance. She was injected with an untraceable poison. But there was one hitch with this scenario: no one explained what happened to the real ambulance crew. It was vital, apparently, that Diana should never reach a hospital alive. She was carrying Dodi's child and the powers-that-be could not allow an Al Fayed-Spencer to survive.

Absence of proper information makes it easier for conspiracy theories to flourish. The twenty-seven volumes of evidence gathered by the inquiry say very little about the medical treatment the victims received. Trevor Rees-Jones' lawyer David Crawford was shown a report on the injuries Diana sustained but it consisted of just one page. Virginie Bardet, who represented one of the paparazzi, told us there were more details in a sealed section of the dossier. All the lawyers of the parties in the case could ask for this to be unsealed. 'I did not do so,' Bardet explained, for an honourable reason. She believed that the sealed material related to the question of whether Diana was pregnant or not. Even the one survivor does not seem to have been told too much about the medical treatment at the scene and immediately after. In his *The Bodyguard's Story*, Trevor Rees-Jones devotes no more than three pages to that.

Technically, the French could have explained that so little information about the medical response was given because the only aim of Stephan's 'instruction' was to find out the causes of the accident and decide who to prosecute. But Stephan himself went further. In the inquiry's final summary, he categorically exonerated all the medical personnel of any blame. This summary, circulated to the parties on September 4th 1999, included a somewhat laboured phrase. The medical treatment was, Stephan said, '*exclusif de toute faute par rapport aux règles de la réanimation prehospitalière'*. The literal translation is 'exclusive of all fault in relation to the rules of resuscitation before hospital'. No one could criticise the treatment Diana received before she reached hospital.

Stephan explained how he had come to this conclusion. The injuries Dodi and Henri Paul received were 'frequent in the case of violent trauma, especially'. But since they had died so fast, nothing could have been done to save them. But with Diana it had been different. Difficult to the last, she did not conform to the expectations of French doctors. 'Lady Spencer', as Stephan called her in this part of his report, had suffered 'quite exceptional' wounds. The magistrate added 'these could be explained possibly by the lateral position of the victim at the moment of the shock'. If Diana were lying down when the Mercedes hit the thirteenth pillar, that would make it too hard for French doctors, alas.

The more I have thought about this the stranger it seems. Witnesses did find Diana lying down, partly on the floor, after the car hit the pillar. That does not, of course, prove she was lying down when the Mercedes entered the tunnel or when it crashed. Further, as we shall see, some crucial evidence I have found suggests she wasn't lying down at all when the Mercedes drove into the tunnel.

I am not the first person to raise questions about how the French medical services performed. When we filmed *Lady Died*, we asked two American journalists, Scott MacLeod and Thomas Sancton, to give us interviews. They had covered the crash for *Time* magazine and had criticised the medical procedures used. They had found three eminent American casualty surgeons – Dr Ochsner of the Alto New Clinic in New Orleans, Dr Wasserman of Columbia University and Dr Philip Brewer of Yale University – who were all willing to comment, and in their subsequent book *Death of a Princess: The Investigation* (Sancton and Macleod), they were harsh; each claimed Diana could have been saved if she had had the same injuries in the USA. The French were wedded to ancient A&E techniques. I expected MacLeod and Sancton would be happy to give us an interview for the film but they refused. They explained they had had too much trouble already due to the fact that they had dared criticise French medicine.

The French Minister of Health at the time, Bernard Kouchner, had founded the international charity, Médecins Sans Frontières. He was anything but a bureaucrat but he attacked Sancton and MacLeod bitterly. He saw their work as an outrageous slur on the competence of French medicine. Sancton and MacLeod were even accused of promoting American health business interests. Their task was to destroy the good name of Paris ambulance crews and doctors so that none of them would dare pick up a scalpel; then, Yankee salesmen would flood in and would insist that the only way French emergency medicine could redeem its reputation was to buy the latest American equipment by the ton.

In such an emotional atmosphere, it was easy to forget that the issue was one of philosophy as well as competence. American emergency medicine practice changed dramatically in the 1980s and 90s. It became routine in cities like Baltimore to 'scoop and rush', scoop the victim up and rush him or her, to hospital as soon as possible. Much American research showed that if you could get victims of accidents to a hospital within fifteen minutes their chances of survival increased significantly. (Berriff, P, 1997).

In France there had not been such a change. The policy was to give patients as much help as possible at the scene of an accident, to stabilise the victims and, only then, to move them to hospital. It has been argued that this works especially well with certain kinds of injuries like fractures. The latest SAMU ambulances are better equipped than most British and American ambulances. The French ambulance service also employs doctors who regularly go out to accidents. They are called specialists in resuscitation. But a SAMU vehicle does not have an X-ray machine and a heart-lung machine. Perhaps if Diana had been X-rayed quickly, it would have been obvious it was vital to rush her to hospital.

Dr Frederic Mailliez

The first doctor to arrive at the scene, Dr Mailliez gave a detailed account of the minutes after the crash to the *Quotidien du Médecin*, the daily paper for France's doctors. He also told CNN the next day that Diana 'looked pretty fine. I thought this woman had a chance and that she was able to breathe.'

The first task was to get Diana out of the car. Petel, Rat and Dorzee had all been able to touch her. By removing the driver's seat once Henri Paul had been laid out in the tunnel, it should have been possible to lift her out. It is never easy to be sure how long it should take to extract a person. There was panic and confusion. Removing Diana from the position she was in is what is called a 'partial extrication'. Dr Vic Calland, one of Britain's leading experts on road-accident medicine, estimates that if the crews were working well it should have been twenty-five minutes. It certainly should not have taken more than forty minutes to prise her loose.

By 12.45 there were four SAMU vehicles at the scene. 'I suspect that the dispatcher (the central controller) discovered at least one person was dead and another person was dying so the fourth ambulance was sent away,' Dr Calland told me.

The Central Paris dispatcher had sent an ambulance with an expert in emergency medicine to the Alma Tunnel. Dr Jean-Marc Martino was used to critical situations like this. He arrived at the tunnel around 12.45 and recognised Diana. Dr Martino realised at once that only Trevor and Diana had any chance. 'She was agitated and crying out, and did not appear to understand what I was saying to reassure her. I asked my crew to take care of the front-seat passenger, who seemed the more seriously injured of the two survivors, while calling for back-up from the SAMU to allow me to take charge of the second victim.'

One of the fire engines sent to the scene also carried a doctor who took charge of Trevor Rees-Jones so Dr Martino could concentrate on the Princess. 'She was still agitated, moving her left arm and right leg, and speaking incoherently and in a confused way. Her right arm was bent behind her – dislocated. With my team I examined her and put her on a drip to allow us to release her from the wreck. She was locked in a medically abnormal position between the back of the front passenger seat and the rear seat. We extracted her with difficulty and taking all the necessary precautions, with the aid of the firemen.'

Dr Martino never confirmed exactly the wounds that Diana suffered but Dr Mailliez did describe these in some detail. He found Diana had a three-centimetre cut on her forehead and that her right arm was fractured. He also reported that Diana's buttock was injured. But Dr Mailliez could not see, of course, whether she had any internal injuries and nor could Dr Martino.

Victims of road accidents are often in a state of shock. The photographer Romuald Rat had said Diana called out for help. The police said later that the Princess had been so upset by one of the photographers she said 'Oh God, oh God' and 'Leave me alone'. Another witness, Arnal, heard her say something similar. Dr Martino, however, said she was babbling incoherently. Dr Derossi, who was in charge of SAMU at the scene, agreed; she was talking but it made no sense.

Diana does seem to have lost consciousness while she was still in the car. The French authorities eventually said that after Diana was pulled out of the car, she was in a class 1 coma, the least profound kind of coma. This is a peculiar state where a patient's sleep and wake rhythms function normally so there is every hope a patient will recover consciousness soon.

Dr Martino insisted everything was done according to the usual procedures. 'Despite this, as this was being done, she suffered a cardiac arrest and I had to intubate her, ventilate her and use CPR to revive her. I got her into my ambulance to carry out a more thorough examination, and to continue her reanimation. She was in a serious condition.' But the ambulance did not carry the equipment needed to find out whether she had internal injuries and how extensive these might be – an X-ray machine.

In the last chapter, we saw the fragility of eyewitness evidence. That is again apparent when one contrasts the account of Dr Martino with that of his ambulance attendant Michel Massebeuf who told the authorities: 'When we arrived the SAMU doctor immediately started treating the princess, while she was in the car. That's when she was put on a drip. The firemen extracted the princess from the crash vehicle. I brought up the trolley, and she was put on. It seems to me she was intubated at that point, to help her breathe. It might have been in our vehicle that it happened. I don't remember very well. We got the princess into our vehicle as is customary, so that the SAMU doctor could take care of her in the best conditions.'

Intubation is a routine procedure. It consists of putting a tube into the trachea past the vocal chords so that the patient can breathe. It is normal to check the breathing sounds. The only problem paramedics frequently encounter is that the tube goes down the oesophagus, adding to the trauma. But an intubation procedure that is badly handled is extremely unlikely to hurt the lungs.

Six pictures show ambulances at work in the tunnel. Two are of Diana on a stretcher with blood on her face but the authenticity of these two photographs has been called into question by *Paris-Match*. But two of the four other photos appear to show someone who has to be Diana in the ambulance receiving treatment. Dodi and Henri Paul were never in an ambulance; Trevor Rees-Jones was extricated later and taken at once to hospital. Either while or just after Diana was extracted from the vehicle, she had a first heart attack. In Britain or America, the ambulance would then have rushed her to hospital. Given who Diana was, they would make certain there was a heart surgeon available. But that did not happen.

One of the key questions a British inquest will have to consider is what treatment Diana received and whether it was appropriate. Diana spent over twenty minutes in the ambulance before it set off.

Which hospital?

The nearest hospital with emergency services was the Val de Grace. The Val de Grace is a military hospital and, therefore, has much experience of emergencies, but it was decided not to use it. Instead Massoni closed all the roads along the Seine so that the ambulance could get as quickly as possible to the Salpêtrière. The ambulance was given an escort. Astonishingly, one photographer, Pierre Suu, was able to follow the ambulance. His presence meant the world would know just how often the ambulance stopped.

Every great city has its great hospitals. In Paris the most famous is the Pitié-Salpêtrière. It is on the left bank of the river just by Austerlitz Station. The hospital is a warren of old and new buildings. It traces its origins back to the Middle Ages. The most beautiful buildings date back to the eighteenth century when the Salpêtrière was the mental asylum for Paris.

The Salpêtrière is most famous for revolutionising the treatment of the mentally ill. In 1789, at the height of the French Revolution, Pinel removed the chains from the 'lunatics' and ushered in the birth of humane psychiatry. A hundred years later, the famous neurologist Jean Marie Charcot demonstrated – the curious term psychiatrists use – every Thursday afternoon a number of hysterical patients, mainly women. Charcot was a great showman and his 'demonstrations' influenced Sigmund Freud who studied with him for a year. Freud left the Salpêtrière convinced that the unconscious mind can control the body. The hospital library is named after Charcot and, in 2000, I presented it with one of my books, a small courtesy that would turn out to be useful.

The ambulance stopped twice after leaving the Alma. The driver, Michel Massebeuf, said: 'At the Jardin des Plantes, the doctor asked me to stop. We stopped for about five minutes so he could carry out a treatment which required absolute immobility.'

We don't know what required immobility but it is very possible that this was getting a central line in. It can be difficult to get access to circulation using the outside veins and so a central line is sometimes put in just below the collarbone. All kinds of fluids can be put in through a central line including blood and adrenalin. But it is a trickier procedure than intubation and it would be considered best practice to do while the patient was completely still.

But this was just the first of two stops the ambulance made. The Jardin des Plantes is quite long and it ends near Austerlitz bridge. Here the ambulance stopped again. It was now just 300 yards from the hospital but something so dire happened that Dr Martino decided to stop for ten minutes about one minute's drive from the hospital. The explanation Dr Martino gave was that 'the patient was suffering a fall in blood pressure'.

Just before 2am, Chevenement joined the chief of police, Philippe Massoni at la Pitié-Salpêtrière. They were astonished the ambulance with Diana had not yet arrived. Massoni worried there had been an accident. Could the journalists have got in the way? He called Marcel Vinzerich, public security commissioner on duty, who was directing the convoy from one of the two cars. Massoni was alarmed to hear the ambulance had stopped on the Austerlitz bridge.

At 2.06 the ambulance finally arrived at the Salpêtrière. Massoni saw Diana as she was wheeled in on a trolley but 'I no longer recognised the woman I had seen at the Alma.' This quote was obtained by Sancton and MacLeod. Diana's condition had deteriorated drastically.

When Diana reached the hospital, she had spent an hour and forty minutes receiving intensive care. Yet it is quite possible to argue that no one realised the extent of her internal injuries or was prepared to deal with them. There is one piece of evidence that suggests this very strongly.

Inside the Salpêtrière, Riou had assembled a very experienced medical team. It is curious however that the Salpêtrière had not grasped that there had to be a heart surgeon on hand since Diana had already had a heart attack. It certainly suggests that they did not know the state of her internal injuries.

The official French records do make it possible to work out some of the treatment Diana received. Riou's team included Daniel Eyraud, a vascular surgeon. He said Diana was unconscious when she arrived but 'she was breathing and she had a cardiac rhythm. That means her arterial BP was very low, but that her heart was still beating.'

Diana was X-rayed at once and that revealed there was a serious haemothorax – bleeding into her chest cavity. I think it is plausible to argue that, until then, the full extent of her injuries was not known. A dam of blood had built up and it now flooded out. If the wound had been seen and clamped earlier, she would have stood a better chance. 'Her heart and her right lung were compromised. The cavity needed to be drained and she required a massive blood transfusion,' Eyraud said. That was quickly arranged.

When the X-ray was analysed, it became clear Diana had a 2.5cm long tear to her left pulmonary vein. The vein carries blood to the lungs and the heart. The wound needed to be clamped. It is exactly the kind of injury that is best treated in hospital because the patient can be kept alive on a heart-lung machine.

The moment Diana was wheeled into the operating theatre, she had a second heart attack. It was timed at between 2.10 and 2.15. Riou and his colleagues then tried the classic method of internal and external heart massage. They were not going to give up easily.

Diana was also given large doses of adrenalin to get her heart going again. One account quoted Nurse Dominique Hagnère as giving her 150 ampoules of 5ml/mgs.

Professor Riou realised he needed a specialist heart surgeon and called for Professor Alain Pavie. But every second counted after Diana had been X-rayed. Without waiting for Pavie, Riou and Moncel Dahman, a general surgeon, opened Diana's thorax on the right side. This would allow them to clamp the wound and stop the internal bleeding.

The moment Professor Pavie arrived, he took over. One doctor said that 'the situation was so grave they discussed what to do as they started to perform a thoracotomy. Fortunately Pavie agreed with the assessment Riou and Dahman had made and he took charge. For the rest of the operation, Dahman would concentrate on giving Diana cardiac massage. 'The Princess's vital functions were being maintained by Dr Dahman.' Pavie also noted that 'the origin of the bleeding was in the pericardia to the left and to the rear.' The pericardia is essentially the cavity in which the heart is.

Professor Pavie soon realised that 'the treatment necessitated an enlargement of the surgical incision'. For some reason they had taken Diana to a facility that did not have everything they needed. Critical as her situation was, she had to be moved again to another operating theatre. I have been unable to find out why. The scene was terrifying. Diana had to have heart massage and, yet, she had to be moved. As nurses pushed her on her trolley, Dahman was trying desperately to keep her heart going using internal cardiac massage.

When they got to the second operating theatre, Diana was close to death. Professor Pavie noted 'bleeding was due to a partial rupture of the left superior pulmonary vein where it joins the left auricle. This wound was sutured. Bleeding was controlled and we continued with resuscitation.'

But, for Diana, it was too late. She could not survive without continued cardiac massage. She did not recover any cardiac rhythm. Nurse Hagnère then observed: 'Even after half an hour of this adapted resuscitation the pressure of expired carbon gases remained depressed. We even applied several electric shocks during the reanimation to get the heart going.' Nothing helped, however.

The critical doctor

I did not think when we started to make *Lady Died* that we would get a French doctor to speak to us but one did agree, Professor Philippe Dartevelle. He is also the brother of Al Fayed's lawyer, Bertrand Dartevelle. He is one of France's best-known thoracic surgeons.

We asked Dartevelle what could be done in a SAMU vehicle. He was precise. 'Nothing, because in a SAMU vehicle you cannot do surgery . . . a wound from the heart can only be treated by a surgeon . . . there is no other solution. Inside a SAMU vehicle the methods are limited.' He repeated that the only way to save her was to transport her to a very competent surgeon. Dartevelle added that even if that had been done she might have died but she may have stood a far better chance.

At around 3.30, the doctors told Chevenement and Massoni that Diana was dead. Chevenement was appalled. But he had to compose himself before giving the bad news to the British ambassador. Sir Michael Jay at once telephoned Sir Robin Janvrin, the Queen's Deputy Private Secretary. Janvrin then rang Prince Charles at Balmoral.

Philippe Massoni left the hospital as soon as he knew. He wanted to coordinate the operation at the police headquarters. This investigation would be politically delicate, he knew. Chevenement and Sir Michael Jay then started to work out the details of how to announce the death. Journalists were gathering outside the hospital, Jay and Chevenement decided the first step was to get the surgeons to make a public statement.

Between 4 and 5am preparations were made for a press conference. 'We were allowed into the hospital. We were in a small room,' Anne Corbet of Radio France Internationale remembers. A mobile phone bleeped. Before making the statement, Riou and Pavie changed into fresh gowns. Police started to put up barriers to stop the public getting into the hospital.

It is surprising how few journalists arrived by the time of the impromptu press conference. Anne Corbet reckons it was about twenty. Chevenement introduced the doctors. Riou seemed confident but terse. 'We wanted to know time of death and how she died,' Anne pointed out. 'We did get to ask questions but the doctors did not want to expand on anything. It was just the confirmation of her death. The hospital was not the place to go into the causes of death.' All Riou said was the following:

'Tonight, The Princess of Wales was the victim of a high-speed car accident in Paris. She was taken into the care of the ambulance service SAMU. When she arrived here she had a heart attack and the left pulmonary artery was torn. Though we closed the wound and performed a thoracotomy and, though she was given internal and external heart massage for two hours, we couldn't restore any circulatory activity and we determined death took place at 4am.'

As Riou read the statement, CNN tracked down Christopher Dickey of *Newsweek* who was in the room. In a whisper, Dickey confirmed to the world the news that Princess Diana had died. It was after that that he returned to the Alma Tunnel to check on the scene there and discover the tunnel had been reopened.

Riou insisted Diana had been alive when she reached the hospital but there have been some doubts expressed. Radio France Internationale had the story Diana was dead from a source inside the hospital shortly after 2.10am. Anne's source was the son-in-law of a colleague who worked there, she explained. 'I was still at the tunnel. My colleague had a son-in-law who worked at the Salpêtrière. She told me he had just phoned her to say Diana was dead. It was three o'clock but the editor of the night did not want to take the responsibility of broadcasting that just on the basis of one phone call. So I was careful to say that certain sources in the hospital said she had died. I hedged my bets. We had a wonderful scoop but we did not use it.'

When we pressed Anne, however, she wavered about the time. 'It was the middle of the night and I was not looking at my watch. I was not shocked when I heard that she had died at four o'clock.'

The British expert

Throughout this story, luck has played a part in my investigations. Every month I get the *Journal of the Royal Society of Medicine* as I am a Fellow of the Society. I don't usually scan it very thoroughly. Early in 2003, however, I spotted a review of a book called *Safety at Scene*. Its author is Dr Vic Calland. Calland is one of this country's leading experts on emergency medicine and road accidents. He also runs MedAlert, which provides emergency services in Lancashire for road accidents. Calland works closely with the police and ambulance services and his own car is an ambulance.

I rang him, expecting Calland would not be very willing to help. I was pleasantly surprised. He saw the question of how the emergency services reacted as a very proper subject to study and he agreed to meet me if I came to Preston. Calland is a tall, very friendly man. He told me there are two sorts of victims who cause paramedics to get so emotional it can affect their ability to perform their roles: children and beautiful women. Calland agreed to review the evidence for *Diana – The Night She Died*. As he usually works in partnership with the police, Calland is used to receiv-

ing the information on a case, however confidential.
He asked me to get hold of the pictures of Diana, the
medical records of the ambulance crew who would
have written up every procedure and detailed diagrams
of the car. He would normally have access to these. I
could not get hold of the medical information of
course, so he had to work on the basis of far more
limited material than he usually does.

Calland had no interest in being sensational and is
very aware of the pressures that paramedics work
under. Everyone would have been trying to do everything by the book. In Calland's opinion one possible
explanation is that something went wrong with the
intubation. It is a routine procedure but it can be very
tricky. It is strange that Martino and Massebeuf do
not agree about where the intubation took place and
that makes it reasonable to ask if something went
wrong when they intubated her. But Calland believes
it is more probable a mistake was made putting in a
central line and that this may even have aggravated
the tear of the pulmonary artery.

One of the reasons Calland's analysis may be persuasive is the language *Juge* Stephan used in the long
summary that was sent to all the parties involved.
Stephan did not say that the ambulance crews made no
mistake but rather that they could not be faulted because
they had adhered to the rules of resuscitation. These
rules stressed the need to provide as much treatment as
possible at an accident site and include putting in a
central line if necessary.

Stephan's very careful phrase makes Calland's interpretation – that the emergency services did stick to the

rules but some of the procedures were carried out very badly – one that the inquest must look into in light of the lack of medical evidence; at the moment, it is not an interpretation which I am in a position to test.

For the French, the question of how Diana was treated became extremely political and what happened that night needs to be set in context. France has the worst road-accident record in Europe. In 2000, there were 8,079 road deaths – well ahead of the 7,503 in Germany, which has 33 per cent more cars and 36 per cent less road space. In 2001 road deaths in France climbed to 8,160. Car accidents kill more French young men and women aged 15–24 than anything else. The French tend to blame the rampant ego of the French male driver who thinks he can corner like Michael Schumacher even after glugging two bottles of claret. On July 14th 2002, Bastille Day, President Jacques Chirac said he was 'absolutely horrified that France's roads are the most dangerous in Europe' and he promised to improve road safety.

But it is perhaps not the French roads that are so dangerous. If they and French drivers were so appalling, you would expect not just the number of road-accident deaths to be very high but the number of road accidents per se. In fact European statistics suggest the very opposite. In 1980, French statistics report 248,461 road accidents; in Britain the same year the number was 257,282; in America it was 2.07 million. Twenty years later, the number of road accidents in Britain and the United States had remained much the same. A small increase in the States led to 2.10 million accidents while a small decline took the British total down to 242,117.

Two countries showed radical changes. In Japan accidents nearly doubled, but in France the number of accidents fell by more than half to 121,223.

In Britain improvements in paramedic practice meant the number of road-accident deaths fell by over 50 per cent to roughly 3,600 a year. In France, fewer accidents did not result in an equivalent fall in deaths. Though there were 120,000 fewer accidents, in 2001 as compared to 1980, France still buried 8,100 road-accident victims as against 10,000 when the accident rate was double. You don't have to be a statistician to conclude that such a heavy death toll might be due as much to flaws in French emergency medicine as in the rampant ego of the French behind the wheel.

In Britain, if you are injured in a road accident you have a 1 in 25 chance of dying. In France the odds are roughly 1 in 14. It seems that French medicine became so defensive after the death of Diana because criticisms touched their insecurities about their accident and emergency procedures.

By 7am many people had gathered outside the Salpêtrière. There was real sadness but also curiosity. The crowd had no doubt who to blame. Anne remembers hearing a perfectly respectable old lady curse one of the photographers. '"How dare you be here? You have no right to be here," she shouted,' Anne said. 'The photographer was quite appalled.'

Inside the Salpêtrière, February 2003

The hospital refused all comment on what had happened.

I managed however to get Serge Demattos to agree to meet me. He is one of the organisers of the trade union at the hospital. He and his colleagues work in a crowded room. They represent the nurses and ambulance staff at the Salpêtrière Hospital. As I start talking to him, he is very wary. I must get the hospital director of communications to agree they can talk. But then one of the secretaries recognises me. She had been working in the Charcot Library when I had been there. She had thought I was very polite to write a thank-you letter and send them a copy of my book on multiple personalities. Demattos relaxes a little. But the line he takes is hard to credit, especially given the dramatic scenes I have described earlier. They see so many emergencies here. He insists none of their members remembers anything of that night. It was the night the most famous woman in the world died on their patch. I can't help being sceptical. When I tell Vic Calland what I was told, he is also sceptical. The hospital told the *Sunday Express* (November 2nd 2003) that they were under strict instructions to say nothing of that night.

But before I leave the trade unionists, Demattos does reveal an interesting fact. He believes that the reason Diana was sent there was because she was a celebrity. If she had been a soldier she would have been sent to the Val de Grace. Certain hospitals usually take certain kinds of patients. Diana was not sent to the Salpêtrière because it was the nearest hospital with a good accident and emergency department but because it is the hospital Paris traditionally uses for celebrities. If she had been less famous, she might have been in an operating theatre much more quickly. I'm staggered by this odd fact.

Demattos clams up again, feeling that perhaps he has said too much. I ring Meresse, the director of communications, some time later but he says there is no point in meeting. He will say nothing and he will allow his staff to say nothing. It's a question of medical confidentiality.

The pregnancy question

At the press conference, no one asked the question that would fascinate the press for months. Was Diana pregnant when she died? It has been suggested that the doctors would routinely have done an ultrasound scan to discover whether or not Diana was pregnant. This question led to hundreds of articles. About three weeks after the crash I was shown documents *Paris-Match* had obtained which appeared to be on the headed notepaper of the Salpêtrière. These were the results of tests which showed Diana was indeed pregnant. *Paris-Match* was intrigued by these documents but they seemed to be forgeries which had originated in Spain. The Salpêtrière always denied the authenticity of the documents.

Christian Curtil, Trevor Rees-Jones' lawyer, told me: 'I never saw the Diana medical file. I just saw the certificate of death.' I asked him if that was normal and he was cautious. 'Usually for a medical file to be taken out was not normal but I can understand the way it was done and it is not shocking to me. Dodi's file was really just a death certificate and also the blood tests. The blood tests disappeared from the file'; he meant both Diana and Dodi's blood tests.

There was so much gossip and speculation that Diana's friend Rosa Monckton finally decided to reveal the intimate detail that Diana had had her period when they were holidaying in Greece in mid-August. She could have conceived later in August when she was on the Riviera with Dodi but, almost certainly, she would not have known herself that she was pregnant. But if Diana had become pregnant when she met Dodi again on August 23rd, it is unlikely that the Salpêtrière would have missed it because they would have found signs of that as they tested her urine. Even home pregnancy tests work 7 to 10 days after conception. There is nothing particular which suggests Diana was pregnant, however.

Last rites and Freudian slips

While Al Fayed had flown to Paris at once, Prince Charles did not. At 11 o'clock he went to church at Craithie with the rest of the Royal Family. Until Diana's funeral six days later, the Royal Family would face unprecedented criticism. They seemed to behave in a callous way. Questions were raised about the future of the monarchy. What most commentators found shocking was that Prince William and Prince Harry had to go to church and act as normal, as if they were in control of their feelings when their mother had just died.

While Prince Charles was praying, complex negotiations were going on. He had already decided to go to Paris without his children. Charles insisted that Diana should leave Paris with full honours. Let the people see her, he said. The standard of the Royal Family was draped over her coffin. To his credit, he did not want her body sneaked away in shame.

At 1pm Diana's butler Paul Burrell arrived in Paris. Burrell has described how determined he was to make Diana look as beautiful as possible for her last outing.

Charles flew from Scotland to Paris. He arrived at the Salpêtrière at 5pm with Princess Diana's sisters. He was greeted by President Chirac who can be seen in the news footage whispering sympathetically to him. Chirac had liked Diana. Then, Charles and Diana's sisters went in to see the body. Charles asked to be left alone a minute with his ex-wife's body. When he came out of the room, it was obvious he had been crying.

Charles then went to meet the doctors. Then just as on his wedding day, he said something bizarre under stress. Charles looked at Riou and Pavie and said *'Felicitations!'* It means Congratulations. The doctors were a little surprised. It could have been a slip of the tongue but according to psychologists who argue there is some merit in Freud, Jung and other psychodynamic approaches, there are no meaningless slips of the tongue.

The most useful text that will help clarify is perhaps Freud's *Psychopathology of Everyday Life*. Freud argued that under stress the unconscious breaks through and that the mind uses many ploys to let the truth get out. Freud wrote a great deal about gallows humour and how some jokes allow us to express taboos and forbidden hostility. Having cried as he saw Diana dead, Charles was in a volatile emotional state. He was not thinking consciously but he was feeling and his feelings came out in the true, but utterly inappropriate word he used. The doctors had made his most secret wish come true, so he congratulated them. He would be free now, really free, to love the woman he had always loved. This analysis does not suggest Charles wanted or planned the death of Diana but he was torn. Yes, he was in tears and, yes, her death was tragic and, yes, he had something to thank the doctors for. The more charitable explanation is that Charles was under post-traumatic stress and he reverted to the role of the gracious grandee. You are in a hospital, you say nice things to the doctors whatever they have done.

There was a final, embarrassing muddle before the cars left. The French waited for the British to leave and the British waited for the French to leave first. Prince Charles sat miserably for two minutes, waiting. Then a woman rushed out of the hospital with a carrier bag. Inside was the dress Diana had been wearing when the car had crashed. Burrell quickly took it. He burned it because he was afraid many people would want to get their hands on it as a gruesome souvenir.

Diana's body was flown back to Britain where an autopsy was carried out – but was it a full autopsy? John Macnamara, Harrods' head of security told me that Diana's body was partially embalmed at the Salpêtrière and that this went against French law which requires such a dispensation for such a procedure. As a result, Macnamara claimed a full autopsy could never be carried out. Then in November 2003, an anonymous source in the French Ministry of Justice told the *Sunday Express* that the embalming story was true and that the British ambassador Sir Michael Jay asked the

French to embalm Diana. The diplomat was relaying a request from Her Majesty's government. The Foreign Office refused to comment. I asked Kevin Perry, who wrote the story, if he had faith in his source. He said he did and added that the leak had come from a middle-ranking civil servant. The French, finally fed up with criticism of their emergency medicine and the inquiry itself, had decided to embarrass the British.

It has been suggested that the reason the authorities wanted Diana embalmed was that she was pregnant. If formaldehyde is used to embalm, it often produces results that look like a positive result for pregnancy. Once Diana was embalmed no one could claim she had been pregnant. Later on in the book I suggest there might be other reasons why the British did not want a proper autopsy. Such questions will have to be raised at the inquest and, indeed, it is likely that the question of whether she was partially embalmed or not – and on whose orders – will now have to be answered.

The Arab press and the first conspiracy theories

Later on the day of her death Princess Diana's brother Earl Spencer issued a statement which summed up the first impression many people had of the tragedy: 'I would say I always believed the press would kill her in the end. But not even I could imagine that they would take such a direct hand in her death as seems to be the case. It would appear that every publication that has paid for intrusive and exploitative photographs of her, encouraging greedy and ruthless individuals to risk everything in pursuit of Diana's image, has blood on their hands today.'

In the Middle East, where Dodi came from, the view was very different, however.

I have argued that psychology can help us understand some of the conspiracy theories that have swirled round this case. Phone-ins on French radio did carry interviews with listeners who spoke of murder. One woman spoke of an execution. But it was in the Middle East that the conspiracy thesis first started. It should be remembered that it was not just Diana who died; Dodi Al Fayed did so too. The Arab press accused the British of conspiracies from the start. On its front page the Arab paper *Al Usbue* asked 'Did the British secret service kill Diana?' The paper suggested that '. . . a feeling of spurned hatred raged among the Royal Family and it is likely that orders were given to the British secret services to put an end to this relationship at any price'. *Al Usbue* added that the Brits had learned some useful lessons, as the secret services decided 'to get rid of her and her friend far from England so as not to attract suspicion'.

The authoritative Cairo paper *Al-Ahram* doesn't usually go for sensationalism but it quoted eyewitnesses saying they believed it was a 'premeditated accident'. One journalist was rather more moderate: Salama Ahmad Salama said 'a conspiracy is out of the question . . . such a plot would be worthy of Saddam Hussein'.

And Saddam's media did not fail. The nicely named *Babel*, then run by Saddam Hussein's son, Uday, said:

'Diana was liquidated by the British secret service because she departed from the norms and dabbled in politics, although she is from a family which is supposed to reign but not govern'. Libya's Colonel Gadaffi alleged the crash was arranged by British and French secret-service agents to make sure that a member of the Royal Family did not marry an Arab. He condemned the 'arranged crash' as 'anti-Islamic and anti-Arab'. The Foreign Office made a formal protest to Libya.

The weekly edition of *Al-Ahram* September 4th–7th 1997 pointed out that, initially, friends of Dodi shrugged off conspiracy theories. They preferred to compare the fate of the couple to a Greek tragedy. But the paper gave plenty of play to the assassination theory. Mohamed Nessim, a former Egyptian intelligence officer said, 'Such an accident is highly unusual . . . [events] don't quite add up to a natural occurrence . . . there are precedents – accidents whose mystery was never resolved'. Anis Mansour, a veteran Egyptian journalist, said, 'British intelligence assassinated her to save the throne – just as Marilyn Monroe was assassinated'.

Irony and exaggeration have always been powerful weapons in debate. The Arab view that Diana had been killed made it easy for many respectable Westerners to sneer at the very idea.

After all, how could anyone believe there was a conspiracy when two of the world's worst crackpot, tinpot dictators – psychopaths with the blood of so many innocent people on their hands – were claiming that.

In Britain, a country surprised itself by how much

it felt. People cried on the streets. It was almost Latin. Diana had died so young. And then, who could have imagined that the Queen Mother would be one of the mourners at her funeral? The national reaction was also taken as a sign. Britain had changed. It was no longer the land of the stiff upper lip and the emotionally inadequate. Diana had taught us something. She had been so open about the good and the bad, the joy and the trauma; she had broken so many taboos, making subjects that were once unspeakable open for discussion. She spoke directly to many women – and not just the young. I had one discussion with a 78-year-old woman from the stockbroker belt who adored Diana, she told me, because she was so brave and had been so obviously hated by the Royal Family. The woman in question is a staunch Tory voter.

Diana's fans, however, did not include Her Majesty the Queen. There has been much analysis of why the Royal Family did not respond well – or perhaps did not respond in a modern, acceptable way – to Diana's death. Anthony Holden argues that the Queen was more frightened than she had ever been in her reign. The mood of the nation was so hostile to the Crown. Intelligence sources apparently warned that fruit might be thrown at the Prince of Wales. Eventually, the Prime Minister persuaded the Queen to appear on television and show the nation she too was shocked, upset, caring. This was never the Queen's style but her broadcast did, at least, make many people feel she was trying.

Everyone assumed that the Royal Family just did not understand why Diana provoked such deep feelings. As a psychologist, I am a little sceptical that that's too easy an explanation. I think it is worth remembering Festinger's cognitive dissonance theory, which I mentioned at the start of the book. Cognitive dissonance would suggest one reason the Royal Family were so cold about Diana when she died was that they knew, in their heart of hearts, they had failed her. Emotionally, one smart way of handling the uncomfortable feelings her death provoked was to convince oneself Diana didn't merit love, sympathy or warmth.

I have searched the archives to see if Prince Charles ever said anything about the death of Diana, the woman he had two children by. I have not found any such statement.

The facts I have uncovered suggest also another reason for the royal disdain. British security forces almost certainly had one piece of evidence which would have only confirmed a negative view of Diana. We saw earlier that the *Sunday Mirror* dropped Andrew Golden's story on how MI6 had prepared a file on the Al Fayeds for Buckingham Palace the moment they knew Diana was hurt. That story quoted a friend of the royals saying Prince Philip had complained about Dodi as 'that oily bed hopper'. There was evidence – and I believe the French authorities soon told the British authorities of that evidence – that Dodi had turned Diana on in more than one way.

5

Dirty Tricks 'Drunk as a Pig'

Before breathalysers existed, the police had a simple test for working out whether a driver was drunk, according to endless music-hall sketches. You would be asked to get out of your car, told to put one foot in front of the other and walk straight. If you could manage about ten yards of the horizontal, you were sober. If you were drunk, you would not have the motor control or the eye-foot coordination. There is strong evidence to suggest that, less than an hour before he drove the Mercedes, Henri Paul would have passed this test easily.

The paparazzi were still in police detention on Monday September 1st. But by the middle of the afternoon, two of their lawyers, Jean-Marc Coblence and William Bourdon sensed a change of mood. Something was up – and it was going to help their clients. They found out quickly. By around 4pm, the Paris prosecutor's office provided 'through the usual channels', as Marmier put it, staggering details to gorge the God of Headlines. The paparazzi were still pariahs. But the real villain of the piece, it was now claimed, was the drunken driver, given the findings of the autopsy.

All this is crucial because, thirty-six hours after the crash, on September 1st, the French authorities changed their story. Now it was Henri Paul who had caused the crash. The office of the Procureur Général issued what would turn out to be the key official statement of the tragedy – and one which the French government has never changed. The Procureur Général's office told the press that the autopsy on Henri Paul proved that he was drunk. Though the post-mortem report had not been finalised, journalists like Nicholas Marmier of *Le Parisien* were told categorically that Henri Paul was three times over the limit. In France, the legal alcohol limit is lower than in Britain. The alcohol in his blood put him just twice over the legal limit in the UK, but this was not all. Henri Paul was also taking at least two kinds of medication for depression. He had been in no fit state to drive. Three people had died as a result.

The Paris police also released the news that the Mercedes had been travelling at 122mph, relying on the fact that the speedometer had jammed on 122 (122mph is 191kph). The police were forced to retract this, however, because Mercedes-Benz insisted that the speedometer reverted to zero if the car crashed and airbags were released, as they had been. But by the time the police had to admit they were wrong, headlines like 'Drunk as a Pig' were fixed in the memory. However, there are many reasons to question the police's claim that Henri Paul was drunk.

Henri Paul at the Ritz

On August 30th, Henri Paul returned to the Ritz at 10.08pm. He spent some of the next two hours sitting in the hotel bar with Trevor Rees-Jones and Kez Wingfield while Dodi and Diana were upstairs in the Imperial Suite. If either bodyguard had seen any sign he was under the influence, it would have been mad for them to let Henri Paul drive. David Crawford, Trevor Rees-Jones' lawyer, insisted to me they saw no such signs. There is some controversy about what Henri Paul did drink. John Macnamara told me the Ritz's bar receipts show it was *anisette*. Crawford told me that Trevor joked Henri Paul had been drinking *ananas* (pineapple) not *anisette* (Ricard) because they giggled about the pun on 'arse' in ananas. (It's been suggested to me that the arse might also be a jibe, given rumours that Henri Paul was bisexual.) Both drinks look yellow. But when you have an anisette, you usually pour the water in yourself so that you can make it weak or strong. If so, it's surprising Trevor Rees-Jones did not see Henri Paul doing that. François Meyer, the lawyer for the Paul family, made the same point. Henri Paul spent the last two hours and seventeen minutes of his life in a very public setting with many people around. None of them noticed that he was unsteady or in any way the worse for drink.

The press and the police dug into Henri Paul's past but none of the digging came up with one thing that psychologists who study dangerous driving might have expected – some past conviction, or even a caution, for a motoring offence. Many drivers who are convicted of causing death by reckless driving have already been found guilty of another motoring offence. A study of 200 fatal crashes in Long Island, for example, found that 51 per cent of the drivers who caused deaths either had had their licences revoked once or else, had convictions for dangerous driving or speeding. I would suggest the true figure for drivers who cause death and who have previous convictions is higher than the 51 per cent in the Long Island study because only drivers who survive crashes can be prosecuted. Henri Paul, however, had no conviction for any motoring offence. Of course, that does not prove he was sober on the night but he did not fit the usual psychological profile of a reckless motorist.

One of the witnesses we used in *Lady Died* was Claude Garrec who is a strange mixture of the cynical and the intense. Garrec is very frank about his attitude to Henri Paul. They had known each other when they were young men in Brittany. Henri Paul was his best friend and had been the best man at his wedding. They played tennis together every week, usually on Saturday mornings. Garrec found it hard to credit the story that Henri Paul had taken the wheel of the Mercedes if he had been drinking.

Garrec is not alone in thinking it would have been totally out of character 'for my sensible friend' to drive when he was drunk. Henri Paul had lived with Laurence Pujol and her daughter, Samantha, for four years, until they moved out of his apartment in 1992. They kept in touch until April 1995. Pujol painted a rather touching picture of the man she had lived with till 1992. Henri Paul did drink but: 'Wine made him joyful, he'd get very happy and do gags to make people laugh.

Sometimes he would make you think he was really drunk when he wasn't. He was a joker. He played around a lot, but never got incoherent on alcohol.' After his relationship with Pujol collapsed, Henri Paul often spent Saturday evening with Garrec and his wife.

We talked to Garrec at the foot of the block of flats in the rue Chambon where Henri Paul lived. The location is interesting. The building houses a gay club and some members tried to stop us filming. Opposite is a bar most of whose customers are lesbians. Henri Paul drank there quite often.

Garrec saw Henri Paul on the morning of Saturday August 30th. 'I took him the day of the tragedy from this door,' Garrec said. (In French he said '*le jour du drame*'.) 'We went to play tennis at Issy Les Moulineaux. After we played I brought him back here and left him around noon. I would never see him again.'

The next thing Garrec heard was from Henri Paul's family, who rang him on Sunday morning to break the news of his death. Garrec was summoned to see the *brigade criminelle* at Paris police HQ. 'They said, would I be surprised to hear that he had drunk a great deal and that there was evidence that he had alcohol problems.' The French distinguish between florid alcoholism and what they call *alcoolisme moderée*. The literal translation is 'moderate alcoholism'. No one ever claimed that Henri Paul was an alcoholic but the Paris police did say he had been given medication because his doctor had told him he was drinking too much and should cut down.

'I was very surprised [by what they claimed] I told the police,' Garrec said. 'Henri Paul was serious about his work.' And he found it 'extraordinary to think he would have agreed to drive if he had been drunk. I don't have an explanation but I never believed that the cause of the accident was what we were told.' This was the beginning of a saga which made Garrec angry because 'Henri was not just pilloried by the police but by the French press too.'

September 2nd became Abuse and Accuse Henri Paul day in all the world's papers. In Britain, the *Daily Mirror* said he was a 'Drunken Speed Freak' and reported 'Bike nut could down nine whiskies a night.' The *Daily Star* claimed Henri Paul was so boozed up that as he left the Ritz he yelled at the paparazzi 'You'll never catch us.' The *Express* said Paul was 'a heavy drinker with a taste for the high life'. The British press reported the driver had been drinking a whisky at 11pm in a bar called the Bourgogne even though the videotapes show him back at the Ritz by 10.08. American and Japanese papers got in on the act as well.

Many reporters descended on Lorient in Brittany where his parents lived. Despite trying very hard, the press could find only one person who claimed Henri Paul had a drinking problem. Most of his friends simply said he liked a drink, as Claude Garrec had done. But there is more objective evidence than the opinion of his family and friends.

Body language again

At the start of this book, I explained that the only time I saw Princess Diana in person was when I was asked to comment on her body language the day her divorce was finalised. Now my body-language skills would again prove useful. The Ritz Hotel made their security video-tapes available to the police. Journalists were allowed to see what we believed was an edited version, so when Francis Gillery started to work on *Lady Died*, he met the Director General of the Ritz, Frank Klein. Gillery persuaded Klein to let him see more of this material than any other journalist had seen. One of the video cameras covered the entrance of the Ritz with its revolving door. Another pointed down the grand lobby. Other cameras were outside the Imperial Suite and you can see a trolley being wheeled in.

When I made *Diana – The Night She Died*, I spent a considerable amount of time reviewing these tapes. I was not sure what I was looking for, but I felt it would be negligent not to study them assiduously. I spotted something interesting. Round 11pm Henri Paul was wandering up and down the lobby of the Ritz, occasionally chatting to people. Then suddenly, he saw his shoelaces were undone. He squatted down to lace them up. His shoelace-tying performance was quite graceful. The video shows that Henri Paul gets down on his haunches, ties the left shoelace, and then, without getting up, he transfers his weight from one leg to another and ties the shoelace of his right shoe. It's almost balletic. He then gets up without a pause. This is not the behaviour of a drunken man with poor motor control. I suggest Henri Paul would have passed the 'walking in a straight line' test.

My conclusions are not bizarre. The two patholo-gists and two toxicologists who reviewed the evidence of the autopsy also concluded: 'We have seen the videos showing Henri Paul at the hotel and his pattern of behaviour in our view is wholly inconsistent with someone having a high level of alcohol in the bloodstream.'

As soon as the autopsy results suggested Henri Paul had been drinking heavily, Madame Monteil's detectives from the *brigade criminelle* came to search his flat. Garrec had one set of spare keys and he was present when the police searched.

It was said by the police that they found *crème de cassis*, Ricard, Suze, port and beer. They also found unopened bottles of champagne and red wine and, in the kitchen, Ricard, Martini Bianco and Four Roses bourbon. Garrec argues this was not the drink supply of an alcoholic but a normal bar. 'I have one much the same,' he said. He pointed out the report did not mention the 240 bottles of diet Cola 'which was his favourite drink. It was not strange that he had it delivered in crates as he lived four flights up, just like he used to have his laundry delivered.'

The police, Garrec said, also looked for the medication Henri Paul was allegedly taking but they did not find any in the flat. Garrec did not deny his friend was sometimes stressed at work. 'He told us sometimes he had to make sure that 300 people who wanted access to the hotel were kept away to protect clients. He had to organise barriers. He had recently become acting head of security as well as the deputy head. All these things did cause stress but they did not make him a sick man.' Garrec added that it was not just his opinion. 'Among the papers I have are papers that state three days before the crash he was in perfect physical and mental health.' The papers Garrec refers to are the results of the medical examination Henri Paul underwent when he renewed his pilot's licence. The doctor said his reflexes and general health were good but that he needed spectacles for long-distance vision. There was no mention of a drink problem. 'His parents are still intimately persuaded that there has been a trick, something that is not honest, and of the innocence of their son. They don't believe the thesis of the speed or the alcoholism.'

Garrec is still angry about the way Henri Paul's funeral was reported. It was said that Henri Paul had so few friends at the Ritz that no one from the hotel turned up. Lies, said Garrec. 'In fact there were many people from the Ritz . . . the Director General of the Ritz was in the church on the first row. It contradicts the story that Henri Paul was not liked in the Ritz.'

Garrec had never before had dealings with the media and he was shocked by their attitude. He was particularly upset, he said, by *Paris-Match*. 'They wanted pictures of my friend. I had pictures of him. I said I would let them use the photos but when I saw the article, I said if that was what they planned to write, I preferred not to let them have the photographs.' Garrec claimed the draft he saw alleged Henri Paul 'woke up in a bad mood and worried about his health, when I had told them he was fine and that I had played tennis with him'. Garrec reckons 90 per cent of articles were 'directed against Henri Paul. *Ouest-France* was more honest.' This hostility still baffles him completely.

The sensational information that Henri Paul had been under the influence led to another media storm.

In some ways, it's not so surprising the French press tended to parrot police versions immediately after the crash. The story kept on changing – and changing fast. First, it was the paparazzi; then, Petel had to be discredited and so police sources insisted to the Credo press agency and others that he was not to be trusted; then, and this was only thirty-six hours after the crash, the new truth was that Henri Paul was drunk.

According to Nicholas Marmier, the information that Henri Paul was drunk came from the 'usual sources', which he identified as the Préfet de Police and the Ministry of Justice. Patricia Tourancheau of *Libération* had the same information and, like Marmier, wrote it up without questioning it. All over the world crime reporters rely on police sources but, in France, the press seems even more dependent. That's a far cry from the stance of the nineteenth-century writer-journalist Emile Zola who exposed the lies against Dreyfus in his famous article, J'Accuse. Today the motto of French crime reporters is more 'Je repeat whatever *les flics* tell me.' The only thing that can be said in their defence is that the story was moving so fast – and there was so much pressure – journalists didn't have much time to think, analyse or check sources.

The hotel management described Henri Paul as a model employee. Grand hotels are exotic places, catering for the good, the great and the extremely rich. It's hardly a revelation that their staff sometimes provide unofficial services to their clients. They get tickets for the best shows in town which are booked out, they recommend night clubs and, of course, they sometimes have little black books with the names of escort agencies and prostitutes. The job that Henri Paul held was not a job for the innocent and it is perhaps not surprising that the more one learns about him, the more he emerges as a mysterious, elusive character. There was much in his lifestyle to wonder at, in fact.

The history of Henri Paul

Henri Paul was born on July 3rd 1956 in Lorient in southern Brittany. His father had been in the army and then went to work for the local council. At school, Henri Paul's record was more than respectable. He got his baccalauréat in maths and sciences, but he also had a gift for music; he even won a number of prizes for playing classical piano. In 1976, Henri Paul did his National Service at Rochefort airbase, where he ended up working on security. When he left the military, he had the rank of lieutenant and he enlisted in the reserves.

The Rochefort airbase suited Henri Paul because he wanted to fly. He got his first pilot's licence when he was twenty years old and he had logged 605 solo hours by 1997. He was instrument rated because Garrec remembered flying with him when it was foggy: 'He could fly in all weathers.' One of his flying instructors, George Bielek, remembers Henri Paul fondly: 'He was a good man. No, we never had a problem with him – he was a very serious and a quiet man.' Bielek liked the fact that Henri Paul always tried to improve as a pilot. In 1985, Henri Paul left Brittany for Paris and got a job at the Ritz as a security officer.

Private flying is not a hobby for the poor and Henri Paul couldn't have managed to do much on his basic salary of £3,000 a month. One of my friends in the 1980s was the late Judith Chisholm, who held the world solo flying record from London to Australia. Judith was always struggling to pay for her plane, its hangar fees, its landing fees, as well as the aviation fuel. Henri Paul was lucky because Dodi had a plane and he sometimes allowed him to borrow it. One picture of Dodi and Henri Paul at Le Bourget shows them whispering to each other. Speaking as a body-language expert, I'd say it is a picture of two men who are close to each other.

Henri Paul soon became deputy head of security, but he was disappointed when he was not promoted to head of security two years later. The job involved some driving and the Ritz already had a link with the car-rental company, Étoile Limousine. In the 1980s, Henri Paul went to Germany for two weeks to do a driving course at Mercedes-Benz. He was well quali-fied to drive the car, even if he did not have the specific qualification which the French authorities require for chauffeurs who chauffeur passengers out in rented cars. Much has been made of the fact that he did not have this qualification but Henri Paul had considerable ex-perience of driving Mercedes-Benz vehicles.

Naturally enough, the press tried to find out every-thing possible about Henri Paul's sex life. It had taken him some time to recover from the end of his affair with Pujol but he seemed to have a new girlfriend who had the keys to his flat. No one had met this new girl, however. Oddly, the police search of his flat also found a gay guide to Paris, but no one thought it relevant.

Experts on grand hotels assumed Henri Paul, the model employee, might sometimes have to tell guests where they could find the best of gay Paree. No journalist and, it would appear, not the police either, seems to have wondered if a man who lived above a gay club, had at least a copy of the gay guide to Paris and who also drank in his local lesbian bar might not be 100 per cent heterosexual. His old girlfriend, Laurence Pujol, says people did make innuendoes about him. He was still a bachelor at forty-one, but he would just laugh when people joked about his sexuality.

Earlier I sketched out how Paul spent Saturday August 30th. He was in the group that picked up Diana and Dodi at Le Bourget, and then he drove the Range Rover carrying their luggage to the Villa Windsor. Ben Murrell, the head of security at the villa, was the only person to suggest Henri Paul had been drinking. Murrell told Trevor Rees-Jones' lawyer, David Crawford, that Henri Paul had a 'very good lunch' and was quite emotional. A good lunch would include a small *pichet* of a quarter of a litre of wine; a very good lunch might well mean having a bigger *pichet* of half a litre, roughly two-thirds of a bottle. But Henri Paul was back at the Ritz around 5pm and no one noticed anything odd about his behaviour between then and 7pm, when he went off duty.

The question of how much you have to drink in order to 'achieve' a certain blood alcohol level is not totally precise. It depends on body size, the rate at which you metabolise alcohol and whether or not you have eaten and how long the alcohol has been in the body. Bailey (Indiana University, 1995) provides a good analysis. An average 750ml bottle of wine contains 9.75 units of alcohol. In France, when you have lunch alone, you often order a 250ml *pichet of* wine. Let us assume that Henri Paul drank far more. The 500ml pichet contains 6.50 units. We also know that he may have drunk two anisettes. Anisette is 20%-40% alcohol by volume dependent on brand, and so two shots would provide one-to-two units of alcohol. Let us assume that the anisettes Henri Paul consumed were larger than usual though that is not what the Ritz bar receipts show. That would mean that Henri Paul could have consumed between 6.50 and 9.75 units of alcohol at lunch followed by up to 2.00 units. We know Henri Paul had lunch so the alcohol would begin to be metabolised around 3 pm. Once it started being metabolised, one unit of alcohol would leave his bloodstream every hour. So if he had drunk a full bottle of wine at lunch – and incidentally he then drove perfectly well round Paris – by midnight there would only be one unit of alcohol left in his body topped up by the anisettes. This would produce far less than the 1.74 mgs blood alcohol reading found in his body. The amount of whisky – one of Henri Paul's favourite drinks – that it would take to produce a blood alcohol level of 1.74 mgs can be calculated, given that he drank two anisettes it seems likely he would have had to have had eleven to twelve tumblers of whisky as well. The blood alcohol level only makes sense if Henri Paul left the Ritz at 7pm and then started drinking seriously in the three hours before he went back to work. But no one saw any signs of any intoxication when he returned to the Ritz.

One of the enduring mysteries of the tragedy is what Henri Paul did for those three hours.

August 30th, 7–10pm: Henri Paul's missing hours

A police investigation of the scale that the French mounted should have managed to find out how Henri Paul spent those three hours between 7pm and 9.53, when videos outside the Ritz show him parking his small car on the Place Vendôme. Henri Paul could not have gone far in those 173 minutes. The most obvious answer was that he had gone home to his flat in the rue Chambon, some ten minutes' drive from the hotel. The police, however, suggested that Henri Paul did not go home but they did not succeed in pinning down where he did, in fact, disappear to. They got only one confirmed sighting of Henri Paul, by the owner of a lesbian bar opposite his flat. As Garrec also said: 'He was seen leaving to go back to the Ritz. He waved to Josie (the owner of the bar) before leaving. Of that we are sure. The rest is of some doubt.'

The police explained their failure to account for the missing three hours very simply. Once it was known Henri Paul was drunk, bar owners clammed up. No one wanted to be identified as the person who had sold him the drinks that made him crash. The police enquiries drew a total blank.

In May 2003, I was given an unexpected lead on this. I was told that Henri Paul had been shopping in a supermarket for some of that time. The information came from a friend of David Carr Brown, my co-producer on *Diana – The Night She Died*. The man said that one of his acquaintances ran a supermarket and had served Henri Paul, but this friend saw no point in getting involved with the police.

David Carr Brown and I were eager to follow up this conversation. It was interesting, but it also had certain surreal possibilities. I imagined a line of commentary in my film which would go something like: 'After nine months of investigation we can exclusively reveal that Henri Paul spent part of the missing, never-before-accounted-for three hours buying carrots, marmalade and deodorant.'

The next day, we went back to the bar just off the rue des Petits Carreaux. It is very atmospheric. You sit at dark old wooden tables, the walls are lined with nineteenth-century ads, there are books on the shelves and the place doesn't ever seem to close. I have had bread, cheese and wine there at four in the morning.

I thought we were going back to fix a meeting with the supermarket owner. I wasn't prepared for the first question:

'How much is it worth to you?'

We said we didn't really expect to have to pay for the information.

'My friend wants fifteen thousand euros to talk,' the barman said.

Obviously, as a source of reliable information, the barman's friend would be useless. He was a mouth for hire. If we offered him 30,000 euros, he would probably say his grandmother had machine-gunned Diana.

We paid for our drinks and, in the classic phrase, made our excuses and left.

MI6's bank accounts and Henri Paul's missing assets

We will return to the question of the missing hours. They are however only part of the mystery of Henri Paul. Once his bank accounts were investigated, it became very clear how he could afford to fly, or do anything else he fancied. Henri Paul had over three million French francs, about £300,000, in thirteen separate bank accounts. Three accounts were at the Banque Nationale de Paris at the Place Vendôme branch where he also rented a security deposit box. He also had three bank accounts at Barclays on the Avenue de l'Opéra, as well as a current and four deposit accounts at the Caisse d'Epargne, near the Louvre. In the eight months before the crash, 40,000 francs (roughly £4,400) was paid into a Caisse d'Epargne account on five occasions, each time in cash. Paul also had two accounts in a bank outside Paris.

When all this money was found, it became obvious that Henri Paul must have been doing something other than his official job. One possibility never raised by the inquiry was that he had indulged in blackmail, something which I will raise in a later chapter. But there seemed to be an obvious explanation.

It is clear that Henri Paul was freelancing for various intelligence services. Claude Garrec said: 'All I can tell you is that he had contacts within the French and

foreign intelligence services. I always knew he had dealings with the secret services.' Garrec added that these
were not only the French services but that he did little
tasks for British and even Israeli secret services, including Mossad. The Ritz had an international clientele, he
added. But Garrec insisted that Paul did not carry out
operations on his own account. 'To know if people
were armed or if they were a threat to the security of
the hotel,' Garrec said was more his line. Some evidence
suggests Henri Paul's espionage was not quite so modest.
His address book contained contact numbers for people
at the *Directoire de la Securité du Territoire*, at the
Renseignements-Généraux and, perhaps most remarkable,
at the Élysées itself – the office of the French President.

Not many people have been willing to talk on the
record about Henri Paul's security connections.

The spy's jigsaw

On January 15th 2003 I travel to Nice to interview
Richard Tomlinson with David Carr Brown and Francis
Gillery. Richard Tomlinson was recruited by MI6 when
he was at Cambridge. He then worked in Russia and
claims to have smuggled nuclear secrets out of Moscow
for British intelligence. Tomlinson was then promoted
to run MI6's operations in Sarajevo when that city was
under siege. He thought he had done well so he was
astonished when he was told his services were no longer
needed.

Though he knew he would be breaching the Official
Secrets Act, Tomlinson wrote a book based on his time

in MI6. It painted an unflattering picture of spooks.
Tomlinson was prosecuted and sentenced to twelve
months in prison. He was released after six months.

David Carr Brown and Francis Gillery have met
Tomlinson before. We've arranged to meet him in a
small hotel, in a back street half a mile from the beach.
This is industrial Nice. The motorway lies between us
and the sea.

Tomlinson is supposed to join us at noon. Well before
that, I start to get nervous. I look up and down the
street. I pace to the kids' playground at the end of the
road. This situation has made me anxious ever since I
started making documentaries. The interviewee won't
turn up. You've come hundreds of miles and there's no
one to film.

David Carr Brown teases me. By 12.10 I'm in full-
frontal anxiety. I need to make phone calls to calm
down. Francis is also a worrier and so he rings
Tomlinson. No one replies. There's going to be a real
mess up. Panic isn't too strong a word. The man was
in MI6, trained to lie and deceive. He won't turn up.

At 12.15 Francis rings Tomlinson again. I want to
grab the phone. I'd rather know the worst than have
to wait. The phone keeps ringing. I hit the Krakatoa
level of stress. Then, finally, Francis nods. He's got our
man on the line. Tomlinson is on his way. I can breathe
now. He just started out late. He's been swotting for
some exams and couldn't answer our first call because
he was on his bicycle.

We fix the camera in the secluded back garden of
the hotel. The sun shines on the eucalyptus leaves and
a cheap imitation Greek statue. The owner says they

serve breakfast here but we won't be disturbed if we film in the next three hours.

Tomlinson has a lean, craggy face and a slightly self-deprecating smile. He now makes his living looking after boats on the Côte d'Azur. He's pleasant but he is in a hurry. He will not be staying for lunch. He's got to get back to his studying. As he was sacked by the security services, some journalists are sceptical about any information Tomlinson gives. Some also suspect him of being paid by Al Fayed. I wonder the opposite. Could he still be working for MI6? British security services could ask for him to be extradited from France, as they did with David Shayler, but Tomlinson doesn't seem worried by that and is planning another book. If the M in MI6 stands for Machiavellian, one would assume Tomlinson is still working for them, but pretending not to. Deep waters, Bond.

The first thing I have to ask is: did he take money from Al Fayed?

Tomlinson is not offended. He explains he wrote to Al Fayed when he got out of prison and that he was surprised not to get an answer. He told the story to a journalist who made contact for him. Coming out of prison Tomlinson was broke. He insists, however, that he never took any payment from Al Fayed but concedes Al Fayed did help him pay for an airfare from New Zealand.

Once we start talking, Tomlinson is very clear. He tells me he knows that Henri Paul was a part-time agent for MI6. When Tomlinson worked for MI6 he asked for Henri Paul's file. His reason was sheer curiosity. Frenchmen are quite willing to spy for Russian,

American, Chinese and other secret services but the historic enmity remains. Most traitorous frogs draw the line at working for Perfidious Albion, as the French call Britain. So Tomlinson was intrigued by a Frenchman who was prepared to work for the British. Tomlinson's story confirms what Henri Paul's best friend, Claude Garrec, had told us.

MI6 would have been extremely interested in knowing all the details of the relationship between Dodi and Diana, Tomlinson tells me. They would have wanted all the intimate details, a sense of how much Dodi meant to Diana, whether they were sleeping together and whether they were likely to marry.

None of that seems to me exactly affairs of state, I say.

Tomlinson smiles at me. 'It was of concern to the head of state.' One of the bedrock duties of the intelligence services is to protect the Royal Family.

Tomlinson adds that he was profoundly struck by another fact. Usually, during August there is very little intelligence activity in Paris. Spies also go for their holidays, it seems. But in 1997, an unusual number of senior MI6 personnel were to be found in the city, including Andrew Langman and David Spearman, senior officers of MI6.

'What does that make you speculate?' I ask.

Tomlinson said he needed more information to speculate intelligently. He made another point though. It was very tricky to mount operations in France which the French did not know about. He had done it himself and there had to be a lot of fancy spook dancing if Paris ever found out. But the presence of senior MI6 people would suggest 'that some sort of operation was going down. It is one piece of the jigsaw.'

I like Tomlinson's image of the jigsaw, though I couldn't draw anything more specific out of him.

Tomlinson had looked at Henri Paul's personnel file, and he told me that part of Henri Paul's job was to bug rooms for British intelligence. He used a simple method. He had at his disposal a number of TV sets with listening devices inside them. When MI6 wanted a particular guest bugged, Henri Paul would arrange for a different TV set to go into his room, a set with a bug built in. Tomlinson painted an amusing picture of Henri Paul ordering the specially crafted sets to be moved from room to room on instructions from his handlers.

Tomlinson suggests Henri Paul was being briefed by MI6 for some of the time between 7 and 10pm. That would explain why he had around £1,400 on him. 'That is just the kind of money paid to an informer of a certain kind,' Tomlinson said.

Other evidence supports Garrec's view that Henri Paul, like all good freelancers, did not depend on just one customer. The American investigative reporter Gerald Posner spoke to two American secret-service officials. They told him, he said, that Henri Paul was in regular contact with the *Direction Générale de la Sécurité Extérieure* (DGSE), the French equivalent of MI6. He also freelanced with the French equivalent of MI5, the *Directoire de la Securité du Territoire*, which is responsible for internal security and with the *Renseignements-Généraux*. Posner's sources told him Paul spent some of his missing three hours with a man from the DGSE.

He paid him the 12,560 francs. Unlike the British security apparatus, the DGSE were not very interested in finding out about Dodi and Diana. There were other guests at the hotel of more concern to them including a number of Syrians suspected of links with French Arabist groups who might be involved in acts of terror against the French state.

Tomlinson felt the French should know about Henri Paul's security links, and that is why he wrote to *Juge* Stephan and asked to be interviewed. 'I expected to be questioned in some detail,' Tomlinson explained, but Stephan seemed to be in a hurry and showed little interest. His assistant Marie-Christine Devidal asked far more questions.

Tomlinson outlined the procedure the *juge* could have followed. Stephan could have asked MI6 to let him see the personnel file on Henri Paul. Such a request would have had to come from the French Ministry of the Interior or the French President's office and it was possible that MI6 would have refused to help. But that would have been difficult diplomatically. That file would have listed Henri Paul's contacts and that might suggest who might have a grudge against him. It might also have shed light on why there were so many senior MI6 personnel in Paris that August. Henri Paul's career as a 'minor MI6 asset' was, as Tomlinson saw it, an important part of the jigsaw.

But Tomlinson had an even more controversial point. He told me that he had seen a position paper drawn up by MI6 which included a plan to assassinate the Serbian President, Slobodan Milosevic, in a tunnel. MI6 often draw up such position papers, Tomlinson added.

It was part of the fun of being a spy and he stressed that one should not read too much into it. Spooks are paid to dream up these plots and most of them never happen. But one of the key points about the Milosevic plan was that it was devised so that his death would look like an accident, because the Serbs would go berserk if they thought their leader had been murdered.

In saying 'I was very surprised however when they chose not to ask me many questions,' Tomlinson was being perhaps a shade naïve. The French inquiry had little interest in exposing the fact that French security services snooped on guests at the Ritz.

Given all this, I found Garrec's last words in our interview rather touching. 'I have followed my job of memory. I try to defend my Henri, my dead friend.' Garrec hopes that some serious journalist will reconsider the issue of Henri Paul's guilt. 'No, he did not die the way it was said that he did. He did not die because he missed the turning because he was drunk. I hope one day that the person who did this and who cannot be very proud of it and that before he dies, he confesses "I did it" . . .' But Garrec has not received any new information. He thinks his friend was the perfect fall guy.

Close observation – the judge interviews Trevor Rees-Jones

It is also no secret that someone else in the Mercedes, apart from Henri Paul, had a history of contact with at least one intelligence organisation.

Trevor Rees-Jones' career is a matter of public record. He worked for a number of years for the 1st Battalion Parachute Regiment in Northern Ireland as a member of a Close Observation platoon. Their job was to keep suspected terrorists under observation. As he describes it in his own book, Rees-Jones had become 'a master at silence', learning how to be still and melt into the background. Close Observation platoons are often told whom to watch by military intelligence. Rees-Jones loved his work and hoped to join an even more specialist unit but that unit was never formed. In 1995, Rees-Jones and his unit returned to Aldershot. He didn't relish a more mundane military life as he felt he'd had enough 'army bullshit' and so, after six years, Rees-Jones left. He answered an advertisement for security officers and joined the Al Fayed organisation in 1995.

The only survivor of the accident was lucky and brave. Trevor Rees-Jones needed very complicated surgery on his face yet his recovery was astonishingly rapid, a tribute to his courage. Seventeen days after the crash, he was ready to meet with *Juge* Stephan. The doctors were concerned the interview might be too much of a strain and it had been agreed that Stephan would ask only twenty questions with a doctor present all the time.

Stephan said he hoped that Rees-Jones would remember something that would explain the many questions that needed explanation. Post-traumatic amnesia usually fades but the transcripts show that Trevor Rees-Jones had little information to offer. He said, 'It was Dodi who changed the original plan, not me.' At times, he seemed to be still a little confused, which is hardly surprising given the extent of his injuries. He appeared to think that the Ritz Hotel was on the Place de la Concorde when it is on the Place Vendôme.

The magistrate asked if he thought the cars or the bikes were closer to the Mercedes. 'I don't know,' Rees-Jones said, though he did recall that one of the cars was a hatchback.

Stephan asked whether he was aware that photographs had been taken as the car drove.

'I don't know,' said Rees-Jones again.

After Trevor Rees-Jones came back to Britain, he returned to France twice to meet *Juge* Stephan, who kept on hoping he would recover some memory. Crawford remembered that this was very stressful because there were so many journalists and photographers. 'When we walked to meet them there was just a wall of cameras . . . and he had not made a complete recovery,' he said. Christian Curtil, who had never warmed to Rees-Jones, was nevertheless impressed by one aspect of his character. 'I think he did not lie, I think he was very discreet, I think he did not want to give any gossip, I think he is a very honest man. He says he remembers nothing and I don't think he lies.'

Juge Stephan eventually concluded that the bodyguard could remember nothing of any value.

But Trevor had made one point, which he has continued to maintain ever since: namely, he had not seen any sign that Henri Paul was drunk. There is a cynical view that Rees-Jones would hardly admit that he had noticed the driver was drunk, but that he had been too frightened of Dodi to make a fuss or insist on another driver. But, as he records in his own book, there is evidence that Rees-Jones did have the confidence to express some doubts about the decoy car plan. If Henri Paul had been drunk, that was far more dangerous.

But this point, the one important fact that Rees-Jones could recall, that Henri Paul did not act as if he was under the influence, was ignored by the inquiry. As we shall see, it was not just Henri Paul's reputation which was not well handled.

6

Anatomy of an Autopsy

Mohamed Al Fayed identified his son's body at 5am. He said Dodi 'looked at peace. He looked like he had as a little boy.' Dodi looked so normal, his father added, he could have fooled himself into thinking his son would wake up again.

Under Islamic law, a body has to be buried before sundown. Al Fayed would find this would not prove easy. During the morning Al Fayed's director of security Macnamara had helpful conversations with his old colleagues at Scotland Yard who promised motorcycle escorts for Dodi's body and with the Surrey Coroner, Dr Michael Burgess. In Paris, the head of the Ritz Hotel, Frank Klein, was at the morgue with Professor Dominique Lecompte, the pathologist. At 1pm the atmosphere became more tense. Dr Burgess rang Macnamara to say there would be a delay in releasing Dodi's body because the French were now treating it as 'a suspicious death'. He did not explain why. Macnamara phoned his Scotland Yard contacts who insisted that the British police had not asked the French to do that. Around the same time, according to Klein, Professor Lecompte became rather worried in the morgue and rushed out to make a phone call. She returned a few minutes later, calmer. I have not been able to find out what this phone call was about.

Mohamed Al Fayed took the coffin to Le Bourget. It was hard to fit it into the passenger section of the plane. Someone suggested they put the coffin in with cargo. Al Fayed absolutely refused. His son's body would not returned as cargo and it was flown back in Al Fayed's helicopter.

The body of Henri Paul had been taken to the Institut Médico-Légal close to the Salpêtrière Hospital. The Institut is the most prestigious pathological lab for France and is linked to the University of Paris. Its head was then, and is now, Professor Dominique Lecompte. Lecompte is one of France's top pathologists and she worked on Henri Paul's autopsy with the toxicologist Dr Gilbert Pepin from Toxlab. Some commentators have made much of the fact that Toxlab is an independent laboratory but, in fact, the French government is virtually its only client. Dr Pepin is a biologist and a doctor of pharmacy. He had performed 4,000 post-mortem analyses and has held the office of President of the French Association for Medical Legal Toxicology. I repeatedly made requests to Professor Lecompte and to Dr Pepin for an interview but these have always been refused.

A number of detective fictions have turned the pathologist into a hero or heroine. In TV dramas like *Silent Witness*, and in the books of Patricia Cornwell and Kathy Reichs, the pathologist is attractive and acute. These laser-brained women will work the bone, blood and gore till it reveals the truth and nothing but the truth. They leave no tissue unturned.

Sadly, the expert witness as perfect witness is something of a fiction in real detection and, certainly, the Institut Médico-Légal does not seem to have lived up to the glamorous image. But this is not a specifically French failing.

Through the night of August 30th and August 31st, all Paris hospitals were busy. By the end of the night, there were twenty-three bodies in the morgue at the Institut Médico-Légal. Henri Paul was in a queue for the services of the pathologists. His corpse did not seem to require special treatment. This was not Princess Diana, nor even Dodi Al Fayed. It was just a driver who had been in an accident.

The autopsy on Henri Paul started on the Sunday morning, around 8.30am. We don't know the precise time because those facts were never recorded as they should have been.

An autopsy is, like a funeral, a last rite and, in theory, all those involved treat the remains with respect. Part of that respect is to use procedures that ensure there can be no confusion. Timing the autopsy is the first of those routines.

Much has been made of the *secret d'instruction* and the *secret médical* in France as if it were routine for lawyers and doctors in the rest of the world to ignore confidentiality. Given that the Ordre des Médécins in France insists on confidentiality, it is surprising that the details of the autopsy on Henri Paul were leaked to the press well before the process was finished. By comparison the details of the autopsies on Dodi and Diana have not been revealed.

★

But it was not just alcohol that made him unfit to drive. The Paris prosecutor also revealed Henri Paul was taking Prozac – it was presumed for depression – and tiapride, which French editors were told is used in the treatment of alcoholism.

It is relatively unusual for a pathologist to have to revisit the body or for a toxicologist to have to take more samples. The autopsy on Henri Paul was very different, however. After the first 'go' on Sunday, more samples were taken on September 1st and again on September 4th.

The autopsy results seemed very definite. Yet, something was bothering Herve Stephan, as his behaviour would show. Magistrates do not usually attend pathology labs. Yet, five days after the crash, on September 4th Stephan did not just request a second set of samples of Henri Paul's blood and urine but he came to the Institut himself. He wanted to watch the process by which the pathologists took the samples. Stephan was accompanied by a doctor, J.P. Campana, Dr Pepin, two members of the police judiciaire and another policeman. The taking of the samples was photographed though these photos have never been released.

John Macnamara was in Paris at the time, still waiting to talk to the police. He told me he believed the only reason Stephan went to the Institut Médico-Légal was to add 'legitimacy' to the autopsy. I think there was a less devious reason. At the start of what he knew would be a controversial inquiry, Stephan wanted to check that the procedures did conform to best practice. He also had some data which had not yet been made public – on the astonishing levels of carbon monoxide in Henri Paul's blood.

On September 4th the judge watched as they took a sample of 'a few millilitres' of blood from the femoral veins. But even Stephan's presence didn't lead to proper recording. The precise quantity of blood taken from the femoral veins was not given in the final autopsy results.

Two samples were also taken from Henri Paul's hair. A further two samples were taken from the quadriceps muscle but, again the information was not as specific as normal records of pathology require. We do not know, for example, whether they were taken from the left or the right arm.

Dr Gilbert Pepin, the toxicologist, took away two sets of samples to perform a second analysis. This is a key point. If anyone other than Dr Pepin ever analysed Henri Paul's bodily fluids, there is no record of it in the paperwork. Jean François Meyer, the lawyer for the Paul family, said the fact that Dr Pepin analysed all the samples made it impossible to have what he called a '*contre expertise*', an opposing or critical expert witness statement. The other two samples – no. 1 also of blood from the femoral vein and no. 4 containing hair – were handed over to the judicial authorities, according to a statement made by Christian La Jalle of the police judiciaire. This was to make sure they were safely stored in case there were any disputes later on. The fate of these 'safety' samples would itself become controversial.

The next day, *Juge* Stephan issued an order for yet more samples. On September 5th, Dr Campana returned to the morgue to observe two more sets of samples being taken from Henri Paul's hair, one from his head and one from his pubic hair.

At this point, there is an interesting detail in the paperwork. An autopsy report has to provide full details of how tissue and other material were taken. The inquiry does not seem to have been entirely satisfied, since on September 8th, *Juge* Stephan asked Professor Lecompte to give 'the exact conditions and the precise place from which the samples were taken'. She may well have replied verbally but nothing seems to have been recorded or given in writing.

The next day, Professor Lecompte took another set of samples from Henri Paul's hair. By now there were five sets of hair samples. Again, however, the autopsy report is astonishingly unspecific. It did not say where the hair came from or whether the hair had been cut or plucked from Henri Paul's body.

Stephan saw samples being taken from the body on the Thursday but he was not present, of course, when the first samples were taken or when the analyses of Henri Paul's bodily fluids were performed.

The results from the second – but not the third or fourth samples – were made known to the press on September 5th. They showed Henri Paul had 1.87 mgs of alcohol per litre of blood. But on the Thursday, the press were also given very precise details of the cocktail of drugs which he was said to have taken. The cocktail consisted of:

Fluoxetine level 0.12 milligrams per millilitre
Norfluoxetine 0.18 milligrams per millilitre
Tiapride 0.006 milligrams per millilitre

Fluoxetine is a constituent of Prozac. Patients who take Prozac are advised not to drink alcohol and, especially, not to drive under its influence. The autopsy did not comment on how recently Henri Paul might have taken that medication. Was it a trace? Or was it a heavy dose, taken recently?

The levels of tiapride were low, but they were immediately trumpeted as yet more proof that Henri Paul was a chronic drinker. Journalists were briefed that the drug was used in the treatment of alcoholism. Clearly, Henri Paul was so worried about his drinking he had gone to get treatment. All this should have been easy for the inquiry to confirm with Paul's doctor but there is no evidence that it ever did so.

Tiapride can be obtained only on prescription in France but research shows that it is far from being a medicine that is principally used in the treatment of alcoholism. The drug has been used since the 1970s to control agitation and, even, physical tics. Studies show it can help in treating tardive dyskenesia, the shakes that long-term psychiatric patients get as a result of the side effects of anti-psychotic drugs like Largactil. Tiapride also has a good record in diminishing agitation and aggression in elderly patients. Tiapride has also been used in the treatment of Huntingdon's Chorea.

Tiapride is hardly a drug you would expect to be taken by a 41-year-old man who played tennis every week. It is also strange, given that he had passed the medical for a pilot's licence three days earlier, that the urine test he had undergone then did not pick up the presence of either drug. But when the press were told Henri Paul had been taking tiapride, no one was sceptical. It should be added that 0.006 milligrams is a very small amount.

A much more astonishing revelation came some seven days after the autopsy. The Paris prosecutor's office then said to the press that Henri Paul had 20.7 per cent of carbon monoxide in his blood. We all have some carbon monoxide in our blood – a normal level in a non-smoker is 2 per cent. In a heavy smoker it can reach between 8 per cent and 10 per cent.

The finding was significant because high levels of carbon monoxide can begin to impair motor perform-ance. There is some controversy about how much carbon monoxide has to be in the blood before a person starts to behave oddly. Professor Derek Pounder, head of forensic pathology at Dundee University, told me, for example, that human beings do not necessarily show severe effects even with levels of carbon monoxide of up to 30 per cent. Other experts put it lower, however.

When the second set of samples was taken on September 4th, the average level of carbon monoxide had fallen to 12.8 per cent. The judge obviously wanted to get some explanation of this inconsistency. The carbon monoxide reading was the only oddity in what seemed otherwise to be a simple autopsy.

The independent experts

At the start, Mohamed Al Fayed did not believe that Henri Paul was drunk. Senior staff at the Ritz talked to the barman and other employees. They established how Paul had behaved and what he had consumed. No one had noticed Henri Paul was under the influence of alcohol and Henri Paul's mother and father also did not believe that their son would have driven the vehicle if he felt he had drunk too much.

In Britain, Henri Paul's family would have had the right to have an independent post mortem carried out. But when they tried to get permission for that, they were refused. The French authorities would not even permit them to have a witness present when more samples were taken from their son's body. Most drastic, the family would not be allowed to access their son's blood and urine samples. The family wanted to do a DNA test to check the post mortem had really been performed on the body of their son. This led to a strange alliance between the two bereaved families. Al Fayed backed Henri Paul's parents in their fight to establish the truth of their son's physical condition. The motives of the two families were very different. As far as the Paul family were concerned, if their son was sober, he was innocent and could not be held responsible for the deaths. As far as Al Fayed was concerned, if Henri Paul was sober, that showed the complicity of the intelligence services; the Paul family accepted Al Fayed's help. He introduced them to their lawyers, Maître Brizay and Jean François Meyer.

The Paul family felt very frustrated. But their lawyer, Maître Brizay did manage to get the full autopsy report by October. At last the family had something to work on. Al Fayed then did something very astute. Immediately after the crash, he had asked Peter Vanezis, then Regius Professor in Forensic Medicine at Glasgow University, to accompany Macnamara to Paris but

Vanezis had not been allowed to witness the taking of any samples. After Brizay got hold of the post-mortem report, Al Fayed hired three other eminent experts, two of the best pathologists in Europe and another toxicologist to scrutinise the official findings on Henri Paul. One of the experts was Thomas Krompecher, professor of pathology at Lausanne University. Curiously, Krompecher had supervised the autopsies on the forty-eight dead of the Solar Temple who were burned in Switzerland. Krompecher had also been one of the pathologists who prepared reports on the bodies of victims of the Lockerbie bombing. The other two experts were Dr John Oliver of Glasgow University and Patrice Mangin of the University of Lausanne. All these men regularly appear as expert witnesses in courts all over Europe.

Al Fayed was taking a risk. In general, medical experts do not like being too critical of one another. These distinguished professionals had encountered Lecompte and Pepin at various points in their career. That makes what follows even more remarkable.

The independent experts first met on November 12th 1997 in London. They filed an interim report, dated February 10th 1999. They then presented their full and final conclusions in November 2001.

I don't expect readers of this book to be passionate about anatomy. Nevertheless, I offer a very detailed critique along the lines of Krompecher and his colleagues because their analysis raises so many questions about the justice of blaming Henri Paul, as the French inquiry did.

The independent pathologists started by noting a

number of anomalies in the autopsy procedures. In February 1999, they raised five major issues:

1. Was Henri Paul an alcoholic?
2. Was he a heavy smoker?
3. Did he have a high level of carbon monoxide?
4. If so, what was the source?
5. How can his apparently normal behaviour be reconciled with certain findings in the autopsy report?

The experts first raised many technical concerns. Some autopsy routines cover how body samples should be labelled and what is called the 'chain of custody' to make sure there are no confusions. No court wants the blood of Mr Smith muddled with the blood of Mr Jones.

The report did not mention the time, the anatomical origin and the quantities and volumes of the body samples that were taken.

Usually, autopsy reports describe the containers in which the samples are stored. Are these made of plastic or glass? Are there preserving agents in the containers? It is recommended that such agents should be used to make it possible to examine the samples again weeks, months or even years later.

In big morgues, like that of the Institut Médico-Légal, a pathologist may sometimes work on more than one body at a time – especially on a busy Saturday night. To guarantee there could be no tampering or muddle, the samples should have been sealed in the presence of an officer of the *police judiciaire*. That did not happen on most of the occasions that the pathology team 'visited' the body. Only on September 4th did the experts find any mention of an official of the police judiciaire sealing the samples.

At the start of this chapter I pointed out that, on September 8th, *Juge* Stephan asked Professor Lecompte for precise details of how samples had been taken. The four experts said: 'We could find no written response to these requests.' The independent experts also noted (February 1999) that 'the reports appear to proceed on the assumption that Henri Paul was a heavy drinker, possibly an alcoholic and we have seen it suggested that this might explain an ability on his part to drink large levels of alcohol yet exhibit no sign of this to others.' If Henri Paul drank so heavily one would expect to see damage to his liver and, especially, of cirrhosis. But when the pathologist looked at the liver, it seemed perfectly normal. There were no signs of serious trouble.

The liver is a complex organ and it can be hard to analyse. As a result, many pathologists believe that visual inspection alone does not make it safe to conclude the owner of a particular liver has an alcohol problem. Some years before 1997, Professor Lecompte herself, the experts said, 'subscribed' to a protocol which said that there should be a histological examination of the liver and of the pancreas. In other words, a detailed examination using biochemical analysis. In the case of Henri Paul a histological examination would give information about his lifestyle and especially his drinking habits. The experts said they would have expected the pathologists to carry out such a histological examination. It was not done, however. Other important omissions were:

- The colour of the '*masses musculaires*' was not mentioned.
- The brain was not weighed.
- No measurements of the skull – especially of the thickness at the top of the skull – were given.
- The contents of the trachea were not mentioned.
- At the thorax, the extent of blood loss did not seem to have been measured and the multiple fractures of the ribs were described without specifying whether these fractures were vital or not in causing death.
- The information given about the abdomen was also less than might be expected. Details about the contents of the intestines were not mentioned. Detailed analysis of all the contents of the stomach and the gut might have provided corroborating evidence that Henri Paul was drunk or of how drunk he was.
- The colour of the renal parenchyma was not mentioned when there seemed to be some sort of haemorrhage there.

The independent experts then turned their attention to the skeleton. They noted that there was no exploration of the medullar bulb in the brain stem, which controls our sense of balance. They also noted that the medullary canal in the femur was not properly explored.

Some of these omissions may be just technical and would not have affected the final conclusions. But some are striking. The failure to weigh or analyse the brain is strange. Just as an examination of the liver might have confirmed whether or not Henri Paul was a habitual heavy drinker. Alcohol literally eats up some of the grey matter so alcoholics often have a lower brain weight than average. Examination of the cortex may also show damage to the ventricles.

But it was not just a question of omissions. The experts went on to complain of actual contradictions in the post-mortem findings.

At the start of the autopsy report, Henri Paul's brain stem is said to be intact while, later, the report states there were important traumatic lesions there. That couldn't happen to the same body.

The report then states there are multiple fractures of the corpus vertebral of C3 and of the vertebra at C5 with 'multifragmentary bursting'. They also noted that there was a clear mention 'd'une section franche de C6 with displacement' – a clear break of C6 [vertebra] that was also displaced. The experts felt this was 'incomprehensible'. They asked what force could have caused a 'section franche' of the body of a vertebra.

Henri Paul's urine was said to be rose coloured but no explanation was given for that while his kidneys, urethra and the pario vesicle were said to have been intact. One would not therefore have expected blood to have leaked into the urine which might have accounted for its colour.

There were also a number of ad hoc additions to the autopsy report. Traditionally pathologists dictate what the state of the organs is at the time when they examine the body. These are the facts; the analysis of what the facts mean is of course different. The experts pointed out, however, that Professor Lecompte added to the record on November 6th 1997. Her note of that date, for example, spoke of a rupture of the aorta and that it was a cause of death.

The carbon monoxide mystery

The finding that most baffled the experts was the presence of carbon monoxide in Henri Paul's blood. It was said to be 20.7 per cent, as we have seen. The four experts were concerned by the figure, and asked, if the measure of 20.7 per cent came from blood taken from the heart, was it taken from the right- or the left-hand side?

Krompecher and his colleagues provided a detailed account of how carbon monoxide and carboxyhaemoglobin travel in the body. It goes from the lung to the left side of the heart from where it is pumped in the blood through the body. It ends up on the right side of the heart. The pathologist's report 'has made the assumption that such circulation as is described above, was in the process of taking place in the body of Henri Paul producing a very high level of carbon monoxide in his heart and a high, albeit lower, level of carbon monoxide in the blood in his limbs. Their arguments and conclusions cannot be sustained for this very straightforward and obvious reason. It is a statement of fact in the report that, on impact, the thoracic aorta was ruptured. The flow of blood from the left side of the heart must have stopped at that moment.'

So carbon monoxide would not have flowed from the left side of the heart around the body. If it had flowed, Henri Paul wouldn't have been dead immediately the car crashed.

The independent experts added that this fact led to an even more fundamental issue. They discovered that blood was taken from Henri Paul's heart using a ladle. This seemed a little strange to them. In their experience, 'this means that it was not taken specifically from the left ventricle but was a mix of blood originating from both sides of the heart. The figure of the 20.7 per cent was therefore an *average* [their emphasis] of the two sides of the heart. This means that the level of carbon monoxide in the left ventricle must have been in excess of 28 per cent to 35 per cent, a significantly high level.' Even Professor Pounder, from Dundee University, would accept that so much carbon monoxide would impair performance.

The experts added that most of the blood in the ladle would probably have come from the right side of the heart as this area had a far greater volume of blood than the left region. If so, there would have been even more than 35 per cent of carbon monoxide in the left ventricle of the heart. In their final report in November 2001, they repeated that point, arguing that 'one can conclude that the real measure of carboxyhaemoglobin in the arterial blood of the left side of the heart was much higher than the average of 20.7 per cent.'

For them, this wasn't an academic mystery but something that had to be explained if the true causes of the crash were ever to be revealed. They pointed to a paper by Dr Charles Winek in *Forensic Science International* (1981) which suggested that as blood decomposes, pigments form which can interfere with the measurement of carbon monoxide. But even on a doctor-to-doctor basis they were never given that information.

Over a year after the crash, on October 16th 1998, Professor Lecompte and Dr Pepin were aware their work was being scrutinised by independent and well-known post-mortem experts. Krompecher and his colleagues had written to them. Lecompte and Pepin countered that these high levels of carbon monoxide were simple to explain. Henri Paul was a heavy smoker. If he consumed two packets of cigarettes a day, he would have something like ten per cent of carbon monoxide in his blood. They seemed to ignore the fact that the actual reading was 20.7 per cent and that, even four days after the crash, it was 12.8 per cent.

But, Krompecher and his colleagues pointed out two difficulties with this thesis. Firstly, the general consensus was that even smoking two packs a day would yield a reading of only eight per cent of carbon monoxide. Secondly, one witness told the judge that Henri Paul smoked five to six cigarillos a day – far less than forty cigarettes.

Pepin and Lecompte then suggested much of the carbon monoxide came from the airbags. The independent experts noted that Murray MacKay, professor of transport safety at Birmingham University, rejected the idea the airbags would produce any significant level of carbon monoxide. Mercedes-Benz made the same point. Yet no one suggested that the levels of carbon monoxide were the result of some kind of 'assault' on Henri Paul.

The level of carbon monoxide would also have made it likely that Henri Paul would have been showing symptoms such as lack of concentration, even stumbling, which would alert the bodyguards. High levels of carbon monoxide make it hard to concentrate, victims can report blurred vision and be unsteady on their feet. Jean François Meyer, the lawyer for the Paul family, said that Henri Paul would have been obviously unfit to drive. In their report of 1999, the experts said 'the combination of an allegedly very high alcohol level and high carbon monoxide level' would make Henri Paul behave in an erratic way. It would have been obvious he should not be allowed to take the wheel. Instead, the Ritz videos show Henri Paul walking normally and tying his shoelaces nimbly.

The independent experts then went on to discuss the final conclusions Professor Lecompte and Dr Gilbert Pepin presented to *Juge* Stephan. Most peculiarly, they noted that the pathologist and toxicologist did not reply to one rather central question Stephan asked. What was the cause and what were the circumstances of the death of Henri Paul? The independent experts concluded by offering four different hypotheses that would explain the presence of the carbon monoxide in Paul's blood.

The first was that the samples were really from Henri Paul's body and that he had been exposed to extremely high levels of carbon monoxide during the last day of his life or that his lifestyle led to such a level routinely being in his body. They noted that Dodi Al Fayed had perfectly normal levels of carbon monoxide. That meant it was unlikely that the car had, somehow, picked up a dose of carbon monoxide which affected the passengers.

The second hypothesis was that the pathologist and the toxicologist made an analytical error. Krompecher and his colleagues noted that the level of carbon monoxide was measured in two separate ways. First Dr Pepin did a spectometric analysis with the blood actually visible; the second technique relied on an instrument called a 270 CO-Oximeter made by Ciba-Corning. International guidelines recommend using two different means of measurement to avoid mistakes. Dr Pepin would have had to fail to notice any differences between the readings taken in these different ways. The experts said this is most unlikely as he signed each page of the analyses.

The third hypothesis was that the samples did come from Henri Paul's body but that, while the samples were being subjected to toxicological tests, there was a mix-up. As a result, the blood and urine which were examined came, in fact, from another body. The four experts found this unlikely, though it was impossible to exclude.

The fourth hypothesis was the most disturbing. There had been a mix-up in the samples at the very beginning. In other words, the blood, urine and other materials were initially taken from the body of someone other than Henri Paul – and, at the start of the process at least, no one noticed. Krompecher and his colleagues ended with harsh words about their colleagues, accusing them of being unscientific and of producing explanations which they as scientists must have known to be fanciful. Their 'attitude is inexplicable,' they said.

In the penultimate chapter, I offer a worrying

explanation of what might have caused the high level of carbon monoxide if the autopsy results do indeed relate to Henri Paul's body.

Juge Herve Stephan admitted off the record to Francis Gillery (who directed the French film I co-produced) that Henri Paul's blood was the great mystery of the affair.

When I made *Diana – The Night She Died*, I drew attention to the report of the four experts. When I went back over the paperwork, I realised I had missed something crucial. It seemed at first to be just an academic and bureaucratic detail.

The search for Andrieux

Krompecher and his colleagues had noted the existence of a document labelled '(D789/1)' which was attached to the report of the autopsy. This document reported samples being taken which were not mentioned in the official autopsy. This document, the four experts said, contained 'inscriptions which seem to have no link with this affair'. This was followed by a name in brackets. The name given was '(Andrieux)'. Initially, I thought that the fact this name was put in brackets meant it was an academic reference. It was only later that I realised that this might have rather more important implications.

The document tagged (D789/1) was not the only additional document. The experts also found it 'extremely surprising' there was mention of a second document which was identical to the first one, but which was 'filled out on September 1st', not on August 31st, the date of the autopsy. This document referred to 'male X' and, then, male X was scrawled over and replaced by 'Paul' in one report and by 'Henri Paul' in a second report. This second document spoke of yet more samples being taken; these included samples of urine, gastric contents, hair and viscera. 'No explanation is given for the reasons that led to the writing of this second document,' Krompecher and his colleagues noted. They added, 'It is impossible to gather all over again, twenty-four hours after a standard autopsy, urine and stomach contents.' So what would be the point of such data?

The independent experts also added it was strange that the number of samples of urine and stomach contents doubled on September 1st, the day after the autopsy was done. In the first report there was one sample of each; in the second there were two.

What might be the meaning of 'male X' and 'Andrieux'? The experts wanted to know. In most situations they were insiders who could call on the police to help but, in this case, it was different. They raised the question of what it might mean but they had no way of pursuing it, for reasons which will become very apparent.

One possible explanation is that there was the body of a person called Andrieux in the morgue that night. In Britain it would have been relatively simple to confirm or deny that. It is likely that there would be an inquest on a dead man whose body ended up in a pathology lab. As I mentioned earlier, I made a *Dispatches* programme for Channel 4 which examined rates of deaths in old people's homes, and I found that the Coroners' Officers were helpful; they supplied me with information about who had died where. For two pounds I could obtain a copy of the death certificate. With the date, a name and the name of the morgue, it would have been possible to get the death certificate of all the Andrieuxs who had died in London between, say, August 30th and September 1st.

I thought I would do the same in Paris. I asked Murielle La Coche, David Carr Brown's wife, who deals skilfully with the French authorities, to help me. She assumed that all she had to do was go to each town hall in Paris and ask to look at the register of deaths for the relevant dates. She started at the *mairie* closest to the Salpêtrière. There, she made an interesting discovery. In France, the register of death cannot be consulted by the public. I was astonished both as a journalist and because, as a teenager, I spent a summer in a French village called Bauduen. I became friendly with the mayor and the parish priest who had given me a demonstration of what history meant. On the shelves of the *mairie* were the bound volumes of records of births and deaths going back to 1577.

But today in France, the registers of death are kept secret for fifty years. You can only enquire about a death certificate if you belong to the same family as the deceased and, even then, you need an identity card and other documents to prove you are entitled.

So, we decided to look at the electoral register. Finding out if the body of a man called Andrieux was in the morgue at the same time as Henri Paul was made harder by the fact that there are about 1.3 million individuals with that surname.

There were twenty-three dead bodies at the Salpêtrière that night. In all these cases samples would have been taken and analysed. It is possible there was a mix-up between one of those taken from Henri Paul and that taken from someone who killed himself using a car exhaust, which would have produced a high carbon monoxide reading. The independent experts say that is a 'strong and plausible hypothesis'. In other words, the corpse with the high alcohol level might not be Henri Paul. François Meyer, the Paul family lawyer, told us '*il faudra trouver une autre explication*' – they will have to find another explanation (for the crash).

One of my police contacts tried to get hold of the names and addresses of the deceased housed in the Institut morgue on the night of August 31st. I wanted to see if there was an Andrieux among them. My contact finally gave up. It was one of the few times he could not bypass the bureaucracy. All the relevant documents concerning the bodies in the morgue that night are now held under strict security in the Ministry of Justice. They can be consulted only by those the Ministry approves.

Krompecher, Mangin and their colleagues added that, as the police had retained samples no. 1 and no. 4 – it seemed to have been the case that all the other samples were lost or could not be traced – that there was still material which would allow a DNA test to be carried out. They said they had taken DNA samples from the mother of Henri Paul. Even if the samples had been poorly stored, it would be possible to get enough DNA to determine whether or not the samples had come from Henri Paul.

On October 19th 2000, the French Attorney General assured the Paul family that Pepin had maintained the samples in such a state as to make it possible for them to be tested again.

The Paul family through their lawyer, François Meyer, claim this assurance turned out to be utterly unreliable. In a deposition made in January 2002, the Paul family lawyers reminded the French court of appeal that Dr Pepin had said the remaining samples were 'in very feeble quantity'. The documents Meyer filed alleged that Dr Pepin had been forced to admit that the samples did not have any preserving agents. Meyer also claimed that the samples had not been stored properly. They should have been kept at forty degrees below freezing but, instead, they were apparently just placed in an ordinary fridge.

The Paul family still do not believe Henri Paul was drunk and their lawyer noted that this error with the preserving agents and the storage meant that whatever blood might still remain would be useless in terms of assessing the blood alcohol level. The statement of complaint also pointed out too that the court had asked for seven samples kept in good condition. That had apparently not been done. Maître Meyer also highlighted the fact that Pepin now said that one set of blood samples was in the possession of another expert but 'of which there is now no trace'. The Paul family still want to get access to their son's blood and urine samples. They claim they had been told the autopsy had been videoed and they wanted to see that video.

Despite what seem to be powerful arguments, the Paul family have got nowhere. The French court was adamant that Lecompte and Pepin had done nothing wrong. The French Attorney General took over the case and Henri Paul's blood and urine samples, in whatever condition they may be, remain the exclusive property of the French Republic. Henri Paul's family are furious they have not been allowed to carry out these tests; tests they have always said would clear their son. Clearing the blood samples issue needs to be looked into by the English coroner.

Again, the differences between the French and British legal systems are interesting. In Britain, the family could have asked for a judicial review of a decision taken by the Home Secretary but French law does not offer that possibility. Corinne Goetzmann who is a *juge d'instruction* like Stephan, refused to start the inquiry that the Paul family and Al Fayed wanted. They demanded a new '*instruction*' – this would in effect be a new investigation of a potential criminal act, that act being the falsification of the expert statements made by the experts in charge of the autopsy and toxicological analyses.

In August 2002, *Juge* Goetzmann noted that Article 6–1 of the penal code states that if someone complains that expert testimony has been falsified during an investigation, legal action can be taken only if that investigation has shown that a crime had indeed been committed. But *Juge* Stephan had decided, on September 3rd 1999, that there was no case for anyone to answer. Henri Paul was dead and could not be accused. The paparazzi were not charged with manslaughter. By the definition of Article 6–1, therefore, there had been no crime and, so, evidence of a crime could not have been falsified or tampered with. So no offence could have been committed. It did not matter if the expert witnesses had been negligent or lying. Goetzmann did not even offer a word of sympathy to Henri Paul's family in their predicament. Her decision in August 2002 closed the case in France.

Geordie Greig, the editor of *Tatler* magazine who has previously called for an inquest hearing (his sister-in-law was lady-in-waiting to Diana), told me in November 2003 that the British coroner has used as an 'excuse' the fact that legal proceedings in France still exist. But there is no law in Britain that requires that.

Henri Paul's autopsy was not the only controversial one. Princess Diana's body was flown home on September 1st. Her remains were taken to Fulham where an autopsy was carried out. The coroners have always refused to comment on the procedures used and what that autopsy revealed. I have some sympathy with their decision for two reasons. The first is the privacy of the dead. One recalls the very intrusive pictures of Marilyn Monroe dead on the mortuary slab. The second is that the one question that obsessed the press – particularly *Paris-Match* – and the public was whether Diana had been pregnant. But there are many other legitimate questions which still need answering. Was there carbon monoxide in her blood, for example?

On June 23rd 1998, another French toxicologist Andre Lienhart and Professor Lecompte set out for London. They went to New Scotland Yard where they met Dr John Burton, the then Royal Coroner, Dr Michael Burgess (now Royal Coroner) and Superintendent Jeffrey Rees. Dr Chapman, the forensic pathologist who had carried out the autopsy on the Princess, was also present.

The autopsy report was handed to the French pathologists for their private and personal use only. Apparently the pathologists said they wondered how the Princess could have survived such terrible injuries.

After the divorce, stripped of Her Royal Highness-title, Diana had no longer been protected by British security services as she had been before. Yet she needed protection. She had started a high-profile campaign to ban landmines. She was having an affair with a man whose family had many enemies. (In 2000, for example, a fax suggested that Mohamed Al Fayed was involved in smuggling nuclear material that could be used to make a dirty bomb. The fax was a forgery; Al Fayed won damages against the *Sunday Telegraph* which printed the story. But someone was keen enough to cause trouble to manufacture this forgery.) Diana became, in terms of her security, dependent on the kindness of strangers. That made her more vulnerable than she had been since her marriage. Ironically, of course, she loved her freedom even though there were moments when she seems to have been very worried about what might happen to her.

7

Drugs and Dirty Tricks –
What Was Found and Not Found
in the Car

Police procedure in Western countries includes keeping a detailed record of what was found in a vehicle which has crashed, and of the possessions found on the victims. In this chapter I outline the discrepancies between the official version of what was found and the facts I discovered later. Twelve hours after the crash, the traffic police were already under intense pressure not to tell the whole truth about what had been found in the car and that pressure came from the Élysée, the office of the French President.

The Mercedes S280 itself, the police soon realised, had a recent history that might have some bearing on the case. It had been stolen in April from outside the Taillevent restaurant in Paris. The Étoile Limousine Company, the owners and also the car-hire company owned by the Ritz, reported the theft to the police.

Some weeks later, the police recovered the car but were very surprised to find that its electronics and its braking system had been ripped out. Neither of these have much value if sold. When Étoile Limousine got the car back, they sent it to be repaired and refitted.

When I met Mohamed Al Fayed, I asked if he thought it was possible the car had been tampered with or poorly repaired. He dismissed the idea with a grand wave of his hand. The car was in perfect condition when it drove away on August 31st. The vehicles Étoile Limousine provided for the clients of the Ritz were always in first-class condition. Nicholas Davies in *Diana: Secrets and Lies* has revived this idea – that the car was sabotaged – arguing the safety belts were tampered with, but this is difficult to sustain because no one knew Dodi and Diana would use the decoy Mercedes till at most ninety minutes before they set off from the Ritz.

However, those who believed that the crash had been planned or was what the French called '*un accident provoqué*' argued that one of the most intelligent ways of achieving this would have been by tampering with the electronics and, especially, the braking system. This would be done by installing a new electronic braking system which had one frill the driver would know nothing about. The new system could be set so that it would respond to commands sent by remote control. The technology is no longer cutting edge; it is a sophisticated version of the kit used on model planes and boats. A chip is put in which starts to operate only when a pre-set command is sent on a particular frequency but, then, when that chip is activated, the driver no longer has control. The problem, of course, is how anyone could have predicted in April when Diana had no particular contact with Dodi that she would ever get in a vehicle associated with the Ritz Hotel.

We shall see that when the French inquiry dissected the vehicle, it found no trace of such a chip or of any other kind of sabotage. The theft seemed utterly senseless.

Tunisia 2003 – every war has its hotel

I have argued throughout that any investigative journalist needs luck and happenstance. You throw the net out but much depends on whom you meet and who will talk to you. That would prove to be the case.

In the autumn of 2002, a Dutch film producer, Ludi Boeken, asked me if I would become the English co-producer of a feature film, *Deadlines*. Set in 1982, the film follows an ambitious American journalist, Alex Randall, who is just a stringer in Paris. When he hears of the bomb in Beirut that killed 231 marines, Randall flies out on spec and gets lucky. This is a tale about luck, which came out of a film about luck. Randall is handed a number of scoops, but it takes him a while to realise that he is sharing a mistress with, and being manipulated by, the corrupt Foreign Minister. *Deadlines* owes something to Evelyn Waugh's classic novel *Scoop* about an innocent journalist, Boot, and something to personal experiences. Boeken had covered the Lebanon war for Dutch TV. His writer and co-director Michael Lerner had reported the war for *Newsweek*, too.

As ex-journalists, Boeken and Lerner thought their film would feel more authentic if the cast included some real hacks. I was asked not just to co-produce but to act. I played the part of the Reuters man in Beirut. (We shot the film in Tunisia because we thought Beirut was still risky, especially for a project with two Jewish producers.) Two other journalists agreed to act in the film, Bobby Buechler and Patrick Chauvel. Buechler often works for CBS TV and has won an Emmy. Patrick Chauvel is a wiry, dark man in his early fifties who still has the build of a good scrum-half. As I have previously mentioned, he is one of France's great war photographers. His portfolio includes some historic shots, including one of a solider in Lebanon leaping out of a burning tank. He too had been in Beirut in 1982.

Chauvel comes from distinguished diplomatic stock. His grandfather was ambassador to the Court of St James's for twelve years from 1958 to 1970 and got on so well with the Queen that she asked de Gaulle to extend his tour of duty in London. Patrick spent a good deal of his childhood in the embassy. On Saturday mornings, suitable diplomatic children would be invited to Buckingham Palace to play with Prince Charles. Charles and Chauvel once had a fight over some chocolate. Years later, Chauvel was at an official reception and an equerry whispered to him that Prince Charles would like a moment with him. Chauvel was taken to the Prince's study. They talked about the past, laughed and agreed the quarrel over the chocolate was bygones. I give this background to emphasise that Chauvel has no animus against Prince Charles and, also, that he is not the kind of man to scattergun allegations for the hell of it. He understood the implications, and the seriousness, of the story he was about to confide to me.

I hoped Chauvel might give me an introduction to some of his paparazzi friends who had been in the Alma Tunnel. But I was nervous about asking. Making a feature film involves hours of waiting, waiting for camera, waiting for sound and waiting for the light. As we waited on various Tunisian hilltops, I started a familiar routine for any hack. I talked to Chauvel about the Diana film. He never seemed to want to pursue the conversation too far, but finally, he said we would discuss the subject properly before he left.

I was getting anxious by the time the filming moved to the smart seaside resort of Hammamet. Chauvel was leaving for France the next day. I still hadn't got anywhere with him. I was beginning to think that I had put him in a difficult situation. Since we were working on the same film, he did not want to be rude, but he really did not want to discuss anything with me.

I was not very hopeful when I finally managed to sit down and drink with Chauvel in the rather garish gold lounge of our hotel in Hammamet. He was still a little diffident, I thought. He asked me to tell him what I had found out about the Alma crash. When I had finished he said he didn't think any of the paparazzi would talk because they had all been too bruised by the accusations made against them. It wasn't much consolation that I had guessed right. Chauvel didn't want to play.

Then, Chauvel's creased face broke into a smile and he said that he did know something which, he imagined, would be of some interest. Two weeks later, we met again in Paris and he agreed to be interviewed on camera. We had lunch first in his neighbourhood restaurant and then went to the flat he was staying in for a while. Even though it was just his temporary home, it was littered with photographs; his own, those of colleagues he liked.

He wanted to set what he knew in context. The behaviour of the photographers bothered him, as he knew more pictures had been taken than people imagined. 'I would never have taken pictures of the woman in the car. But I don't think the paparazzi behaved so badly. They were under pressure.' Chauvel reminded me Dr Mailliez had said that the photographers had not stopped him helping the injured. And then he got to the heart of his story.

Two years after Diana died, Chauvel was making a film about French drivers for France 2 TV, the French equivalent of BBC2. He was spending long days and nights with the traffic police in Paris. 'The film took a long time and finally I became friends with them,' he told me. The traffic policeman's lot is not a happy one. 'They feel lonely, they pick up bodies every night, and they see horrible things, so they started talking. They talked about the usual stuff and, then, soon really, about the famous, or infamous, accident.

'The traffic police arrived with the ambulances but they didn't see much. They didn't see the paparazzi, as the press said, the way it was told,' Chauvel said. 'They could see immediately that if the Mercedes was going fast, there was no way that the paparazzi in small cars could have been close. And if anyone had been following close behind the car, they would have become part of the accident. They could not have braked and kept out of it.' Chauvel added that the traffic-police investigators found no traces of braking. One detail the police revealed made Chauvel a little uncomfortable because it showed the paparazzi were pushing it. Chauvel said: 'Lady Di reacted to the flash (of one of the cameras) and her last word was leave me alone.'

As the traffic police started to trust Chauvel more, they began to share with him much confidential information. 'One of the guys I was talking to said' – here Chauvel paused, searching for the right word in English, 'it was all under reserve . . . confidential . . . he doesn't want to say who he is, or who he works for. He said to me there was a lot of pressure about certain things.' Chauvel added that it was ridiculous in a way, 'because there was not a lot to talk about. They had pressure from the Élysées and they were told to keep it low. They didn't think it was a big deal.' As far as they were concerned, the Alma was just another crash.

But the political instructions from on high did not go down well with the traffic police and, in particular, with one of the officers Chauvel had become friendly with. 'This guy was pissed off because of the pressure and he told me if ever this goes bad, I'll leave this photo in my office and you can take it.' He added that it was a photograph which sections of the press would pay handsomely for. His friend showed him it one night. Chauvel had all the time he wanted to study it and he is a man who understands photographs.

The photo was clearly taken by a flash camera outside the tunnel, Chauvel said. 'It was a photo taken by the flash . . . there is a speed camera outside the tunnel . . . there was a flash . . . the camera is gone now.' It was lucky that I had taken a shot of the outside arch of the tunnel the *one* night we were filming there. That was where the speed camera had been positioned.

Chauvel went on: 'The flash is a frontal flash so you can see the people in the car. And you can see all the people in the car and you could recognise all the people in the car.' He recognised Diana at once. 'The driver was normal. I didn't know his face before. The guy on the right was a little bit tense, he seems a little afraid. Maybe the car is going a little too fast.' That 'guy' was Trevor Rees-Jones. But the first truly interesting detail is this. 'The people in the back are laughing their heads off and having fun . . . they seem to be having fun. They seem to be pretty happy.' It seemed some consolation to Chauvel that 'Dodi and Diana died happy'.

Chauvel's evidence is important for another reason too. It was suggested by many people that Dodi was in a state of panic that night because the photographers were after them and that he ordered Henri Paul to drive very fast. A man who is laughing with the woman he is involved with is unlikely to be in a state of panic, and I say that with the confidence of someone whose PhD thesis was on the psychology of laughter (Cohen 1985).

Chauvel's account is important for two reasons. First, in his summary of the inquiry's findings, *Juge* Stephan makes no mention either of a speed-camera photograph or of the photograph reproduced on the inside of the cover of this book. I explained in the last chapter that Stephan, however, did stress that the medical services were in no way to blame for Diana's death, they had had to deal with the extraordinary injuries Diana suffered because she was lying down when the car crashed. It was suggested her head rested in Dodi's lap. Chauvel is adamant that he could recognise Diana. That

means she could have not have been lying down because
he would not have been able to see her face.

A number of conspiracy theories claimed Henri Paul
lost control of the Mercedes as flashes fired at the car
from inside the tunnel blinded him. Commandos do
have military-style flashguns and they have been used
to shock and stun in certain operations like rescuing
passengers held hostage on planes. Some of these flashguns produce a burst of light seven times more intense
than the sun. For me the deadly flashgun theory is a
shade hard to believe. Why did no one spot at least
one commando?

Chauvel's description of the photograph gives a
more prosaic explanation. It seems that there was a
flash just outside the tunnel but it was a perfectly
ordinary speed-camera flash. It had been triggered
automatically because the Mercedes was doing more
than 60kph. There is no evidence that such flashes
disable drivers or cause them to lose control of their
vehicles.

I asked Chauvel why the police had never made this
picture public. He replied; 'I have no idea why this
picture was not released. That for me was a mystery. But
maybe it was because when they made their first
comment to the press, the official comment was that the
flash didn't work.' But this denial soon became suspect,
Chauvel added, 'when they found out that a guy who
was driving in his normal car ten minutes before (the
crash) got his ticket fifteen days later.' That would suggest
the flash camera outside the Alma had been functioning
a few minutes before the Mercedes entered the tunnel.
Why should it have started malfunctioning? So the police

claimed the camera had not been on.

Chauvel is sure that the photo he saw had the speed on it but it was not what interested him most. A number of things would seem to follow from what he says. The police would have seen a speed-camera photo by midday on August 31st at the very latest. Then, the decision was taken to deny the existence of any such photograph even though it was valuable evidence. The photograph would have cleared up immediately the question of the speed the Mercedes had reached. We would have known whether it was belting along at 122mph as some headlines blared or whether the speed was much slower.

But the existence of this picture was not the only revelation Chauvel made to me.

I asked Chauvel if the traffic police had also told him anything of what had been found in the car but not mentioned in the log of effects of the victims. I hoped to get confirmation that they had found Dodi's mobile phone. Chauvel paused and said, in a very matter of fact way, 'Yes, they found stuff. They found cocaine in the bag.'

I was stunned, and asked in whose bag the cocaine had been found.

'There was only one woman in the car,' Chauvel smiled ruefully. He repeated what the traffic police officer told him. 'He did say there was cocaine in the back of the car.' He added that 'it was nothing special' and he wanted to make two things clear. First, the traffic police often found drugs in cars that crashed. In the case of the Mercedes, however, the drugs could not have been the cause because the cocaine, he added, 'had nothing to do with the driver, it was with the passenger'.

I also asked Chauvel if his police contacts had said anything about Dodi's missing mobile phone. He added he was unable to say anything specific about Dodi's mobile phone. He told me: 'I don't see anyone stealing anything in the car.' There were policemen around and Dorzee was keeping an eye on the car because he was worried someone would steal Diana's jewels.

'The guys who were investigating . . . he's a normal investigator and he does his job honestly but these people don't like to be pushed around. The personalities involved made it a hot potato.' (Chauvel speaks English well and it was his phrase.) And the traffic police experienced considerable pressure. It was because of this that the traffic police officer said to Chauvel, '"If things go bad, I'll leave it (the photograph) for you to find in my office."' Chauvel then tried to persuade the officer to appear in my film but the man refused. This was not unreasonable because he would risk losing his job.

I thought Channel 5 might not want to broadcast Chauvel's claims at their most hard-hitting so I did a second version of the portion of the interview relating to cocaine, a version in which Chauvel used the more general word 'dope', rather than cocaine. That was the version we eventually used in the film but I taped both versions. When the *Sunday Express* reported on my film they linked this to Dodi's history of taking drugs but Chauvel said nothing of that.

I walked out of Chauvel's flat with a good feeling that any documentary filmmaker will know. You have something really unusual in the can, something that will make your film. I went straight to an editing suite and made a number of copies of the tape. This was not one to lose.

The claim that drugs were in the car is, of course, dramatic. But Chauvel is a responsible man. Nevertheless, any allegation that is made by just one source should be treated with caution.

And then, I had another piece of luck. My friend David Carr Brown was asked to make a series of films about a Paris suburb and, among other things, how it dealt with crime. The project had the full cooperation of the French Ministry of Justice. David met, and then introduced me to, one of the policemen based there. He had been in the narcotics squad in August 1997. This man confirmed to us Chauvel's story. Drugs had been found in the vehicle and there was great pressure to hush it up. The same officer was also perfectly aware of the photograph Chauvel had seen. It is now locked in a safe at Paris police headquarters, he alleged.

The news that there was cocaine in the Mercedes, and that it was in Diana's handbag, would have been passed quickly up the chain of command. Senior officers would have reported it to their political masters. A few hours later, their instructions were clear. The French Republic at the highest levels did not want this to leak out. I have pointed out earlier that Dodi's mobile was, astonishingly, not found at the crash scene or logged in the list of the effects of the victims. It is possible that, as Dodi was known to buy cocaine, his mobile contained records of conversations with people who were known to the police as drug dealers.

The question is, when did the French tell the British? I don't have an answer to that. But I find it hard to believe that the British authorities did not learn the truth quickly. MI6 had many staff in Paris that August and were preparing a briefing on the Al Fayeds for Buckingham Palace. They would have been talking with the French. Scotland Yard was being kept abreast of developments and would have pressed the French for every detail.

The fact that Diana had been carrying cocaine in her bag created a dilemma for the powers that be on both sides of the Channel, I believe, both an ethical and a political dilemma. No one wanted to cause more pain to Diana's children. But there was also the issue of how the British public would respond to such information, especially as the Royal Family was under attack. The Royal Family, and even the Queen, did not seem to feel the sorrow the country was feeling. It is not hard to imagine the outcry there would have been if the news that Diana had cocaine in her handbag had been made public. Many people would simply not have believed it and would have seen it as a very nasty piece of 'spin', an attempt to blacken the memory of Diana. Bureaucratic instinct prevailed, and that instinct was 'to keep it low', as Chauvel said.

This decision was taken quickly and obviously under pressure. No one thought clearly about the implications it might have for holding inquests into the deaths of Dodi and Diana.

The delayed inquest

The last inquest held by the Royal Coroner was into the 1972 plane crash which killed Prince William of Gloucester. The Royal Coroner has to convene an inquest when a member of the Royal Family dies in untoward circumstances, as Prince William did.

The coroner can decide to hold the inquest in front of a jury and members of the jury can sometimes ask questions. The jury can return only one of a set number of verdicts – natural causes, suicide, death by misadventure, unlawful killing or an open verdict. Despite this limitation, a well-conducted inquest can ask and answer questions that matter deeply to the bereaved.

It is surprising how many deaths in the United Kingdom are considered by a coroner. If a doctor feels there is the slightest doubt about certifying someone has died of natural causes, he or she has to inform the coroner's officer. About forty per cent of all deaths in the United Kingdom are referred to a coroner's officer.

Until 1983, if a body was returned to the United Kingdom for burial, the coroner could use his discretion to decide whether an inquest was needed. But then, the law was amended. The family of a nurse who fell to her death in Saudi Arabia sued the local West Yorkshire coroner to get an inquest into her death. The authorities thought this was unnecessary but they lost the argument in court. Since then the law states inquests have to be held on British citizens who die abroad in mysterious circumstances if the body is returned to the UK. The coroner does not have any discretion.

The bodies of Diana and Dodi were brought back

to the United Kingdom on August 31st 1997. Four days later the *Daily Telegraph* reported that the Royal Coroner confirmed there would be an inquest and said it would be held in a normal time frame. Dodi Al Fayed lived in Surrey and the Surrey coroner, Dr Michael Burgess, also said there would be an inquest into his death. The inquests were finally opened – and adjourned – only in January 2004.

For six years a number of reasons have been given for the delay. The first was that Mohamed Al Fayed tried to get the two inquests joined so that there would be one single inquest on Diana and Dodi. Al Fayed lost that case in the English courts in 1999. He is now demanding a public inquiry through the Scottish courts. A second reason given for the delay was that there were still proceedings going on in France. Neither of these reasons holds as the Coroners Act of 1988 does not insist all other proceedings are ended before an inquest begins. The act says in fact the inquests should be held 'as soon as practicable'. The coroner must have judged it 'practicable' when he said he would give a date for the inquest in a week's time. So what changed then? As I said earlier, friends of the coroner say he has been put under intense pressure by the Royal Family. The only legal proceedings in France since 1999 concern allegations of malpractice at Henri Paul's autopsy, and even these were settled more than eighteen months ago. Al Fayed then started a case for invasion of privacy against the paparazzi – a case he lost in November 2003 – but that had nothing to do with the causes of the accident.

I believe the suppression of evidence I have outlined earlier has implications for any inquest. The inquest

system is not perfect, but it is public. Coroners have
the power to compel witnesses to give evidence. An
inquest will mean that all the technical evidence about
the car crash and all the medical evidence concerning
Dodi and Diana will be examined in public. The
coroner, in fact, has called Scotland Yard to everyone's
surprise, to help him sift fact from fiction. It will be
hard for the French police, the doctors and the pathologists to refuse to come. There would be a diplomatic
outcry if they stayed away.

Since the issues and allegations are complex, I think
it sensible to summarise them. The inquest cannot legit-
imately avoid evidence which shows that one or more
of the passengers had taken cocaine or had it in their
possession. It cannot avoid asking why the speed-camera
photograph had been suppressed. It cannot avoid the
question of why Dodi's mobile phone had disappeared,
and how that might have happened. Such revelations
might embarrass powerful people affected by this
tragedy. Again at the risk of seeming pedantic, it seems
useful to spell out the potential embarrassment.

Mohamed Al Fayed had no illusions about his son,
but he has become very protective of his memory.
When he showed us round Harrods, he took us to see
the shrine in the department store's basement he has
built as a tribute to Diana and Dodi. Again, he spoke
of them having been 'executed'. He watched as we
filmed and, then, walked away. His mood changed
swiftly. All of a sudden, he pointed to the huge golden
statue of the Sphinx and asked with a smile if I recognised the face. It was much like his own, he laughed.
If you despise Al Fayed as a mountebank, you would

think that was perfect hypocrisy. If you don't despise him, you think a man can only spend so much time thinking about the death of his sometimes wayward son. And, then – and you don't need a PhD based on your research on the psychology of laughter to do this – you remember one of the tried, tested and very human ways of coping with trauma is to make jokes.

Al Fayed would not have wanted the stories about cocaine to surface because there had been much press coverage of Dodi's link with the drug. He complained to the *Sunday Express* that my documentary was vicious in suggesting any link between illegal drugs in the car and his son's missing mobile. We made no link of that sort, in fact. Al Fayed would have been in a position to publish the full details of the autopsy on Dodi but they have never been made public.

Buckingham Palace may have had its own reasons for not being keen on an inquest. The honourable one is a wish to protect Prince William and Prince Harry but I do not believe that was the only reason. Some royal advisers might be pleased that telling the world about the cocaine would damage Diana's reputation. Some in the royal entourage had always believed Charles has never had a fair press because Diana kept winning the publicity wars. But some advisers to the Royal Family were also only too aware of the political risk of being seen to tarnish Diana's memory. In dealing with this tragedy I have complained that too much has been covered up. I certainly was not going to ignore Chauvel's evidence, especially as I have made two films about unexplained deaths and in both the families believed it was important to get the whole truth on the record.

The French authorities too would hardly want it known that they had apparently suppressed the last photograph of the Mercedes before it crashed and put political pressure on the traffic police to 'keep it low', as Patrick Chauvel put it.

8

The Wreck of the Car and No-Go Areas

The wreck was driven away from the tunnel and taken to the IRCGN forensic laboratories (the *Institut de Recherché Criminelle de la Gendarmerie Nationale*) soon after 3am on August 31st. As stated earlier, we were told that on the night none of the team who would eventually study the vehicle was available, so when the inquiry asked two of France's leading forensic experts, François Nibodeau and Bernard Amouroux, to tooth-comb the vehicle, neither of them had seen it on site and neither had been able to collect forensic evidence personally. But by 4.30, of course, the Alma Tunnel was opened to traffic. These experts started their work the day after the crash away from the tunnel.

Nibodeau indicated during the making of *Lady Died* that he was very nervous about certain aspects of the investigations. He let it be understood that he had been very concerned about interference with his enquiries, not by the judge but by security services, especially foreign security services. He would not say more than that.

To help the forensic experts understand what

happened to the Mercedes, *Juge* Stephan ordered a number of 'reconstructions'. The first took place seven weeks after the crash. *Juge* Stephan had the Mercedes returned to the Alma Tunnel and placed in the exact position in which it had come to a final stop. The Alma was again surreal. Searchlights lit up the bare tunnel. The 'reconstruction' had been announced and it drew a large crowd; the police erected barriers to keep onlookers well away. The press didn't get close so news crews had to film on long lenses; the footage of the night has a spooky, shadowy feel as officials who are mere shapes walk and sometimes bend down. With this quirky lighting, the only person who is easy to identify on the footage is Stephan's fellow magistrate Marie Christine Devidal.

Months later, in June 1998, the inquiry rented a race-track outside Paris at Montlhery in Essonne. The idea now was to research how fast the car could go and whether motorcycles like those the paparazzi were driving could keep up. The official top speed of the Mercedes was 131mph according to the manufacturers. The police guarded the track while Nibodeau and Amouroux supervised a series of races, in effect. The situation was a little bizarre. Only one of the paparazzi arrested had been on a bike, the others had been in cars, and ten months on, it was generally accepted that the paparazzi had not been close enough behind the Mercedes to cause the crash or to have overtaken it. The driver closest behind the Mercedes, Erik Petel, had finally given his version of events to the inquiry.

In theory, the tests at Montlhery showed that the motorbikes could have overtaken the Mercedes but, if the drivers were not of Grand Prix standard, they would have had some trouble managing the curve that dips into the Alma Tunnel. The logic is a little Alice in Blunderland, as a flat racing surface like Montlhery is not the most obvious place to test whether motor-bikes can overtake a car on a stretch of road with two tunnels, each of which one drives down into. Ottavioli, the ex-head of the *brigade criminelle* who had been hired by Al Fayed, was not impressed by the expert-ise and suggested that the experts were '*experts de la merde*'.

After the racing experiments, it took Nibodeau and his colleagues a further three months to hand in their report, which they did on November 1st 1998. I am going to be pedantic because the issues are highly tech-nical. The report was very thorough and dealt with issues like tyre pressures, the lines of force that caused the damage and the trajectory of the car. By the time they reported, it was accepted that the Mercedes first hit the right-hand wall of the tunnel, bounced back and hit the thirteenth pillar and, then, wheeled round again to finish as it did. The main conclusions of the experts related to four questions:

- Was there any evidence of sabotage on the car?
- How fast had the Mercedes been travelling?
- Did it brake?
- Was there any evidence that the Mercedes had hit or been hit by another vehicle?

Sabotage

The experts concluded that there had been no sabotage and that the Mercedes was in perfect working order when it crashed.

More recently, Nicholas Davies in *Diana: Secrets and Lies* has claimed that Diana was killed because her seat belt was faulty as a nut had been filed off by rogue members of MI5 and the French security agency, DST *Directoire de la Surveillance du Territoire*. I have already suggested that involving French agents in a plot to kill the mother of the future King of England would give Paris endless power to blackmail the British and, is therefore, unlikely.

But there is a simpler problem with Davies' theory. Since the decision to use the second decoy Mercedes was made at the very last minute, the agents would have had to improvise at speed and run the risk of being caught in the act. Davies also seems to presume that wherever spooks go, they carry the metal-cutting equipment needed to cut bolts. In addition, Davies claims Henri Paul had been told all the speed cameras would be switched off, which was why he could go as fast as he liked to avoid the paparazzi. But I do not suppose the question of whether or not a speed camera caught him so that the Ritz had to pay a fine for speeding bothered Henri Paul too much.

The speed of the car

The inquiry was either not made aware of the speed-camera photograph Patrick Chauvel saw or it came under pressure, as the police had been, to bury that fact.

But the speed camera was not the only camera which could have revealed how fast the Mercedes was going. John Macnamara told me he had always wondered why all the CCTV cameras from Concorde to the Alma Tunnel were switched off that night and there are certain conspiracy theorists who claim that was to allow agents to infiltrate themselves in front, beside and behind the Mercedes without leaving any evidence. Neither Macnamara nor Al Fayed has any proof of this but it is true that no CCTV footage was ever produced or mentioned by the police. I suspect the truth was more bureaucratic. Once the police said that the speed camera at the Alma was malfunctioning, the disinformation spread and was exaggerated in a way very familiar to those who study rumours. Soon the story spiralled into the 'fact' that all the cameras on the route were out of action that night.

I said earlier that the police had first claimed that the car had been doing 122mph because the speedometer needle was stuck there. This was a remarkable error for traffic police to make. Accident investigators know that where a needle finishes after an accident does not matter because instruments get jolted and where they end up may bear no relationship to the speed of the car at the moment of impact. Christopher Wain of the BBC reported that almost immediately after the crash. Instead, accident investigators look for a phenomenon known as *needle slap* – a mark which *can* be made by the speedometer needle on the face of the instrument at the point of impact. Nibodeau did not mention finding such a slap.

So the inquiry had to resort to different techniques. Usually when accident investigators try to work out the speed of a crashed vehicle, the method they use is called backtracking. For this, they find the first point at which they can see traces of braking and then they measure the distance from there to the point of impact and use that to work out the pre-impact speed. In some news footage you can spot the backtrackers at work; two officers push a unicycle to trace the path of the car and its speed. They consult watches and other measuring devices as they run their quaint one-wheel machine back and forth to the thirteenth pillar.

In addition, accident investigators use a formula which also allows for the reaction time of the driver. Nibodeau assumed Henri Paul was drunk and that always leads investigators to suppose reaction time is slower, but there are two problems with this model. If you know how long it has taken a car to cover a hundred yards, you can, of course, work out its speed; but no one was timing the Mercedes. This explains why the judge decided to do something most investigations simply cannot afford. *Juge* Stephan asked Mercedes-Benz to carry out tests in which at least two S280s were crashed at different speeds. The logic was to see at what speed a car would have to be travelling in order to produce the kind of damage Dodi and Diana's Mercedes sustained.

There is considerable literature on single car accidents. According to Kruger, an independent oil engineer and engineering expert, in an accident in which there are no skid marks and a collision has occurred with an object, say a tree, 'a speed calculation would be based on the amount of energy which would be expended crushing the front of the car. If the car hit basically dead centre on the hood, the crush can be measured and using the stiffness coefficient for the vehicle (the vehicle acts somewhat like a spring) a calculation of the energy necessary to cause the damage can be made.' The stiffness coefficient measures the strength of the vehicle and once you have measured the damage, you can work backwards to calculate the speed at the time of impact.

Afterwards, one can calculate the speed with any rolling or sliding friction, which can be ascertained from the vehicle's approach to the tree to work out the velocity at the time that the vehicle lost control or left the road.

The theory is impressive but it depends on having enough information, and it shows how much they had to struggle that Nibodeau and Amouroux were not able to solve the puzzle definitively. Their conclusions outlined three possible speeds which could have caused the wreck to be in the shape it was. They were: 95kph, 115kph, 155kph; i.e. there was no way the Mercedes could have been going at its top speed of 131mph

In every case the car was going too fast but the experts leaned towards the slower of these speeds. The claim that the car was going insanely fast was not proved and, in fact, contra-indicated.

I use the word 'insanely' deliberately. The accident investigators went further claiming 'that Paul's brain which had been shown to have been under the influence of drugs and drink had been overloaded with information' (Gregory 2000). The dossier added that 'when this phenomenon appears we notice that the driver does the opposite of what he should do and an accident is inevitable.' Psychologists have studied information overload for years; one of the great authorities on the subject was the late Donald Broadbent, the first psychologist to be elected to the Royal Society. He recreated in the lab the kinds of situation that often happened in planes and cars. Information overload depends on the number of stimuli the brain has to process, the speed at which they appear and whether they are all in central or peripheral vision. Information overload does not affect the brain as simply as the French experts seem to suggest – and that is a subject I will return to at the very end of the book.

Did the car brake or not?

The story of the braking is not easy to work out. If Henri Paul had braked well before entering the tunnel, either because he feared he was going too fast, or because there was some unexpected obstacle or emergency, it would suggest he was in control of the car and not drunk. There were long skid marks in the tunnel, which the police first assumed had been caused by the Mercedes skidding. But the experts concluded that the skid marks had been made earlier by another

car. Again, all the forensic evidence relating to this
would have had to be gathered in about ninety minutes,
after the Mercedes had been removed and before 4.30
when the tunnel was reopened.

On the basis of that short search, Nibodeau and
Amouroux reported that the Mercedes did not brake
until sixty-nine metres from the point of impact. That
would mean the car braked only five metres before it
entered the tunnel as the thirteenth pillar is sixty-four
metres inside the tunnel. I shall argue that this 'conclusion' was forced on the experts by two errors in
procedure. First, the police ignored Erik Petel's evidence
about the 'implosion' even though it was corroborated
by at least one other witness. Second, the rapid re-
opening of the tunnel meant the site was not searched
as it should have been.

The Mercedes S280 was fitted with anti-lock braking
or ABS, which was seen as a major road-safety break-
through in the early 1990s. Anti-lock brakes are
controlled by a computer chip which senses when a
wheel locks up, or is about to lock up. The computer
orders the brake sensors to apply intermittent brake
pressure to prevent that happening. Alert drivers do the
same when they pump the brakes, but computer-
controlled sensors do it much faster than any man at
the wheel.

It was often said in the press that ABS does not leave
traces but this is not true. The traces are just harder to
identify for a number of reasons and that is not common
knowledge. The electronic wheel sensors either stop
the wheels locking or limit lock-up to only a split
second. Generally when wheels lock, wheel marks are

left which are essentially straight, prominent from end to end, and stop rather abruptly. When ABS brake marks are left, they resemble the straight-line skid of conventional vehicles but they are far fainter and are, therefore, harder to detect. Traffic conditions, weather and rain can wash away these marks fairly easily.

Old-style brakes leave tyre marks, which are solid continuous streaks if they are not interrupted by pedal pumping or irregularities in the road surface. They often begin and end abruptly. ABS marks, on the other hand, may follow an intermittent light and dark pattern. The reason for this is that sensors relay wheel speed information back to the microprocessor in the vehicle's computer. There is a slight delay in the feedback system, which allows the wheel to cycle from higher to lower brake force in a consistent pattern. For both these reasons – the lightness of ABS traces and their intermittent pattern – extra care is needed when an accident scene is searched. This was precisely the opposite of what happened in the Alma Tunnel. It is especially not hard to imagine traces of braking were missed on the dip that leads down into the tunnel.

The question of how ABS braking works also fits in with the evidence reported in Chapter 2 of a very loud noise that was heard a few seconds before the crash. Petel described this as an implosion. Clive Gourovoodou, a professional driver who was on the Place de l'Alma, said he had heard the engine whine. Crawford suggested to me that the loud noise was very similar to the sound made when a car is put into neutral by mistake. If his foot was on the accelerator that would make the engine rev up abruptly and that could lead to such a noise.

But the loud noise may have another explanation. It could have been produced by the Mercedes as Henri Paul tried to slam the brakes on very fast. The literature on ABS describes two sorts of noises that can occur when the system is engaging and neither sounds like a typical squeal of brakes. One is a loud groaning sound and the other is a loud grating sound. If Henri Paul had been braking too hard as he entered the tunnel, this would have set off the ABS system and produced a noise like that Petel heard as an 'implosion'. By 1995, insurance companies in America claimed that ABS was not the marvel the car makers had promised because many drivers often did not understand how it worked. They often panicked when they heard that noise and did not respond correctly because they thought it meant something was wrong with their brakes when, in fact, they were working correctly. The insurance companies had at first offered discounts on premiums for cars with ABS, but two big companies now proposed to stop those discounts because cars fitted with ABS had as many accidents as other cars (USAA, America's fifth largest insurer was one of the critics).

Petel's evidence and that of Clive Gourovoodou suggest the noise of this was heard before the car reached the mouth of the tunnel. And here the failure to gather forensic evidence properly caused real problems. In ninety minutes, the police could hardly search the sixty-four metres inside the tunnel to the thirteenth pillar; they had no hope of also searching the incline down into the tunnel for light tyre-tread marks and intermittent patterns which could show where the Mercedes had started braking. But that was not admitted in the dossier.

Henri Paul had been travelling faster than the speed limit so it is not that likely he braked so hard because he saw a speed camera. One of the most common reasons for slamming on the brakes is, of course, when a driver sees an obstacle in the road.

Was the Mercedes hit or obstructed by another car?

In the week after the crash, the Credo press agency interviewed Patrick Riou of the *police judiciaire*. Riou assured them that the police had found nothing else of any forensic interest in the tunnel. So there was some surprise when, on September 18th, the police story changed again. Now there was a new 'cause' of the accident. The police announced that they had been studying shards of a red taillight picked up in the tunnel. The pictures in the French inquiry dossier are dramatic.

Stephan did not explain in his summary how these shards had been found. One rumour was that an off-duty policeman had gone down into the tunnel to help and had found these red shards neatly piled in a heap. I don't think this is necessarily a sign of any conspiracy but it suggests that tidying the tunnel was as important as finding forensic evidence. It is another indication of how poor the search was.

The *Institut de Recherche Criminelle de la Gendarmerie* said the red-light shards came from the rear light casing

of a Fiat Uno manufactured between May 1983 and
September 1989. The scientists also found two sets of
scratches on the Mercedes – there were hardly visible
black scratches on the front door of the Mercedes, and
much larger white scratches on the wing mirror and
right side door. These were one to four centimetres
wide and 124 and 80 centimetres long. Étoile Limousine
insisted the car had no scratches before it left the Ritz
that night – and they were believed. The Mercedes
must have been in contact with a vehicle after leaving
the Ritz. The black scratches contained deposits of
polypropylene, which is used to make the bumpers of
many kinds of cars. The white scratches, however, were
more useful as they showed traces of white paint – and
that paint was relatively uncommon. This compound
known as Blanco 210 had been used on white Fiat
Unos made between 1983 and 1987.

The lower scratch was 81.5 centimetres from the
ground. The bumper on Fiat Unos is also 81.5 centimetres up from the ground. Suddenly a good deal of
evidence suggested that the cause of the crash was not
just that Henri Paul was drunk, but also that the
Mercedes had hit or been hit by a white Fiat Uno.

Madame Monteil and the *brigade criminelle* started the
search for this vehicle. There were also, as stated before
in Chapter 3, three witnesses who claimed to have seen
a white Fiat Uno at the scene. The first was the lawyer,
Gary Hunter. Hunter said he was looking out of his
hotel window and saw a white Fiat disappear into the
tunnel followed by a white Mercedes. He was interviewed on television but the French police did not
bother to talk to him and nor did the magistrate. Hunter

had spoken of a Fiat Uno before any of this forensic work was publicised which means his evidence could not have been influenced by what people imagined had caused the crash.

Two days after news of a Fiat was first reported, however, two other witnesses came forward after the police announced that they wanted to find the driver of this car. Georges and Sabine D were very specific in their description of the car and the driver. They saw it come out of the slip road that exits the tunnel. The Fiat was 'old and shabby' and it was zigzagging, while the driver was stocky, between thirty-five and forty years of age and apparently disturbed. He was looking in the rear-view mirror, which seemed very odd to them and he was going very slowly too. In the back of the car, there was a big dog that they thought might be a German shepherd; strangely, this dog had a shawl tied round his head! The couple even offered details of the colour of the handles on the car doors and Georges appeared to remember that the registration number might have included 78. In France, that indicates in which *departement* the car is registered.

When witnesses come forward with such detailed testimony after an event has been publicised, their evidence does need to be treated with caution, not because they are being dishonest but because their recall may well be influenced by what they imagine will help the police. Research by Dr James MacKeith and Gisli Gudjuddsohn of the Institute of Psychiatry (1997) has found that some individuals have a personality make-up that can make them eleborate what they saw, and not out of malice. It is just that such individuals are very suggestible and want to please persons they perceive as being in authority. They pick up cues from those who question them and, unconsciously, give back to interrogators what they think they want to hear. Sometimes they make false confessions to crimes they could not have committed; often they create utter confusion in investigations because they make up so many details. In the space of less than ten seconds Georges and Sabine noticed almost too many interesting details about the white Fiat Uno and its driver, it could be argued. This had nothing to do with conspiracy, but a lot to do with psychology.

Stephan had no choice but to order an intensive search for any Fiat Unos in the *departement* 78 to the west of Paris. The police actually contacted 40,000 owners of Fiat Unos in the area around the city but they did not reach out further. No one ever explained why they limited the search area.

The most promising lead for a few days was a Vietnamese plumber called Lee Van Than. Madame Monteil was especially suspicious because his car had been resprayed red the day after the crash. After six hours of intensive questioning, however, the police realised this was the wrong man. Lee Van Than had a good alibi as he had been working as a nightwatchman at the time and a number of witnesses vouched for the fact that he did not leave the premises he was guarding between 11.00 and 7.00. He could not have been at the Alma.

A few people have never accepted the reality of the white Fiat Uno. But even those who argue that the crash was an accident pure and simple, like Martyn

Gregory, who made the *Dispatches* programme, often seem to accept there was some such vehicle. In his *Diana: The Last Days*, Gregory suggests the driver, if there was one, got scared and then may have dumped his Fiat in a river or canal where it has never been found. François Nibodeau in his analysis certainly accepts the presence of a white Fiat Uno in the tunnel as he concludes, 'The Mercedes was more likely to have gone off course as a result of trying to avoid the Fiat, rather than being knocked off course by it.'

Meanwhile Al Fayed had hired the two recently retired policemen, Ottavioli and Kerbois. They did not confine themselves to the area west of Paris and given their contacts it is likely they could access the records of all Fiat Unos in France. They have never admitted exactly how they worked but I suspect their logic was simple. Did anyone who was known to have been interested in Dodi and Diana possess such a car? It did not take that long for them to get the name of such a person.

9

James Andanson and His White Fiat Uno

Mohamed Al Fayed knew the names of all the paparazzi. It would have been basic police technique to search a database of registered owners of Fiat Unos and to see whether any of the paparazzi came up as owners. I suspect this is what Kerbois and Ottavioli did on behalf of their client. It is surprising the official inquiry did not do this as well, especially as the paparazzi were still charged under France's Good Samaritan law.

In Chapter 1, when describing Diana and Dodi's last days around Sardinia and Corsica, I mentioned that one of the most aggressive photographers in the press pack was James Andanson. He was not content just to snap Diana on a long lens from another boat and he had hired a helicopter to get closer to her aboard the *Jonikal*.

Al Fayed's team soon learned that James Andanson had a white Fiat Uno and that it was usually kept on the farm he owned in Lignières in central France. It certainly fitted George and Sabine's description as it was old and shabby. 'When we found this Fiat in a garage because he had sold it a month after the accident, our agent was arrested for interfering with police

enquiries,' Macnamara told me. His eagle-eyed investigators spotted the fact that the car had been fitted
with a new rear light, which would make sense if the
taillight had shattered.

Macnamara alerted the French police that there was
a white Fiat Uno owned by a man who had been
following Diana for much of the summer. Just as
Martine Monteil was suspicious because Lee Van Than
had had his Fiat resprayed, Macnamara was suspicious
because Andanson had sold the Fiat and it was not clear
on what precise date he had done so.

I suspect the fact that Macnamara brought something to the attention of the French police provoked
some turf and pride problems. The French were
certainly not going to allow the man from Scotland
Yard to have the last word and suggest that he was a
better detective. The recently retired chief superintendent was told that if he interfered again with French
police enquiries, he would be charged with a criminal
offence.

The doyen of the paparazzi

James Andanson is, like Henri Paul, one of the mysteries
of this affair. He was born in Clermont Ferrant in 1946.
His real name was Jean Paul Gonin but he adopted the
name of Andanson when he married his wife, Elisabeth.
No one commented on the fact that it is very unusual
for men to change their names to that of their wives,
especially when the person is as macho as Andanson.

Andanson had started working for a living at the age

of seven, in a newspaper kiosk after school. He then worked as the motorbike rider for a photographer who covered the Tour de France. By his early twenties he was working in the darkroom for *l'Equipe*, the French sports paper. His ambition was always to be a famous photographer. In the 1960s, he started to take pictures of variety performers and singers at Olympia where Edith Piaf had sung. In 1971, Andanson took an iconic picture, possibly the best known of all his work, of a Coca-Cola bottle on the Great Wall of China. He also managed to get the only picture of Aristotle Onassis on his deathbed. People loved, and hated, Andanson. He was something of a bully and a show-off but he was also a very determined man.

Andanson was one of the founders of the Sygma photo agency and by 1997 he was one of the most successful paparazzi in the world. The rich and famous were his territory. In 2002 I watched a twenty-minute programme about him, made by M6 TV, one of the most commercial channels in France. The film is an engaging portrait of Mr Hustle among the royals and the celebs. Andanson always bustles with energy; but to his social betters, he is deferential, always calling someone Prince or Lord or Highness. One sequence shows Andanson running along a quay and trying to attract the attention of the Crown Prince of Jordan who just wants to be left in peace in his speedboat. 'Prince,' Andanson nags to get Abdullah to look up at him, 'Oh Prince'. The polite Abdullah finally caves in, smiles at the lens and even gives a friendly wave for the camera. 'Thank you, Prince,' salamaleeks Andanson. In another sequence, Andanson arrives by appointment at the home of the exiled King of Italy who gazes forlornly across the bay at his kingdom. The King is not allowed to set foot in Italy. Ah Majesty, sighs Andanson with sympathy, one day you will be able to eat your pasta in Rome. When he was filming actors like Daniel Auteuil, Andanson was a bit less obsequious. The film showed him photographing Auteuil in his home and sometimes teasing him.

Some of the rich and famous were not quite so cooperative, it has to be said. For example, Diana's friend Elton John waved him away grumpily. But most of Andanson's glitterati subjects seemed pleased enough to be captured by him on camera and the M6 film showed how close he could get to them.

Andanson was hard-working and an excellent craftsman. He kept up with all the latest technical developments and was one of the first to use satellite technology to send pictures to papers. But he also loved the fun of getting the negatives there in person before the deadline. An exciting sequence in the M6 film tracked him as he raced on his bike as if he were competing in the Isle of Man grand prix. The negatives had to get on the last plane. By the seat of his pants and the speed of his Yamaha, he got them there.

The most revealing sequence for me in the film was to do with a car. It started with an exhaust pipe and the next shot revealed the exhaust pipe belonged to Andanson's white Fiat Uno. It was old and shabby indeed. Driving through a village, Andanson smiled that he loved this car, which had seen him through 325,000 kilometres and would see him through more. Andanson was a good storyteller and he explained why he had

every intention of continuing to drive it. One day at
the smart Riviera resort of St Jean Cap Ferrat, he caught
Giovanni Agnelli, the boss of Fiat. The great industrialist was diving nude off his boat, the *Capriccia*. The
next day Agnelli recognised him in town and said,
apparently, 'Ho Mr the Artist, what are you up to?'
Andanson replied, in his usual butter-up-the-celebs
style, that he loved his white Fiat.

Agnelli examined the battered Fiat and went into
mogul mode. He promised Andanson he would make
him a present of a brand new Fiat when he had
completed 500,000 kilometres in his old banger. 'I am
only afraid that this car won't last the next 175,000,'
Andanson confided to the camera.

At an early stage in the making of *Lady Died*, the
director Francis Gillery had gone to meet Elisabeth
Andanson. She did not want to appear in our film, and
she rejected any suggestion that her husband had
anything to hide. She insisted that the police found that
the paint on her husband's Fiat did not match the paint
on the Mercedes.

I remained sceptical about any part Andanson had
played, till I got to know much more about the photographer through a man I will call Harold. Harold is a
senior officer of one of the French security agencies,
the *Renseignements-Généraux*. I said in Chapter 2 that
this is an idiosyncratic security agency. It can officially
investigate and arrest people but usually they just
research them unofficially. Officers of a certain rank
then write essays, which are seen only by the director
general who reports to the Prime Minister. Harold is
a long-serving officer in the agency. He trained as a

lawyer and that does show in some of his replies. He works for it full-time and at one time was a specialist in information technology.

The spy who was ready to talk

When I started to make *Diana – The Night She Died*, I approached a number of contacts I had kept in touch with from the film I made on the Order of the Solar Temple. One had been an agent of the French government in the Far East. Through him and another source, I was told there was an officer who might be willing to meet under conditions of anonymity. I seized the chance. I first met Harold in the restaurant of the Terminus Nord Hotel in Paris near the Gâre du Nord. I had just come over on the Eurostar with a number of my colleagues on *Deadlines*, the film on which I had met Patrick Chauvel. Many of us involved had worked as journalists and when I told Ludi Boeken, Eric Dussart and Michael Lerner I wouldn't be joining them for dinner, they assumed I had a hot date. I replied severely I was for an evening of Diana business, not funny business.

I left them at the railway station and crossed the road to the Terminus Nord. The restaurant is a large old Parisian brasserie. Harold was waiting, but as I sat down I was worried that he seemed rather nervous. He is a slight man in his thirties with a rather academic manner. He had brown hair and was wearing glasses. I was afraid he would clam up. We had an aperitif. Then, the *maître d'* said we had to move to another table.

Suddenly I felt a lurch in my guts, as Harold and I were led to the other dining room. At one of the tables there, Ludi, Eric and Michael were ordering their dinner. My *Deadlines* colleagues were also hungry and, as luck would have it, the only empty table was the one next to theirs. Disaster was on the menu. Harold would not be impressed with my assurances that everything he told me was confidential, if I couldn't even arrange to have dinner without running into friends. But Ludi, in particular, had experience of secret journalistic assignments as he had worked for the *Panorama* programme and he did not acknowledge my presence once. The others followed his example.

Fortunately, Harold too was on a mission that night. Three years of research had persuaded him that Andanson was a complex man with many secrets. Having ordered a bottle of Sancerre and a bouillabaisse, Harold launched into the definitive lecture on his favourite subject, the life and times, the sins and skills of James Andanson and, as he did so, he relaxed. He admired the man in many ways. Andanson 'was at the height of technical progress because he was always trying to send his stuff as rapidly as possible and he was a perfectionist,' he pointed out.

As a senior officer in one of the French security services, Harold dissected Andanson. 'He operated in three spheres,' Harold said. 'The first sphere was that of show business; then second was politics. He was one of France's most famous photographers of political people and did many pieces for *Paris-Match*. He had been the official photographer of the French Prime Minister, Pierre Bérégovoy.' For Harold the link with

Bérégovoy mattered. Bérégovoy came from rather modest origins and worked as a railwayman before becoming a trade union official. François Mitterand had picked him up out of relative obscurity in 1982 and made him, first, a senior official of the Socialist Party and, then, a Minister. In 1992 Mitterand appointed him Prime Minister. Bérégovoy in turn appointed Andanson as his official photographer. It was a fabulous entrée to the corridors of power for a hack.

The relationship between Andanson and Bérégovoy was more than official, Harold continued. Bérégovoy sometimes dropped into the Andanson house at Lignières for a spot of lunch; sometimes the Prime Minister even took friends along. Andanson boasted of how much time they spent together. Remarkably, Bérégovoy was not the only French Prime Minister Andanson was close to; there is also a photograph of him on his motorbike with Lionel Jospin, the socialist Prime Minister. Such high-level contacts made Andanson quite arrogant.

I was relieved to see that Harold had absolutely no interest in the diners around us. He continued, saying: 'The third sphere Andanson operated in was that of business. We find there men linked to the arms trade such as Jacques Monsieur, the famous Belgian Colonel who spent time in Iran after he and the ayatollahs had a disagreement about arms supplies and, of course, Adnan Khashoggi.' As I pointed out earlier, Khashoggi was the brother-in-law of Mohamed Al Fayed but the two men fell out in the 1970s, when Al Fayed and Khashoggi's sister divorced. Khashoggi blamed Mohamed, but he did stay close to his nephew. Dodi lived with his uncle at one time and could always seek his help. Monsieur was Andanson's neighbour at Lignières and the two men knew each other quite well.

Harold then explained some key history. The socialist party Bérégovoy led lost the Parliamentary elections of March 1993 and he had to resign, but what hurt him very personally was that his mentor, François Mitterand, abandoned him completely. According to Harold, Andanson saw a great deal of Bérégovoy in the last months of his life. Bérégovoy died two months after the elections on May 1st 1993. The ousted Prime Minister was found by a canal near Nevers in central France with a bullet in his head. Some people do not believe he committed suicide; indeed, a book argues he was assassinated. Others claimed Bérégovoy just felt a total failure, the working-class star and hero who had suddenly lost everything and who could not bear it. On top of that, he may have used his political position to borrow a million francs – about £100,000 – to buy a property and he feared that would be exposed.

When Bérégovoy's body was found, some documents were missing. His diary was not recovered for nine years after his death. Some commentators believe it contained embarrassing facts about family people. Nine years on Bérégovoy's family claim they made sure the diary was not found as it listed meetings Bérégovoy had with his mistresses. Many people don't think that is the whole truth. One of Bérégovoy's friends, Gerard Carreyrou, said something very different – and of far more interest, which again suggests how ruthless French political life can be. The man who had made him, François Mitterand, 'no longer took his calls'. Bérégovoy was now an embarrassment. 'He had a meeting with a major industrialist a few days later and so it was important to make his diary disappear. There were a number of people who had an interest in certain things remaining hidden.'

Harold claimed there were direct links between Andanson and the death of Bérégovoy. 'There are witness statements that Andanson was there at Nevers on a different photographic assignment on the day Bérégovoy died; later Andanson's wife Elisabeth said he was at Nevers on the day.' The forensic evidence suggested Bérégovoy was shot from some distance; that did not fit with the official conclusion that he put a gun to his head and then fired.

Harold now introduced the macabre twist into his revelations, a twist that brings us back to the tragedy of Dodi and Diana. 'When you look at the people Andanson photographed there were a number of violent deaths among them. You can't prove he was responsible, of course. But you have Dodi Al Fayed, Diana, the painter Bernard Buffet, who killed himself, too.' Harold continued the catalogue of Andanson's subjects who met a violent end soon after being photographed by him. The list included Lolo Ferrari and the singer Dalida. And the pop star Claude François who had recorded the French version of 'If I Had a Hammer'. Harold used an unlikely word to summarise all this: 'intuition'. Andanson 'had strong intuitions and he had the art of approaching people who died suddenly'. Harold phrased it a little strangely, but, gradually, he would make very clear what he meant.

'At the *Renseignements-Généraux*, we came to the

conclusion that James Andanson did not work alone but that he was manipulated, or led by a service or services,' Harold told me. By services Harold meant security services and these could have been French, British or those of other nationalities. 'And that he [Andanson] was sometimes tasked to eliminate or to hamper or to compromise certain personalities.' Harold argued that it all suggested James Andanson worked as an informer at the very least – and possibly as someone who provided information which helped plan 'eliminations'. His job as a 'people photographer' gave him wonderful access, as he could get really close to celebrities. 'It is completely different from being at a press conference. The people photographer moves into your kitchen, he becomes your intimate, and friendship develops and he learns the private habits of famous people. And that makes him remarkably useful for certain agencies.' I had seen very clearly in the M6 film how close to celebrities Andanson could get.

The *Renseignements-Généraux* authorised Harold to pursue his investigation into Andanson before Diana died. I pressed Harold on the status of that inquiry. The inquiry was not a police inquiry, he conceded, 'but it was conducted by officials who were employees of the state and we were tasked to find out whether Andanson was really just a photographer or something else too. After eighteen months or so, we decided the evidence was that he was more than a photographer. An inquiry of this sort does not have the power a police inquiry has of obliging people to talk to you but it also doesn't have the limits a police inquiry has. It is the kind of inquiry that is not minuted and that official sources can deny ever took place but it tends to be more wide ranging. We quickly noticed that, behind Andanson, something was well organised and that he was a meticulous man,' Harold said. 'During these enquiries we got the listing of his work which is really a remarkable document with twenty-thousand entries.'

The 'rabbateur'

The second time I met Harold he came to London – I paid for the tickets but put him up in my own home – and he brought along sheets of computer papers. This was the document with 20,000 entries. It showed in minute detail the times and places where Andanson had photographed celebrities. As Harold spread the sheets on my dining-room table, I was being shown not just interesting information on Andanson but proof of the ability of security services to snoop on an individual. Harold had compiled lists of Andanson's meetings, public and private, going back ten years at least. There are civil-liberty issues here, but in February 2003 they were not what interested Harold or me.

The word Harold used to describe Andanson was '*rabbateur*'. He explained that it was a hunting term. A *rabbateur* is a beater. 'You have a pack of paparazzi but you have one person who is more focused, more aware of what the target is.' Harold explained. 'If there is a target who it has been decided will be executed by someone, for example – he handled information that was of the greatest use on their habits, their tastes and so on.' Harold added that such a man would provide valuable information if one were conspiring against someone, whether one was planning to kill or blackmail them.

As Harold took me through his computer sheets of 20,000 entries, he pointed to names like Lolo Ferrari, Grace Kelly and her daughters Princesses Stephanie and Caroline of Monaco. He pointed to show-business personalities who were linked to the Order of the Solar Temple like the French singer Colette de Real, a close friend of Grace Kelly's. There are a number of other celebrities on that list whose links to the Order of the Solar Temple have never been made public.

'You could see that from July 1997 Andanson had focused his work on Dodi and Diana as if he had a certain intuition. He normally spent his summers at St Tropez and in Cannes but in the summer of 1997, he devoted himself to following Dodi and Diana.' Elisabeth Andanson said later that was just an accident. Harold begged to differ.

The most surprising allegation Harold made was that Andanson had actually spent some time on the Al Fayed yacht in the last weeks of Diana's life. Harold did not know, incidentally, if Al Fayed had any idea Andanson might be on his yacht and the *Jonikal* is a large yacht. He insisted, however, his claim was based on reliable information from reliable witnesses but he could not reveal their names because that could put them at risk. We included this claim in my Channel 5 film and it provoked no reaction or denial from Al Fayed.

Andanson was so successful partly because he was so persistent. He had hired a helicopter to get the best pictures of Diana and Dodi. Andanson's persistence made it seem very bizarre, Harold argued, that the photographer should have suddenly stopped chasing the couple twenty-four hours before they died. Harold did not think that made any psychological sense. Yet no paparazzi had seen Andanson at the Place Vendôme in the evening. 'Why should Andanson deny being there? I find it especially strange because he always boasted of being where the stars were and suddenly he has a pretext . . . And he is not there.' The bullish photographer suddenly becomes a shy and retiring fellow who can't be bothered to hare after Diana because he has to look after his vines. If no one saw Andanson at the Alma, Harold suggested, Andanson was taking care not to be seen.

Harold had talked to witnesses who had been at the Alma Tunnel and to some officials who had investigated the crash. On the basis of what he knew and what he had been told, Harold came to a simple conclusion. 'He [Andanson] said to people he knew, people and neighbours in whom he had confidence, that he caught the last moments of the Princess in the tunnel. Andanson also had an exceptional collection of sound recordings. He apparently boasted of having photographed the last moments of Princess Diana. He said that to his circle of intimates.' He added: 'I am sure Andanson was there.'

One further fact which would suggest the presence of Andanson is a second photograph of the Mercedes taken inside the tunnel. I have not seen the photograph but I have seen a photocopy of one, which seems to be very similar to the one Curtil described, which is reproduced on the inside of the cover of this book. In that photocopy, however, only the front seats are clear and you cannot see the back seats. I saw it in the dossier of the French inquiry.

When I interviewed Trevor Rees-Jones' Paris lawyer, Christian Curtil, he was adamant that he had seen the original of the photograph whose photocopy is reproduced. 'It was taken in the Alma Tunnel,' he insisted. I pressed him on how he could be sure. He said he could not be certain where in the tunnel it was taken, but he added that he had seen the original, which only *Juge* Stephan had. 'In the original it is much more evident it was the tunnel,' Curtil said. He remained adamant that this second picture had been obviously taken from in front of the car and that 'it was obviously taken somewhere in the tunnel or at the beginning'. As Trevor Rees-Jones' lawyer he had no vested interest in making an allegation of that sort. This photograph did not mention, as a speed-camera photo would have done, the date and the speed of the car. This would suggest at the least that it is very possible Andanson took this picture.

And luck again played a part in our investigation. I was able to get confirmation from within Andanson's 'circle of intimates', as Harold called them. Francis Gillery, who directed *Lady Died,* started his career making television profiles of artists and writers. One of the subjects was Frederic Dard, a best-selling writer of detective stories who saw Simenon as his main rival. His series *San Antonio* used so much slang that readers needed a glossary to understand some of the dialogue. Gillery stayed friendly with Dard and his wife after he made his film. Luck again: Dard was friendly with Andanson because Andanson often took pictures of him for publicity purposes.

Frederic Dard died in 1998 so Francis contacted Madame Dard when we made *Lady Died*. She agreed to give us a sound interview but she did not want to be filmed. In that taped interview Madame Dard insisted that Andanson had told her and her husband that he had been in the tunnel at the time of the crash. As we have seen at least two witnesses claimed a Fiat was zigzagging on the road in front of the Mercedes. It was typical of the man that Andanson boasted he had been very cunning and clever and got away before the police knew he had been on the scene. '*Il était malin*,' Madame Dard said: he was cunning.

I now had two sources that placed Andanson in the tunnel. I was to meet a third. Pierre Blois is a well-known investigative journalist who often writes for *Voici* and *VSD*. He is also a well-connected man, married to a woman who is an important executive for Radio France Internationale. Blois's father-in-law is the chairman of the CNRS, the committee that supervises scientific research in France. These connections have not made Blois stand-offish, and especially not so when you share an aperitif with him – which is what I was doing in a bar near the Pompidou Centre.

I first met Blois during the making of the film about the Order of the Solar Temple. He then wrote a long piece on the Grace Kelly film and tried, at first, to discredit our research. Eventually, he had come to the conclusion our story was true. We stayed in touch.

When I started to make *Diana – The Night She Died*, I rang Blois again. I thought we might be able to work together and, to some extent, he agreed. This was in 2000 but he pointed out that Al Fayed had offered a

£1 million reward for information. Blois hoped he might land some of that bounty. Nevertheless, Blois shared one crucial fact with me. Andanson had not been alone in the Fiat Uno and he, Blois, knew where to find the person who had been driving with him. Blois was friendly but he did not want to tell me more. He explained why. First, he wanted a guarantee of a substantial sum of money. Second, he did not want to approach the man who had been in the car with Andanson yet. He wanted to be able to surprise him and confront him with real proof and he needed better evidence of what Andanson might have been doing in the tunnel. To doorstep the man too soon could end very badly as he would just deny the allegation. We could not agree how to proceed and Blois would not trust me with more information. Yet, he too was certain Andanson had been at the scene. Chester Stern, Al Fayed's director of press, says they have video evidence which shows Andanson was outside the Ritz earlier in the day.

Harold added a new element at our second meeting in London. 'I met an investigator who assured me he had talked to witnesses who spoke of a Fiat Uno stopped outside at the end of the tunnel. [By 'the end' he meant the far end that the Mercedes was driving towards when it crashed.] The driver was wearing a bomber jacket and he was corpulent. This description fitted Andanson,' he said. This description was similar, but not identical, to that given by Georges and Sabine, who gave the elaborate description of the car and the dog on the back seat.

I asked Harold if it was his professional opinion that

Andanson was spying on Diana and Dodi. The lawyer in him emerged and he phrased his reply with care. He told me: 'People have talked about his links with French and other services. I cannot prove that but these hypotheses can't be excluded. They stemmed from the exceptional people he knew, some were in the arms trade, some in show business,' Harold said. Others were people of great influence in the running of the French Republic.

The police interrogate Andanson

When the French police had their attention drawn to Andanson's Fiat by Al Fayed's detectives, they went down to his house, les Manoires, at Lignières, 160 miles south of Paris. When she talked to us for *Lady Died*, Elisabeth Andanson was very matter-of-fact about what had happened. The police asked questions but they did not bother them much or take very long about it. The white Fiat was soon eliminated from their enquiries. 'James stayed very calm. Eventually the police said they were satisfied the car was not the one that was supposed to be involved in the crash,' Elisabeth Andanson said.

The reason the police gave was apparently that the paint on the Fiat Uno did not match the paint found on the Mercedes. Stephan insisted on this in his final summary but this is not the only conclusion about the paint to be found in the twenty-seven volumes of the dossier. Another expert testimony argues the very opposite, stating 'the comparative analysis of the infra-red spectra characterising the vehicle's original paint (the paint that was on the car at the time of the crash, *Blanco 210*) − and of the trace on the rear-view mirror showed their absorption bands are identical.' The same went for the traces of black polymer on the Mercedes (Gregory 2000).

The fact that these matched did not prove, of course, that the Fiat hit or was hit by the Mercedes, but it was possible. Taken together with the rest of the evidence, however, it makes it quite likely Andanson's car was in contact with the Mercedes. At first, that seems to have been a likely scenario as the police saw it. If the forensic evidence showed Andanson's Fiat Uno had never encountered the Mercedes, why did the police examine his alibi in some detail? Moreover, the records I have found in the files suggest the interplay between the police and Andanson was complicated and, at times, bad tempered. I have located and filmed transcripts of a series of conversations between Andanson and Eric Gigou, a policeman with the *brigade criminelle*. Gigou rang Andanson to try to arrange to come and see him. Andanson refused and said he had better things to do than talk to the police. He said he would only talk to the military police − the gendarmerie in France. He was powerful enough and arrogant enough to do that and Gigou accepted it. He did suggest rather humbly Andanson should talk to his chief, Vyerere.

Gigou then recorded how Andanson changed his story twice. First, Andanson said he was at home on the night of August 30th with his wife and with his daughter, Kimberley. He had had to get up in the middle of the night to drive to Orly airport to take a plane to Corsica. He left his house at 3.45am and got to Orly in good time for the 7.20 flight to Bonifacio in Corsica where he had to take pictures of Gilbert Becaud, a well-known French singer. Becaud died a few weeks later of natural causes.

In the dossiers, I also found photocopies of pages of Andanson's diary, which we filmed, and they show that he had made a date to see Gilbert Becaud on the 26th, four days before the crash. It would have made sense as the yacht was near Bonifacio on the 26th and so it would have been reasonable to film Becaud there and then.

Harold added that Andanson usually carried a good deal of cash, yet he paid for the road tolls by credit cards. He also had the relevant receipts, which he used to establish his alibi. But then, Gigou's notes show, Andanson changed his story and said he had been in St Tropez the night Diana died. The police files also record that his son, also called James, thought his father was grape harvesting in Bordeaux and rang home at 4.30 that morning.

For Harold the catalogue of contradictory alibis means: 'It is reasonable to assume that Andanson lied and that was in his character. He provided airline tickets but all the tickets mean is that he was at the airport for the take off around eight or nine in the morning. He could have gone to Lignières from Paris and then back to Orly. It is not incompatible at all,' Harold told me.

The story Andanson told the police about his Fiat Uno was also contradictory. Originally Andanson said that it had done 372,000 kilometres and he sold it in June, even though, as we have seen, Giovanni Agnelli, the boss of Fiat, had promised him a new car as a present when he had driven 500,000 kilometres. In a second statement, Andanson said he had not used the Fiat Uno for some time and that it had been sold in October 1997. He had not driven the Fiat since 1995, he insisted. Andanson told the police he was now successful and he had 'reached the stage of the BMW'. He had been keeping the Fiat in a barn and used it to store all kinds of rubbish. By October 1997, he had decided it was time to dump the Fiat. The police seem not to have probed this story any more than they probed his contradictory alibis.

I asked Harold if there might be any interest on the part of the French Republic in not investigating Andanson's role in the death of Diana fully. Again he phrased his reply with care as if he were preparing a position paper. 'It is not to be excluded if you assume Andanson was also informed of certain things. At that point he would have received a certain leniency on the part of the authorities.'

It is not hard to imagine how the British press would have reacted if a man who had been close to one French Prime Minister and had been pictured sitting on a motorbike with another – Lionel Jospin – turned out to have been at the Alma when Diana was killed.

The French police did not press Andanson too hard about any alibi. In his final summary, Stephan was just happy to note that the white Fiat Uno had never been found despite a most intensive search. He never mentioned Andanson.

Interesting as Harold's evidence is, there is one question I can't avoid asking. Why did Harold speak to me at all? Any reasonable investigative journalist has to be sceptical about the motive of his sources when they work for intelligence agencies. Harold had seen *Lady Died* and liked it but that does not, of course, exclude the possibility that he had been told by the *Renseignements-Généraux* to talk to me. He claimed that he was willing to talk anonymously because he was in dispute with his superiors. Additionally, he believed it was important to explore the role of Andanson in all this and he had it in mind to write a book about the photographer. I agreed to tell Harold anything further I found out. Since I interviewed him, Harold has settled his dispute with his boss.

Harold raised, as we have seen, the possibility that Andanson worked for security agencies. The ex-MI6 agent Richard Tomlinson told me that MI6 often use people who have a normal career. 'Most of the time they do their work as barristers or journalists or accountants but then they are called up to do a particular mission.' Henri Paul fitted into this pattern. Tomlinson went on to say that 'MI6 did have on its books one paparazzi photographer' though he could not give his name. Like Harold, Tomlinson argued that being a photographer was a marvellous job for a part-time spy. You had an entrée and an excuse to go anywhere. If an accountant decides to visit Kosovo, people might ask why but it is quite normal for a photographer to take off anywhere in the world to get the shot and get the story.

I would like to return now to the photograph taken in the Alma Tunnel and reproduced on the inside cover of this book. There were no cameras in the tunnel in 1997 nor in 2002 when I filmed inside. It could have been taken by a speed camera outside the tunnel or it could have been taken from a stationary vehicle inside the tunnel or one that was moving slowly. The definition of the faces inside the car is so sharp it seems unlikely it was a picture of a car travelling at around 60mph taken from another car moving fast. Every witness who said a Fiat Uno was in the tunnel mentioned it was moving slowly. It has to be possible that Andanson took that picture leaning out of the Fiat while someone else drove.

Conspiracy, cock-up or cover-up

As this is a complicated story I should like to list a number of points I believe it is safe to make so far.

- A number of investigations were set up by the French after the accident. There were clearly turf wars between different agencies of the state.
- Cocaine had been found in the car in Princess Diana's handbag. No mention of this was made in the official reports. Chauvel reported there was pressure from the office of the French President to suppress evidence of this. So did the policeman I met through David Carr Brown.
- The French Ministry of Justice have now leaked the fact that they felt under pressure from Britain to embalm Diana's body before a proper autopsy was carried out.

- A completely trustworthy witness and child-hood friend of Prince Charles claimed to have seen a speed-camera photo. The French authorities have always denied the existence of such a photo, which would have solved the issue of how fast the car was going.
- The controversy concerning the authenticity of Henri Paul's blood samples has never been resolved.
- The inquiry did not probe the security connections of the driver, even though they had good evidence of that from two sources at least.
- The inquiry exonerated the French medical services of any blame. The inquiry suggested the surgeons found that Diana was particularly hard to treat because she had been lying down in the car. The speed-camera photograph Patrick Chauvel saw contradicts this.
- The inquiry took seventeen days to release news of the shards of glass from the taillight of a Fiat Uno found in the tunnel.
- There is sufficient evidence to suggest James Andanson was at the tunnel in his Fiat Uno and possibly working for either French or British security forces.

None of this proves there was a conspiracy to murder either Diana or Dodi but it does show the French authorities had a good deal to hide.

As the story developed it became even more obvious that we were not getting the whole truth. I asked Harold what the official attitude was among law-enforcement agencies.

'When this happened it upset the French government considerably, it upset President Chirac, that the Princess who was so young, so popular, lost her life so in the middle of Paris. I think it was embarrassing and troubling in terms of public opinion. It was troubling in terms of relationships with the British. It was inopportune to investigate areas which opened out into avenues other than a pure accident.'

I asked Harold whether, in his experience, security agencies and the police received instructions from politicians about how to conduct inquiries, instructions not to probe excessively that man, this line of evidence, in that direction.

Harold smiled and, for once, he dropped that lawyerly caution.

'Never in writing,' he said. 'An inquiry should not exclude anything and on the Fiat Uno, on Andanson [whether he was there or not], yes or no, one has the impression that it was decided not to worry James Andanson too much about this business.'

And, then, the story took a very dramatic turn in June 2000.

10

Death on the Plateau

On May 3rd 2000 James Andanson visited the Sipa Agency in Paris, the agency that distributed his work. 'He had just finished a reportage on the Countess of Paris. He had many projects in hand and he was earning good money. He seemed perfectly normal. He even told me to be happy,' said Goksin Sipahioglu, the director of the agency. 'Then he went out to have lunch.'

Andanson had specific reasons to be cheerful. He and his wife Elisabeth had just sent out 150 invitations for their daughter's first communion, a very significant event for a Catholic family. And, in general, the family lived well. Andanson loved the forty hectares of land they owned in Lignières and his herd of Charolais cows. There is a sequence in the M6 film where he drives a tractor over his land with quite as much brio as he rode his motorbike.

At 11.30 on May 4th 2000, James Andanson told his wife that he had to post some letters but that he would not be long as he had to prepare for an assignment the next day in Lille. He had arranged a shoot with the actress, Martine Aubry. Elisabeth Andanson would say later that he had received four phone calls that morning. He scribbled a letter quickly and got in his car. The four calls were later traced to a public call box near his home.

Andanson also mailed a letter to the Sipa Agency in Paris. It said that all the rights in all his pictures should belong to his wife, and he added, 'if something strange should happen' to him. Andanson had been a professional photographer for nearly thirty years and French law is very clear. If a person dies, their heirs inherit all the copyrights in his work automatically. Writing such a letter seems strange and unnecessary.

Andanson never made it to Lille to photograph Martine Aubry and no one knows for sure what happened to him between 11.30am and 10.30pm that day. The police version is that he drove into the town of Millau about 600 kilometres south of his farm at Lignières. He then bought a jerrycan of petrol. Then, in his BMW – for the old and shabby Fiat had long been sold to his mother-in-law and dumped by a garage – he drove north to the plateau du Larzac. Such plains make you realise how large France is. Dull fields stretch for miles. Villages are far apart. Coming across a herd of cows is an event. Elisabeth Andanson said that she had been told the Larzac reminded her husband of Ireland. She could not think why he would want to be reminded of Ireland. The police said Andanson chose the Larzac deliberately because it was a peaceful spot, though peaceful is an odd description for a number of reasons.

The army uses much of the area for military exercises. To win the Larzac back for the people, a group of socialist intellectuals settled on the plain in 1973. They also wanted to live the wholesome natural life as peasants had once done and to stop the army grabbing more of the people's land. One of their leaders, Jose Bove, became very influential in the anti-globalisation movement. One of the assignments Andanson had in his diary in May 2000 was to photograph Bove.

Andanson reached a point just on the edge of the army land. It was halfway between the village of Nant and that of La Cavalerie. He parked, then apparently poured the jerrycan of petrol, containing forty litres, inside the car. Then, he made himself comfortable in the driver's seat. He then set fire to his BMW. With so much petrol it would have burned intensely.

Harold had continued his inquiry for the *Renseignements-Généraux* and he said with irony, that Andanson was apparently a very careful driver to the bitter end. 'He put on his seat belt and then we are asked to believe he set fire to himself and sat quietly while the flames burned him. The pain would have been unbearable.' Harold added that the 'appalling way the man died' was one of the reasons Andanson aroused so much interest at the *Renseignements-Généraux*.

Elisabeth Andanson is a woman who seems used to staying in control but as she explained what had happened, she was obviously still shocked. On the filmed interview, you can see her control a shudder at the thought of the agony her husband must have suffered. She said she was flabbergasted by the sequence of events as they were related to her. Her husband had apparently headed south for 600 kilometres to kill himself in a spot that meant nothing to him, a spot as far off the beaten track as it is possible to get in France.

In the isolation and desolation of the Larzac, no one noticed a car burning. At the end of a day's military exercises, however, a group of soldiers spotted something. They went to have a look and found the burning shell of Andanson's BMW318. No photos of the car were ever released but a local farmer, Julian Christian, said: 'The car was badly melted. The glass had shattered and you can still feel the heat, and the driver's body . . . it was hardly there.' Elisabeth Andanson was told all the seats in the BMW had been burnt down to the metal frames. She added that must have taken a great deal of fuel. It had been suggested to her that one jerrycan of petrol would not have produced enough heat to destroy so much of the car, so much of the body.

Initially it was said that the police found the skull, some bones and that there was enough of the jaw left to be able to identify Andanson through dental records. Gery Plane, the commander of the Aveyron group of the gendarmerie, explained that the fire had burned so fiercely inside the car 'which explained, the complete destruction of everything that was in the car'.

Commander Plane also told the press that it was a clear case of suicide because Andanson was depressed and had serious personal problems. This contradicted everything Andanson's family and friends said. The only obvious problem he faced was that he had been helping his son launch his career as a Formula 3 driver and that he needed to keep on making money, which he seemed to be succeeding at.

His wife, Elisabeth, is sceptical about her husband

committing suicide because she is struck by the sheer difficulty of burning yourself to death in your car. She is astonishingly matter-of-fact about it but very interesting. It would have been an atrocious way to die. He wasn't a masochist and had no reason to kill himself.

Harold led what he calls 'a restrained' inquiry into how Andanson had died. It was unofficial or, at least, deniable. But it was staffed entirely by individuals who worked for various state agencies. I pressed him on the status of the inquiry and whether it was approved by the *Renseignements-Généraux*. It was state business, Harold assured me, which did not mean we would ever be able to trace a record of it.

The not-so-secret instruction

The official procedure, once Andanson had been found dead, was similar to that with the Alma crash. There was no inquest but the Procureur for the area, Alain Durand, appointed a *juge d'instruction* to enquire into the death.

Remarkably, given how secret investigations are in France, we were granted an on-the-record interview with the magistrate in charge of the inquiry into Andanson's death. The French Attorney General had given permission. *Juge* Marty, a 35-year-old woman, was charming but very firm. The police inquiry had been very simple and it had been concluded by June 7th 2000. There was no question of Andanson having been murdered, *Juge* Marty said. She also dismissed as fantasy another rumour that had come to her attention – that

Andanson was still alive, having faked his own death because France had become too dangerous for him. That belonged in the movies, she smiled. She was much given to smiling and did so even when we asked how the police had identified Andanson.

'There are methods of forensic analysis that allow us to be certain,' she said. There was enough DNA to make a positive identification. She smiled when she was asked just where the DNA came from or how much there was. That was part of the *secret d'instruction*. This contradicts the police statement that Andanson had been identified through dental records.

But *Juge* Marty wanted to make it clear that one school of thought did not impress her at all. She was not surprised friends and relatives claimed that Andanson had not seemed to be suicidal or told anyone he intended to burn himself to death. Determined suicides do not always advertise their intentions. People do often commit suicide in such a way, she assured us with a smile, and everyone close to them is taken by surprise. Many suicides don't leave a note for their loved ones. Trust me, I'm a *juge*, she said.

The psychology of suicide is complex and does not offer many hard and fast answers. I was struck by the fact that if Andanson had killed himself he had chosen to die, like mediaeval martyrs did, with the flames devouring him. Cars are often used in suicides but the usual method is to run a pipe from the exhaust back into the vehicle. If you run the engine, you will die of carbon monoxide poisoning but the method is supposed to be relatively painless. There is literature on people who burn themselves to death in great pain but they nearly always come from the Middle East and Asia where that is part of a cultural tradition. The Indian government, for example, has banned the practice of *suttee* in which widows burn themselves. The Royal College of Psychiatrists, in a survey of clinical experiences (May 2003), pointed out that there were differences in suicide methods among different ethnic communities and that one difference between different cultures was that nine per cent of South Asian psychiatric patients who committed suicide did burn themselves to death. Even among the profoundly mad, there were virtually no European examples of that. If *Juge* Marty was right, James Andanson had not just chosen a painful way to die, but also one which was extremely unusual for a European.

'From the first day it's not clear if it was Andanson at all,' Harold said, and with a certain macabre expertise that may come from working for intelligence agencies, he added, 'allegedly only ash was found and you need more than a jerrycan of petrol to reduce a body to that. They should have found a burned skeleton. But here we only had ash. And this was a shock to many people.' Those who were shocked included the funeral director who came to get the ashes. 'He said all this was just a masquerade. He was given a pot with ash and earth in it and told these were all the mortal remains of James Andanson.'

Harold was ironic: 'The death was something of a mystery and one wonders what were the instructions on the death of Andanson but it seems the judicial authorities did not show an exaggerated interest in this subject.'

The question of where Andanson bought the petrol became something of an issue. *Juge* Marty claimed that the police had proved to her that Andanson had bought a jerrycan of petrol in Millau. The *Renseignements-Généraux* came to a very different conclusion. 'We did take a close look at this and made enquiries. We spent a lot of time in Millau trying to trace the petrol-pump attendant who had sold Andanson the jerrycan,' Harold told me.

Millau is not a big town. There are about 35,000 inhabitants and maybe five or six petrol stations. 'Yet we could not find this elusive petrol-pump attendant.' Harold added he had finally lost confidence in the efficiency of the local police when it turned out they made a mistake about the colour of Andanson's BMW.

Harold was also surprised when he was told that the jerrycan was bought on Andanson's credit card. His own inquiry found that this card had certainly not been reduced to ashes. Harold told me: 'It was used three days after Andanson had died and then again seven days later.' And that was strange too, Harold pointed out. 'Andanson paid for nearly everything in cash. He carried bundles of 500 francs with him.' A short sequence in the M6 TV film shows Andanson flaunting a huge wad of notes. Harold wondered 'why should he have decided to use a credit card. We would have liked to have had some explanation of that.'

Elisabeth Andanson raised the possibility that her husband had been killed by MI6 but she did not offer any evidence for that or any possible motive. Harold agreed that Andanson's 'death is more like an elimination' but I am not sure he agreed with Mrs Andanson that MI6 might be to blame. Harold was not sure whether Andanson's death was linked to the deaths of Diana or Dodi or to something else. But it is striking that here was yet another man with secret-service connections who was at the Alma and who was now dead. Harold added that 'Either it is an assassination which took many precautions to make it look like a suicide or . . .'

By now I felt Harold was very much on our side. We were thinking possibilities out together so I was surprised when he suddenly became wary again. I asked him if he thought it might be possible that Andanson and Henri Paul knew each other. Many of the people Andanson photographed were typical of the clientele of the Ritz after all. Harold became very general. It was one of the few times he waffled vaguely, speaking of the fact that hotel staff were good people to recruit as spies.

I noticed that Harold did not reply to this point and that a few minutes later, a little nervously, he asked if he had told too many secrets.

'No,' I said.

'You made me talk like a lunatic,' he said.

I promised him that we would conceal his identity.

'You can't say there was or wasn't a result but I assure you it was not a banal inquiry,' Harold said.

Andanson's funeral was very poorly attended, given his contacts. 'When they bury Andanson only thirty-five people were there . . . no one from politics, no one from show business, why did no one go to his funeral?' Harold asked.

Elisabeth Andanson said that a few days after the

death three men came to collect photos of Bérégovoy from her home at Lignières. She felt their attitude was threatening though they took nothing else.

The raid on the Sipa offices

This was not the only raid on Andanson's archive. On June 16th 2000, just days after his death, three gunmen wearing balaclavas burst into the Sipa offices. They shot a security guard in the foot and held staff hostage for three hours. The police were never alerted and, eventually the raiders left, taking with them a few hard disks, some laptop computers and some cameras. The thieves took nothing of any resale value but much of this material belonged to Andanson. The police have not caught the thieves. But yet again in this saga material that could have provided hard evidence disappeared.

The *Renseignements-Généraux* obviously kept the family under observation after the death of Andanson. 'We did notice that an internet letterbox was set up with a stupid name which tried to link the suicide of Andanson with British secret services. It was called the Suicide Squad 007. And we decided to find out who had set this up,' said Harold. He claims they discovered it had been set by Andanson's own son and that the website would make it possible to find out who logged on and, therefore, who wanted to know who was interested in his father's suicide. Harold found that strange but I find it quite understandable.

I have argued throughout that the French inquiry into the death of Diana was inadequate. It denied

Andanson played any role in Diana's death. Harold's revelations as well as the much more limited evidence of Madame Dard and Pierre Blois suggest otherwise. Then, of course, when Andanson burned in his BMW, the investigation came to the conclusion that it was suicide in the almost record time of seven weeks. *Juge* Marty told us that, of course, if we had new evidence which sensibly suggested Andanson might have been murdered, she would consider re-opening her inquiry. She said that with her sweet girlish smile.

In the next chapter, I want to deal with the many areas that her fellow investigating magistrates did not seem to pursue.

II

What the Inquiry Did Not
Want to Investigate

When I first talked to Trevor Rees-Jones' lawyer, David
Crawford, he suggested the problems with the French
inquiry were not exceptional as France has a history of
judicial scandals throughout the twentieth century. The
first was the infamous Dreyfus affair when a Jewish
army officer was framed. The philosophy of the French
Republic argues that the Republic is the people and
if, therefore, the Republic has to bend the rules and
dispose of its enemies, these morally regrettable actions
are essentially for the good of the people. No one puts
this down in black or white, of course. Crawford
claimed this has allowed all kinds of skulduggery which
would never be tolerated in the United Kingdom.

There are a number of modern murder cases – the
Domenici affair for example – which suggest the state
does not investigate too thoroughly.

Crawford's list of unexplained murders is far from
exhaustive. In 1962, forty Algerians died in Paris at the
hands of the police; many bodies were dumped in the
Seine. No one was ever even criticised for these deaths.
Renaud Marhic, a well-respected journalist from

Brittany, in his book on the Order of the Solar Temple points to the still-unsolved killing of an Inspector Massie and his family at Auriol; Massie was a policeman and a member of the SAC, the *Societé d'Action Civile*, and he had begun to question what it was doing and whether it was breaking the law. The SAC was a very right-wing organisation which was formed after the student revolts of 1968. Its founder was Charles Pasqua who then became Minister of the Interior in the 1980s and is still a force in Gaullist politics.

It is important to understand the very different atmosphere in France in 1968, too. In Britain, 1968 was fun with The Who and The Beatles strutting their stuff and the odd demonstration. The students never took over Whitehall; the Crown was never at risk. In France, however, the stakes were very different because politicians feared the students who had strong links with the very powerful French trade union movement. At the height of the riots of 1968, de Gaulle left Paris and made sure he could still count on the army to support him. Panic gripped the French governing class and that made them take – and justify – extraordinary measures. One was the creation of the SAC which has often been accused of being involved in unexplained murders. Fear of both the far left and of the far right have influenced French politics profoundly and the French far right – first the Poujadist party and then Le Pen's – has been far more important than far right British parties.

The French can be matter-of-fact about all this. Bob Denard, who was a French mercenary leader from 1960 to 1985, explained to me that he had often been commissioned by the French state to arrange for the disposal of individuals who were politically inconvenient. Denard was very frank with me about his activities outside France – in Yemen, the Congo, Tunisia – and it is a matter of record that he staged a coup on the Comores Islands in the Indian Ocean and had its president killed at the behest of Paris.

In other words, the French political system has allowed a surprising amount of violence to protect itself.

Some unsolved murders had a sexual twist. In 1973, the chauffeur of Alain Delon was killed in what came to be known as the Markovic affair. A number of journalists claim Markovic – the chauffeur – was going to blow the whistle on sexual scandals involving showbusiness celebrities and the then President of the French Republic, Georges Pompidou. In 1995, deaths at Versailles were linked both to French security services and allegations of child abuse. It is not just that there are many unexplained deaths in France but that many of the dead have been people of some political importance.

I do not mean to suggest that Britain has an impeccable record by contrast. There are guns for hire in London too. There was real shock when the links between Lord Boothby and the Krays were exposed in the 1960s, for example. Nevertheless in Britain strange deaths of politically connected people usually lead to a proper inquiry. Stephen Ward's death in the Profumo affair provoked an inquiry by the famous Lord Denning. The most recent controversial death is that of David Kelly who worked for the Ministry of Defence. Lord Hutton required the Prime Minister to give evidence in public, and he has already exposed the workings of the government in a very damaging way. In France the President cannot be charged with a crime and he can afford some protection to his advisers. Such lack of scrutiny has made it easier for links to flourish between criminals and government and business circles

David Crawford has much of the bluff Northerner in him. He loves France and yet is very critical of its judicial system. He had nothing against *Juge* Stephan who had always been very 'kind and considerate to me personally. They worked very hard on it but I don't think they got fully to the bottom of it.' Crawford's colleague Christian Curtil shares that view and so does a man they have battled against: Mohamed Al Fayed. The club of the dissatisfied is even larger, as Al Fayed's lawyers, the Paul family lawyer, the lawyers of a number of the paparazzi and Petel's lawyer, Maître Desguines, all believe that the inquiry stopped well short of the whole truth. And that this was no accident.

Mohamed Al Fayed has been snubbed and sneered at in Britain but in France Al Fayed has a better reputation. France was the first country he lived in when he left Egypt, he told me. He has three homes there – one at St Tropez, the flat at rue Arsene-Houssaye and the villa Windsor. He compared France very favourably with Britain because the French were 'less racist' and they had had the good sense to abolish their monarchy.

'*Juge* Stephan started very fair and then he stopped.' Al Fayed claimed that the magistrate stopped because he had been influenced 'by the intelligence services'. Al Fayed mentioned MI5, MI6 and secret societies in France, which had existed 'since the days of Napoleon'.

He told me he accepted the importance of security services but he was still shocked by their behaviour. Stephan, he claimed 'investigated Andanson himself and he knows what Andanson did and Stephan has completely ignored that and I'm sure he was instructed to do all that. I can't believe this can happen in France,' Mohamed Al Fayed alleged.

Though there was huge media interest in France, the press were not very critical of the inquiry. Christian Curtil, the Paris lawyer for Trevor Rees-Jones, explained: 'The media don't know anything because no one can verify what is in the file. It's very frustrating for them. They wanted evidence, and since my client did not want to speak, I couldn't say much more than what I said because I was bound by the secrecy of the investigation.' With the passing of time however, Curtil obviously feels more can be put on the record, as we shall see.

Curtil and Crawford wanted the inquiry to investigate the case against the company the Mercedes had been rented from – Étoile Limousine. The Ritz are major shareholders in that company so, in effect, they wanted Stephan to turn his attention to Al Fayed. The car had been stolen. Had it been fixed properly? They also raised an issue that John Macnamara had raised when I interviewed him and he said he was worried that the Ritz's own security procedures had not been followed. One of the guidelines that the Al Fayed organisation wrote itself – number 1629 – stated that there always had to be a back-up vehicle when someone who needed close protection was on the move. Al Fayed himself never travelled without such back-up. In their books both Ken Wharfe and Martyn Gregory suggest that Al Fayed and his companies had failed Dodi and Diana by not providing them with proper security.

There is also the question of who had the right to drive the Mercedes S280. Under the byelaws of Paris, when a car is hired out 'for reward it must be hired out with a driver who is an employee of the car-hire company,' Crawford told me. Henri Paul was an employee of the Ritz, but not of the car-hire company. Second, Paris transport regulations require anyone who drives a rented car for reward to have a particular driving licence; Henri Paul did not possess that special licence.

These two points mattered, Crawford explained, as 'there is a general French offence of putting others in danger and that can be made out simply by irresponsible activity or any form of failure to comply with the law. We said that offence was made out because Étoile Limousine had not respected the rules in these two ways.'

The terms of reference the inquiry created for itself 'only concerned the photographers,' Curtil told me. 'It was never extended to anyone else or anything. I tried to get it extended to involuntary manslaughter by the Ritz and Étoile Limousine because I believed there was negligence on their parts; but obviously the magistrates did not want to investigate that.'

Both Crawford and Curtil thought they had a very strong case and that it might well lead to very substantial compensation for their client. They wrote asking for an inquiry into the car-rental company.

Under French law, an investigating magistrate has five days to decide how to proceed after he has received a request to open an investigation. If he decides not to do so, he has to explain why in writing. Crawford told me, 'We had complained that the couple and Trevor Rees-Jones had been put in danger by not respecting these rules.' Crawford and Curtil were amazed by the magistrate's unusual response. They were not notified after five days that there was no case to answer and, in fact, the directors of the Étoile limousine firm were summoned and questioned on the record by both *Juges* Stephan and Devidal, exactly as if an inquiry had started.

Months later, however, it transpired there was no such formal inquiry. When Crawford and Curtil asked why, it was explained that there was no case to answer. It was alleged that the passengers in the Mercedes had been put in danger by the negligence of Étoile Limousine, but Crawford told me: 'Mysteriously the *Juge* dismissed that on a technicality because the passengers were all dead or had been injured; they had not been put in danger . . . because the danger had been realised.' David Crawford does not believe this is very reasonable reading of the law.

I said that ruling that people had not been put in danger because they died seemed 'utterly perverse'.

'I think your description perverse is apt. Why did *Juge* Stephan not say this in the beginning?' David Crawford asked. 'It was only after he interviewed the directors of Étoile Limousine and only in his judgment of September 4th 1999 that Stephan said the offence was not made out because one victim was injured and three were dead.'

There are three other points that emerged which do not make for confidence in the inquiry.

The attack on Curtil and political pressures

David Crawford went to see Christian Curtil in August 1998 shortly after they had made the complaint against the Étoile Limousine company. 'I was rung by Curtil on my mobile phone and Curtil said that I should tell my children not to be shocked by his appearance because he had been assaulted,' Crawford said.

Curtil's face was black and blue when they got there and he had a nasty tale to tell. A man in a turban had started to hit him inside the building where he worked. The man stole nothing, demanded nothing. Crawford was adamant that Curtil did not know of any enemies who might have done this. 'We don't know why and he knows of no one who has a particular axe to grind.' Curtil confirmed that this happened just at the moment that he was pressing to open inquiries on Étoile Limousine but he did not want to talk too much about it. He dismissed it as 'not important' but Crawford had been shocked and he stressed that his colleague had been shocked by the violence.

The second small mystery concerns a reward.

Al Fayed's reward

In one of my early meetings with the French journalist Pierre Blois, he told me that he had had a funny experience and he wanted to see what I made of it. He had become aware that Mohamed Al Fayed had offered a reward of $1 million to anyone who could provide information that led to the conviction of the killers.

Blois went to see Al Fayed's lawyers in Paris. He admitted very frankly to me that he wanted that million or, at least, enough money to pursue his enquiries. What he had to offer Al Fayed, he said, was the same information he had offered me – who was in the Fiat Uno with Andanson and where to find him. Blois had an enthusiastic reception from the Al Fayed organisation at first, but then, nothing happened. It is not unreasonable that Al Fayed was careful because he had been conned out of £15,000 soon after the crash by a man who claimed falsely he had good information on how MI6 had planned the assassination. But Blois is well known in French media circles as a journalist with solid credits. Still, he made absolutely no headway and, soon, Al Fayed's lawyers were refusing to answer his calls. When Blois decided to visit their offices, he was greeted with courtesy but he did not obtain one penny to help him investigate further. He began to wonder if Al Fayed had matters that he did not want probed too deeply. Blois was not the only person to raise that question.

It was put to me that Al Fayed could have made a complaint against X for *homicide voluntaire* – murder. You do not have to name X when you ask a *juge d'instruction* to start an investigation because in theory the investigation should reveal who X is.

When I made that point to Al Fayed, he replied that it was very difficult under French law to make such a complaint. John Macnamara, who was always present when we filmed, added that under French law unless you have good evidence you commit a criminal offence yourself by making the complaint. He went on to point out they had hardly been inactive as they had filed complaints for involuntary manslaughter, invasion of privacy and, with Henri Paul's parents, for falsification of the samples at the autopsy. None of their interventions had met with much success.

Martyn Gregory in *Diana: The Last Days* is very critical of Al Fayed and suggests that one reason why Al Fayed adopted such an aggressive attitude was to deflect any criticism of himself and that these 'diversionary tactics' went very far. They included attacking Dominic Lawson, editor of the *Sunday Telegraph*. He quotes Al Fayed's claim that Dominic Lawson was an MI6 agent. Al Fayed certainly handed me a fat file titled 'Adverse *Telegraph* and *Sunday Telegraph* articles' and Dominic Lawson was clearly one of his *bêtes noires*. Nevertheless, I wonder why a distinguished TV producer like Gregory never seems to ask himself whether Al Fayed might be so angry and aggressive for decent personal reasons, like guilt and despair. If you feel that you could have done more and, especially if you are the kind of man who believes he can shake the world which, right and wrong, true and vain, I suspect Al Fayed does, then it is hard to admit to yourself and to the world that you have failed. If the person you have failed is your wayward son who has died, perhaps you don't always behave in a proper way, stiff upper lip curled, emotions repressed. A friend of Al Fayed's told me that Al Fayed does not always respond sensibly to questions because he is so emotional about the death of his son. I don't think that sinister, but it adds to the confusion.

Both David Crawford and Christian Curtil, the lawyers for Trevor Rees-Jones, share some of Gregory's dislike of Al Fayed but they are more measured. They had seen that at first Al Fayed wanted total control of the case. Curtil told me that he had even had to battle to see his client alone; Al Fayed's lawyers asked to be present. Curtil also fought to make sure Trevor Rees-Jones was not driven to meet the inquiry in a car provided by Al Fayed. He thought that would be quite inappropriate as his client might end up suing the Ritz. 'I was very much pressured by the Al Fayed organisation in the beginning but they found out I could not be pressured so they stopped.'

Both lawyers also claimed that they had never been paid all their fees as Al Fayed had promised. Curtil said he had received the money for only one invoice while Crawford eventually took Al Fayed to court and won £16,000.

The third point concerns the Spencer family itself. But we now ran into another silence – and this time it was aristocratic.

The family does not wish to express itself

When we made *Lady Died*, Francis Gillery and David Carr Brown had filmed a brief, but interesting encounter. Maître Alain Toucas, like every other French lawyer involved in this case, is one of the stars at the

Paris bar. (Maître is the honorary title all French attorneys are addressed by.) He was retained by Diana's family. He regretted he could not give us an interview for *Lady Died* but, somehow, we were given to understand where he would be at a particular moment and, of course, if the cameras were there, accidentally on purpose, he would have to deal with that. We had the impression that he was a man with something on his mind.

David and Francis met Maître Toucas as he got out of his car. He was charming but very firm. 'The family does not wish to express itself,' he said, but when Francis pressed the point of whether there were questions to answer, Toucas did not hurry into his offices. He allowed David to place him in a spot where the light was better for the camera and said that he was sorry, but he could say nothing. Except for one thing. He did agree that there was an 'interrogation'. It was a *'fait notoire'*, a fact for the lawyers, an issue on the record, that there were questions to be asked about the inquiry. He was far from certain we would ever know the truth. But as his instructions were to say nothing he had already said far too much, and there was nothing more he could say. Finally, with a grin, he did then walk through the door and into his offices.

Toucas was also one of the club of dissatisfied lawyers, it seemed. Some of the pressures *Juge* Stephan and *Juge* Devidal faced were mundane – the inquiry was taking too long, costing too much. But when I asked Curtil how good he thought the inquiry was he was careful, saying: 'It's a difficult question. I think it has been very rationally done and quite properly done in a way that many elements that had to be inquired on have been, but it always becomes frustrating when the investigators don't want to go further . . . the investigation has been very well done to the extent that the investigator and the Procureur Général wanted it done.'

Curtil remained frustrated that the inquiry had refused to open the case against the Ritz, since he believed they had a case for negligence to answer. 'So we tried to re-orient the investigation another way but by that time the investigating magistrate and the Procureur wanted it to come to an end. No one would know the real truth anyway and it had to be stopped and it was stopped.' Curtil added that there was a feeling 'it was too late and no one would speak any more . . .'

The precise stage at which the inquiry decided it would never know the whole truth may be earlier in the proceedings than imagined. When I asked David Crawford if he had any evidence of political pressure, he said no one had taken him into his confidence, and then added: 'I was informed at a fairly early stage that there would be no trial of anybody.' Crawford refused to tell me who had said this to him but it must have been someone close to the inquiry. A little later he returned to this theme. His words do come from a man with an ingrained suspicion of the French judicial system, and he pointed out 'any political pressure was difficult for me to perceive. Whether one is making too much of it to say he [*Juge* Stephan] was promoted . . .' Stephan is now head of the defamation division of the courts.

'He was very kind to me and sympathetic and a top

Paris *juge d'instruction* who you would expect to be promoted,' Crawford added, 'but I do feel that the French have a system unlike ours, which we call the accusatory system. Over there they have an inquisitorial system, where an officer of the state conducts the inquiry and all officers of the state are paid by the state and beholden to the state and one is sceptical whether there can be interference from above.'

Crawford speaks from a British perspective but even Curtil did not dismiss the notion of political pressure. Smiling, he said that while in theory judges were independent, in fact 'no one is completely independent . . . they have an ear and listen to what people say or what the Ministry says'.

French legal history shows that many infamous cases were all plagued by interference from above. And this was just what Chauvel had been told by the traffic police had happened in this case. One man who might have been in a position to discuss these issues was Jean-Pierre Chevenement, Minister of the Interior. I wrote to him requesting an interview but he declined and let a French journalist we both know explain his reasons to me. Chevenement had more serious issues than the crash to bother with because that was all such trivia.

Failure to investigate every nook and cranny is not proof of conspiracy. David Crawford believes that 'if we are ever to get to the bottom of this affair I think it will be through the two British inquests. The whole evidence will be gone over twice more and we shall see whether that brings anything else to light.' We shall see sometime in 2005 if this is true.

I believe I have shown clearly that the French inquiry

was flawed, that James Andanson was at the Alma, that he had links with security organisations and that the evidence suggests his death was not suicide. It is also clear that he had a white Fiat and that while that was not fast enough to overtake the Mercedes, Andanson did not turn up in the Alma Tunnel just by luck. He knew Dodi and Diana were likely to be coming that way.

I now want to return to the start of my story – and the evidence of Guy with which I began this book.

Guy, the Gucci bag and the Order of the Solar Temple

In September 1982 Grace Kelly was fifty-two years old. She was in good health though she was plumper than in her days as a Hollywood star. For the first time in twenty-six years, however, she had made a film. It was a modest short in which she played a woman who loved flowers. The film was directed by Robert Dornhelm and starred Edward Meeks, who told me Grace hoped she could now persuade Prince Rainier to let her do some proper acting. She had missed it terribly.

Grace Kelly's heredity was good. Her parents lived into their eighties. On September 13th Grace and her daughter Stephanie set out from the family mansion at La Turbie just outside Monaco to drive into the principality. The road down from La Turbie is dramatic; hairpin bends twist their way down as you look over the Mediterranean.

Two minutes after leaving her house, however, Grace lost control of her car. It swerved off the road at one of the bends. The car tumbled into a piece of land just below the hairpin and ended up upside down,

according to press pictures of the time. Her daughter
Stephanie survived but Grace died twenty-four hours
later. Grace Kelly's death made headlines all over the
world. There was intense speculation as to the cause
of the accident; some journalists suggested Stephanie
had been driving. Mother and daughter, it was said,
had had a row and Grace drove badly because she was
upset her daughter was involved with yet another
unsuitable man.

At the start of this book I suggested there were interesting parallels between the crash at the Alma Tunnel
and the crash in which Grace Kelly died. In this chapter, I outline evidence which claims that Grace Kelly
was killed on the direct instructions of Jo di Mambro
using a technique that may have been used to kill Diana.
There is a further link; the man who claims he was
hired to kill Diana had carried out a number of 'operations' for the Order of the Solar Temple. What makes
these allegations less than far-fetched is that it is a matter
of record that seventy-three people associated with the
Order of the Solar Temple died in mysterious circumstances. Sixteen of them were found charred on an
isolated plateau near Grenoble in France called the
Vercors. The investigating magistrate, André Fontaine,
declared this was a mass suicide but he had to re-open
his inquiry in September 2003 because new evidence
proves at least some of the sixteen were murdered.

When I made my film on Grace Kelly for Channel
4, we explained how di Mambro had lured her into
his cult. We included the allegation that Grace Kelly
had experienced a curious initiation ritual which
included acupuncture. We explained that she had

refused to pay di Mambro more money and that he vowed revenge. If the great and the good did not pay they had to be punished.

Channel 4's lawyers did not allow us to put the whole story in the documentary in 1997. They suggested we did not include the allegation that a man who owed gambling debts he could not pay was offered a deal. (He had been lured into a high-stake game of poker with some very professional card players; at first he kept on winning and then his luck 'changed'.) This man was told he would not have to settle these debts if he planted a bug in Grace Kelly's car. The bug, however, was actually a small device that could release a toxin when triggered from a distance. The toxin would produce blurred vision and loss of motor control.

The official explanation given for Grace Kelly's crash was that she had a very sudden stroke. All Princess Stephanie remembers is that her mother lost control of the car. By a remarkable coincidence, the car tumbled on to land belonging to a member of the Order of the Solar Temple. I talked to one of the local senior police officers and he amazed me by saying he and his colleagues were rung from Paris and told not to proceed to the site of the crash for the next ninety minutes. The accident was outside Monaco so the French had jurisdiction there.

After the film was broadcast, one of the engineers who went out to Monaco to study the car wrote to me. He claimed that the car he examined, the car he was told Grace Kelly was driving, was not the car which the press pictures showed as the one that had crashed. Austin Rover's engineers first agreed to talk to me and then changed their minds under pressure.

And all this does have links to the Order of the Solar Temple.

At the start of this book I described the way I first met Guy, who had worked for the Order of the Solar Temple. I explained how he had asked me to come to Switzerland three weeks after the death of Diana. He insisted that in July 1997, he had been asked to collect and launder $500,000 in Divonne les Bains. Guy claimed to have laundered money for the multi-millionaire John Latsis and he was used to such operations. I took Guy seriously partly because in 1996 he had told me he had laundered money for staff working for the World Health Organisation; years later that scandal surfaced.

'I had no idea what the first pick-up of $500,000 was for but it was quickly and easily done,' Guy told me. A few weeks later, he was rung up and asked to do a similar job. His client was a man I will call Roland who had been in the East German secret services and had gone to live in Cuba after the fall of the Berlin Wall. Roland had done some freelance jobs for Jo di Mambro, the leader of the Solar Temple, which was why he had turned to Guy for help. These freelance jobs included setting up road accidents of two men di Mambro saw as his enemies because they were causing problems for the Order.

When I first started to make my film on the Order of the Solar Temple, I learned about its mystical beliefs and was astonished that intelligent people could be taken in by such mumbo-jumbo. The Order was mystical and elitist, as we have seen. In his excellent book, *Le Mystère du Temple Solaire*, author Renaud Marhic names some of its 1,000 'disciples' who included many rich and powerful people like Guy Berenger, a nuclear physicist who worked at CERN in Geneva, and at least two millionaires – Alberto Giacobino and Camille Pilet, the marketing director of Piaget watches.

In this chapter, I outline evidence that Prince Charles spent a number of holidays at Le Barroux in France, a small village where the Order had a centre. Prince Charles has made no secret of his interest in two areas in which the Order delved – spiritual insight and alternative medicine.

The Order claimed it was based on Templar traditions. Even in the twenty-first century, there are at least fifty Templar Orders who all insist they are the true heirs of the medieval Knights Templar and who are either still looking for the Holy Grail or keeping it safe and snug in a secret place. Di Mambro certainly knew how to manipulate the spiritual cravings, and vanity, of the rich, famous and insecure. There were eight grades in the Order and the more enlightened you were, the closer you were to salvation – and the more 'saved' you were, the more you paid in monthly contributions.

The Order's second in command, Luc Jouret, was a doctor who was an often effective healer; he was also an authority on alternative medicine. Jouret was born in Belgium and was based in Canada where the Order attracted hundreds of disciples. It owned a number of houses and 'sanctuaries' near Montreal. Di Mambro traded constantly in property there. The Canadian 'connection' would prove important.

Guy had been close to Jo di Mambro since the mid-1970s and knew his history well. Di Mambro started life as a jeweller and ended up in jail in France for fraud. He did nothing to hide his love of the high life. He had fast cars, pretty women, a thousand and one bank accounts. 'He used to come to the bar I owned at Divonne les Bains and we became friendly,' said Guy. 'He often invited me to go on trips with him and during one of those we went to Thesiers, where there were thousands of people who had come to meet a guru. Di Mambro was impressed.' Later, Guy lost the bar because he had failed to pay his taxes and he worked as di Mambro's driver among many other things. He smiled as he recalled that visit to Thesiers. 'Di Mambro told me then that creating a cult was the most lucrative con he could think of.' Di Mambro set about it with some imagination. He started the Golden Way Foundation in Geneva and was soon honoured as a spiritual guru who had deep insights, a combination of Freud and St Francis of Assisi. Di Mambro did not think small either, as he told his followers he was in constant touch with thirty-three invisible spiritual masters who held the fate of the world in their hands. These 'masters' were so advanced they could be in two places at the same time. Di Mambro told his disciples that the masters lived at the same time underneath Zurich and in the Himalayas. And they did not pay taxes in either the East or the West.

Thierry Huguenin was a dental technician when di Mambro met him in 1978. The way the guru treated the 28-year-old shows a supreme con man at work. Thierry had just inherited a serious amount of money. He was told that he was the reincarnation of St Bernard of Clairvaux and, at other times that his body housed an Egyptian deity. He was excited by this revelation.

Thierry is an intelligent man, but he hankered after a higher truth and believed every word of it. Camille Pilet, marketing director of Piaget watches and therefore unlikely to be unworldly, was told he was the reincarnation of Joseph of Arimathea.

Di Mambro believed the faithful needed signs and wonders as well as fine words. He invested in a device that could project holograms. Often, members were praying in one of the Order's chapels when, lo, heavenly music tinkled, and white-robed spiritual masters and saints would loom out of the dark in a pool of light. Thierry described these apparitions to me in detail and, for years, was utterly convinced by them. Guy often did additional *son et lumière* effects which added to the atmosphere. Needless to say, di Mambro played up these visits of saints, angels, cherubim, seraphim and much of the cast of Milton's *Paradise Lost* as signs and wonders which showed God blessed the Order. The miracles helped the cash flow. Sometimes, the adepts saw objects of legend like Excalibur, the Holy Grail and even the Ark of the Covenant. You probably had to pay extra to see the Ark, Guy laughed, and said that one of the reasons he stayed with di Mambro so long was that the guru never tried to pretend to him the spiritual stuff and guff was anything but a con.

By the early 1990s, Guy told me he had got fed up of the bullying and also it seemed di Mambro was not as forceful as he had once been. They parted amicably but stayed in touch. Guy told me di Mambro had called him a week before the deaths at Salvan in October 1994. 'He asked me to drive him to a Paris suburb because he had an important meeting there. Di Mambro came back to the car, very upset. He then made a number of phone calls when they reached Lyons. It obviously hadn't worked,' Guy told me. This makes Guy wonder whether di Mambro was not in a state of crisis just before the fifty-three members of the Solar Temple died in 1994.

Thierry Huguenin eventually discovered the apparitions were produced by lighting tricks and clever holograms. He was so attached to the Order, however, that it still took him over a year to walk out. When he did so, he claims he was still owed 500,000 Swiss francs by Jo di Mambro and he wanted it back.

On October 4th 1994, Thierry drove to the Swiss skiing village of Salvan because di Mambro had telephoned to say he could come and collect some of his money. It shows of the power di Mambro still had that Thierry dropped everything at once and rushed 200 kilometres from Geneva to meet him. Thierry did not know that, the day before, di Mambro had started proceedings against him, alleging he was trying to extort money with menaces from the Order.

At midnight, firemen were called to a blaze at Salvan. Inside two skiing chalets belonging to the Order of the Solar Temple, they found twenty-five people dead. All but one had been poisoned. This was just one of three tragedies. At the same time, a fire also started at an organic farm the Order owned in Chiery, an hour's drive away in central Switzerland. Twenty-three bodies were found there. All but two had been shot. As the news got out, the Sûreté de Québec announced there had also been five deaths twenty-four hours earlier in Morin Heights near Montreal. Four adults and a baby were stabbed to death in one of the houses the Order owned there.

The Swiss authorities announced on the evening of the fires at Salvan and Chiery that it was probably a case of collective suicide by a mad cult. A letter the press received said that the faithful had decided to leave the 'all too corrupt earth'. When I started to make a film for Channel 4 in 1995, however, it was far from clear what happened or that it was mass suicide. One of those who had lost family was Rosemarie Jaton, a lean, careful woman who lives in Lausanne. Her brother, Daniel, had been a member of the Order of the Solar Temple and was one of the fifty-three dead. Daniel's wife and their two teenage children had also died. Rosemarie Jaton was convinced that the victims did not kill themselves. None of the dead had an obvious motive for suicide.

The Swiss police found only one gun outside the chalets in Salvan. They claimed all sixty-five bullets had come from it but said it had no fingerprints on it. They eventually concluded it belonged to Joel Egger, whose body was also found at Salvan. The investigating magistrate (because the Swiss have a system much like the French) eventually said Egger had been in Canada and murdered the five victims at Morin Heights. Egger then flew to Switzerland and drove from Geneva airport to Chiery where, apparently, he passed the gun round from person to person; everyone was quite content to shoot themselves apparently. From this macabre scene, Egger drove on to Salvan where he killed himself with the other members of the Order. Before doing so, someone remembered to make phone calls to trigger 'incendiary devices' which caused the fires that started at midnight at Morin Heights, Salvan and Chiery.

One fact was not made public. Two French policemen, Jean-Pierre Lardanchet and Patrick Rostan had
been seen near both Chiery and Salvan the night of
the mass deaths and they were brought in for questioning by the Swiss. They did not reveal anything and so
the Swiss police felt they could not hold them longer
or charge them. When the police set the two men free,
they gave them back their service revolvers. No information about this was released at the time.

A day after the deaths, the Swiss police recruited a
historian who worked in military intelligence to help
their investigation. Jean-François Mayer had spent some
months in 1987 'infiltrating' the Order. He told me that
his purpose was academic research and that he was not
carrying out surveillance. I am sure that was partly true
but it is also a fact that he worked for Swiss intelligence services. We met in his parents' extraordinary
house near Fribourg, a house full of ancient statues and
swords – virtually a museum of the esoteric and the
spiritual. Nothing Mayer saw when he was inside the
Order suggested a group set on self-destruction, he told
me. He attended lectures in 1987, which preached a
mix of ecology and spiritualism. He had enjoyed one
ceremony on the night of a full moon, which he
remembered, was 'very relaxed'.

The day after the deaths, Swiss and French media
got 'suicide' letters in which the Order claimed that
they had left for the star Sirius. Earth had failed; Sirius
was paradise, the new world. Two days later, a letter
was sent to Charles Pasqua, then the French Minister
of the Interior. It claimed: 'Everywhere we went the

police and authorities intimidated and harassed us keeping us under constant surveillance.' Mayer told me that they had found a version of the letter to Pasqua in the wreckage of the computers at Salvan. Pasqua's office denied ever having received the letter.

Though the Swiss authorities insisted the leaders of the Order were paranoid, there were many well-informed people who were not so sure it was a collective suicide. The most persuasive sceptic is Roger Facon. Facon is an inspector in the gendarmerie and he is also a well-known author with seven books to his name, including *Murders of the Occult*. Facon told me he was approached ten months before the deaths at Salvan and Chiery and asked to write a book exposing the Order and, in particular, di Mambro and Jouret.

During these discussions Facon learned about the French policeman seen near the chalets and that both Lardanchet and Rostan were members of the Order. Facon was not sure whether Lardanchet was a true believer or working undercover for some branch of the French police.

Facon said he had other things to write but he was approached again in July 1994. The meeting was more urgent now. He was told 'Operation Faust' was being planned and he had to prevent it. He agreed to go to a meeting in Paris and he agreed to be blindfolded so that he couldn't know where he was going. Facon hinted to me that someone he trusted in the police had given him assurances of safety but Facon did not share with me everything he had been told. He would not say who the people who approached him were but hinted there were some links to French security agencies. The most remarkable revelation was that the people Facon met knew a tragedy was going to happen – and wanted to stop it, it seems. The question is who was planning that tragedy.

The historic suicides of Jews at Massada and York, as well as those of cult members at Jonestown and Waco in more modern times are not hard to explain. At Massada and York, a group of Jews faced a cruel enemy – the Romans in AD68 and the English mob in 1190, respectively. The Jews preferred to die by their own hand than to be butchered. At Jonestown and at Waco the cults were under clear threat. Politicians were coming to visit Jonestown after complaints that people had been kidnapped; the FBI were surrounding David Koresh's compound at Waco.

But no one was surrounding the chalets of the Order of the Solar Temple. Jean-François Mayer told me that at Salvan they had found drafts of publicity material for meetings the Order was to hold in May 1995 – something the Swiss did not publicise at all. There seemed to be no reason for so many members of the Order to kill themselves and to decide to do it so suddenly.

It has been suggested that di Mambro had started to believe the mumbo-jumbo he preached. If so, Guy saw no sign of it when they drove the length of France a week before the deaths. Many other people saw di Mambro at that time. He was depressed and worried some followers were asking him to repay the money they had invested in him and the Order but he was used to dealing with disappointed disciples. The policeman Roger Facon reminded me di Mambro was a wily survivor and he had managed to make sure discontented disciples like Thierry and Camille Pilet stayed loyal. He used flattery and if that didn't work, blackmail. When Camille Pilet threatened to stop paying his monthly subscription, di Mambro threatened to reveal he had had a gay relationship with Jouret.

Facon told me: 'Di Mambro was used to conflict and quarrels. There is no logic in suggesting he'd kill himself because there were quarrels in the Order.' The Swiss police did not find anything which explained why so many members of the Order should decide to die in October 1994.

As with the French police at the Alma Tunnel, there was a lot of evidence that the Swiss police had not done their job well or swiftly. It took them over ten weeks to make contact with the Treasurer of the Order of the Solar Temple who lived in France. This woman was easy to find – her name and address were given by Thierry Huguenin. As there were rumours the Order had laundered millions of dollars, she was an important witness. When the police came to interview her and her husband, however, they were only interested, she told me, 'in getting answers which showed that it was a manipulation . . . had I been asked to sleep with my neighbour. If I said anything which didn't fit their ideas, they just didn't write it down.'

The Swiss police also did not follow correct forensic procedures. Rosemarie Jaton found that for eight days the house where her brother lived was unsealed even though he had on the premises documents and other evidence about members of the Order. For eight days, anyone could have breezed in and removed or tampered with these. A French journalist Bernard Nicolas went to the burnt-out chalets and found records of the payments di Mambro made with his American Express card. At Morin Heights in Quebec, where there were five deaths, evidence one would expect to be removed for forensic examination was left – unanalysed – at the sites. A Canadian researcher, Yves Casgrain, who works for Infosect, a group which provides information about cults, was astonished to find books and documents lying in the ruins of the Order's house.

I was flabbergasted when I went to film at Salvan more than a year after the deaths and found manuscripts, documents and tapes still lying around in the debris. These documents included bank receipts and manuscripts of what seemed to be mystical texts. I had one restored and discovered it was a less-than-mystical porn movie. When, at a press conference, I asked the Swiss police why they hadn't cleared the sites properly, the investigating magistrate snapped back: 'Should you be asking me questions or should I be asking you questions?' He said the police had taken away everything that could be useful. How could they know if they hadn't analysed the tapes I found? I replied.

There was another bizarre fact which was reminiscent of the inquiry into the deaths at the Alma Tunnel. Rosemarie Jaton was not allowed to see the autopsy reports on her family members and she was furious that for eighteen months the Swiss magistrates told her that it was a collective suicide. She then discovered that each of her relatives had been shot a number of times in the head. 'You can't kill yourself by putting three, five, seven and nine bullets in your brain,' she said.

In August 1995, ten months after the first set of deaths, Thierry Huguenin warned the Swiss police the remaining members of the Order were at risk. The police claim they took his warnings seriously but, somehow, even though the Order had houses and members in France, they never communicated with the French authorities.

On December 22nd 1995, sixteen members of the Order were found dead in the forest of the Vercors in France. The victims included the French policemen Lardanchet and Rostan whom Facon had been asked to expose, as well as Edith Vuarnet and her son Patrick Vuarnet. She was the wife of Jean Vuarnet who had been the world skiing champion and had become a millionaire, and Patrick was their son. Some of the dead had been killed by bullets shot from the guns that the Swiss police had allowed Lardanchet and his colleague to keep.

A French inquiry was appointed. I talked to Frederic Barthelmey who gave evidence to the *juge*. Barthelmey and his wife are well known in the area because they make walnut wine. They live in a tiny and very quiet village from where the main road leads to the clearing in which the dead were found. Mrs Barthelmey is a devout Catholic and her husband is still extremely sharp in his early eighties. They agreed to see me even though they said they did not want any trouble. The story Frederic told was troubling. A week before the sixteen bodies were found he had been walking his dog at around midnight. He saw three large Mercedes drive at great speed down from the Vercors. He told his wife about that at the same time because it seemed so odd. When the bodies were found, it was clear they had been dead for some time. Barthelmey went to the local police. They told him they were not interested in this evidence and that, in any case, they were not allowed to study the scene of the crime. When Barthelmey gave evidence to the *juge*, he alleges he was told that his story was crazy and that he would be wise not to repeat it. Mrs Barthelmey was shocked by the rudeness of the magistrate. The inquiry concluded this was another case of mass, mad suicide by a paranoid cult.

Some of the families of the dead never believed it was as simple as that. Alain Vuarnet, whose mother and brother died at the Vercors, fought for a number of years to get the bodies of his mother and brother exhumed. The Vuarnets wanted proper forensic tests performed. The French authorities were again not helpful but, finally, in August 2003, Alain Vuarnet won his case against the investigating magistrate and got permission to dig up the bodies of his relatives. It shows how little Vuarnet trusted the French authorities that he insisted the body samples be sent to British pathologists as well as French ones. The pathologists reported that the bodies of both Edith and Patrick Vuarnet contained a high amount of phosphorus. Somehow the first French autopsies had missed the fact.

The best explanation for the phosphorus is that flame throwers had produced it. This is not a known method of suicide. So yet another French investigation has been made to look inadequate. Some, if not all, of the sixteen dead at the Vercors were murdered – and oddly, like Andanson, died a terrible death consumed by fire. One

of those who has not been very surprised by this
turn of events is Guy.

Guy, May 5th 2002

In 2002, I persuaded Guy to let me film what he had
told me in 1997 just after the death of Diana. His story
did not change over time. His old acquaintance Roland
who had worked for the East German secret services
had been paid $40,000 to formulate a plan to kill a
celebrity and had then been paid a further $500,000 in
July, which Guy had laundered. In the West new laws
oblige banks to watch for drug money and report large
deposits. I have once had my own account blocked
when I sold a property. You can no longer turn up at
Nat West or even the Bank Vontobel in Luxembourg
with a suitcase of dollars and pay them into an account,
no questions asked.

In July, Guy arranged the pick-up of the payment
of $500,000 outside the casino at Divonne les Bains.
'A very British-looking gentleman with a tweed jacket
and smart brown shoes handed me a dark red Gucci
bag. The exchange took half a minute,' Guy said. He
did not ask Roland what the $500,000 was for. He took
his fee, made sure the notes weren't fakes, arranged for
Roland to receive his money when it had been
'legalised' and said goodbye. Strangely he hung on to
the Gucci bag.

Guy heard nothing more from Roland till early
September 1997. Then, Roland telephoned to ask him
to collect and launder another $500,000. This time the

pick-up would be on the Swiss/French border at
Ferney-Voltaire. Again Guy had some minders on watch
and they waited in the town on market day to meet
another stereotypical Brit with another briefcase of
dollars. They waited. No one showed up. Thirty
minutes went by, then an hour. There was still no sign
of the bagman and the dollars.

'Roland had a mobile-phone number to ring in case
of emergencies. He dialled it. He did not get an engaged
tone or the unobtainable and when he rang the operator, he was told the number wasn't just dead, but that
this number had never existed,' Guy told me. They
now became very nervous. I said earlier that Guy has
a sense of drama. He walked me round Ferney-Voltaire
explaining how they got more and more anxious. After
ninety minutes, they gave up. Something had gone
badly wrong.

At this point Guy still had no idea what 'operation'
the pay-off was for. But he could see that Roland was
agitated, even frightened. That was very unusual for
him. Guy told me: 'I decided it was safest to go back
to my flat. Roland was very scared.' There, Roland
explained whom he had been hired to kill. It was Diana.
Guy told me: 'I said he had been mad to accept the
assignment as the world would hunt Diana's killer for
ever.' The fact that the final pay-off hadn't been made
meant trouble and Roland better disappear using his
old East German spy skills and contacts.

Guy claims that he was also told the method that had
been used, but I stress that he did not witness any of
this. The plan Roland had devised was the following.

When I had met Guy at Divonne les Bains three

weeks after the crash, no one had suggested that Henri Paul lived above a gay bar or that he might have some homosexual tendencies. Guy explained to me then he had been told that Henri Paul was bisexual. That made him vulnerable. The first part of the conspiracy Guy revealed to me was to get someone close to Henri Paul, so Roland set him up with a beautiful young transvestite who called herself Belinda. 'She was very beautiful, Roland said,' Guy added. Henri Paul had fallen for her and spent most of the missing time between 7pm and 10pm with his new lover.

After leaving the Ritz at 7pm on August 30th, Henri Paul had a date with Belinda. They flirted, they kissed and, when Henri Paul was told to go back to the Ritz, she went with him and planted a tiny pin-like device on his clothes without his knowing it. This was the instrument of death. It is interesting that the Ritz videos show Henri Paul parked his car at 9.53 but did not walk through into the Ritz till 10.08. What was he up to in those fifteen minutes? The inquiry never asked. One possibility was that he was with Belinda.

The pin-like device, Guy was told, carried a bubble-head with a small amount of the nerve agent VX. VX was first made in 1936 at IG Farben in Germany. The scientists there felt it was a major advance in the technology of death. VX is far more lethal than mustard gas. It wreaks havoc with the way brain cells communicate with each other. Usually messages pass from neuron to neuron across what it called the synapse; synapse is Greek for a clasp and it is a bridge between cells across which electrical signals pass. These signals needed to be eased across the bridge and they are helped by

chemical substances the brain secretes called neurotrans-
mitters. One of these is acetylcholine. One of the effects
of VX is to destroy acetylcholine in the brain. Academic
papers refer to VX as a synaptic disruptor. If brain cells
don't communicate, you lose the ability to perceive and
to act.

In the 1980s, research showed that one of the causes
of Alzheimer's disease was loss of acetylcholine in the
brain and various therapies tried to remedy this.
Alzheimer's often takes years to destroy a person. VX
acts very fast and one way of understanding its effect
is to imagine it causes an instant attack of some of the
most devastating symptoms of Alzheimer's, such as confusion, inability to speak, loss of fine motor control. It
also very quickly leads to blurred vision. The press often
refer to VX as immediately lethal but, as we shall see,
that is not totally accurate.

The claim that Guy made to me was that once Henri
Paul had been asked to drive by Dodi, a fairly simple
plan went into action. Belinda hugged Henri Paul and
fixed the pin with VX on to his clothes. She then said
she would meet him later. Roland had posted men
outside the tunnel and organised for a car to follow the
Mercedes at a distance. At what seemed a good
moment, they triggered the device. The VX made
Henri Paul lose control.

For this scenario to be credible, we have to believe
that VX could be bought, placed in a small bubble-
head pin, and that it could be released at a distance.
The most lethal way of using VX is to get it on the
skin. If inhaled it takes longer to work.

Guy told me in 1997 and, again in 2002, that it was

perfectly possible to buy VX on the black market in the Romanian town of Brasov. There have certainly been cases reported of VX being smuggled across Turkey. The Japanese cult Aum Shinrikyo managed to make a small amount of VX and to handle it safely, as well as the large amount of sarin they released in the Tokyo subway. That freelance agents should get hold of a small amount of VX is feasible. By 1997 there was nothing cutting edge about miniaturised weapons or triggering them at a distance by remote control to release a nerve agent. An ex-army officer who specialises in munitions told me that it was perfectly possible to trigger explosions at a distance. He added that the Tokyo subway deaths showed that careful amateurs could acquire and handle small quantities of VX. He said that there were many refinements because of progress in miniaturisation.

It is surprisingly easy to track down some information on VX. On-line medical references show 135 research papers have been published since 1980 on the nerve agent but these mainly report experiments on rodents, chickens and dogs. Only one paper in the *Lancet* (September 9th 1995) describes the effect on a human being, though there are a number of papers on antidotes. The material detailing the effects on humans remains classified. Doctors at Keio University in Tokyo saw a 56-year-old man who suffered from VX poisoning and described the severe symptoms he suffered including blurred vision, loss of consciousness and temporary muscular paralysis. The paper notes that the doctors thought the patient survived because he breathed in VX but not a drop of it landed on his skin.

As a vapour, the paper claims, VX is far less effective in gas form than sarin. (It is not inconsistent that Trevor Rees-Jones could have survived or that Diana survived for over three hours because, in vapour form, VX is not necessarily lethal.)

Nearly all the literature on VX concentrates on the symptoms and on how to treat VX poisoning. But some studies suggest that VX leaves some traces of cyanide and the post-mortem effects of cyanide are much like those of smoke inhalation. In other words, this could explain the high level of carbon monoxide found at the autopsy of Henri Paul – if the autopsy was carried out on the right body.

In October 1997, Guy said Roland might be willing to talk to me because he was now terrified and he was more terrified of his assistants (who, I was told, were Yugoslavs) than of the forces of law and order. His collaborators might not believe he had not received the second $500,000 – and they were dangerous men it was dangerous to let down by not paying them in full. Guy told me that when Roland carried out operations for di Mambro he was cold and impersonal. Now he was very different.

On October 15th 1997 I talked on the phone to a man who claimed he was Roland. He had a deep voice and he was obviously nervous. He told me he had been living in Cuba when he was first contacted for this 'contract'. It was important that it didn't look like a murder, his clients said. At first Roland did not know who the target was but he was told it was someone high profile and paid an advance of $40,000 to devise a plan. When he eventually discovered who he was supposed to murder, Roland didn't have any particular quibbles. He was adamant that Diana was the target, not Dodi.

At first Roland could not work out how to get near to Diana. But, as her relationship with Dodi developed, he reckoned the Ritz and Henri Paul offered a good chance. Roland told me that he had often used prostitutes to get close to people he was targeting – sometimes for blackmail, sometimes for murder.

The details of the story told to me six weeks after Diana's death were extraordinary. Roland confirmed what Guy had said to me three weeks earlier. He had employed Belinda, the transvestite prostitute, to befriend Henri Paul who had just quarrelled with his girlfriend. When Guy told me this story for the first time, no one knew apart from a few members of the Paris police that Henri Paul lived above a gay bar and had gay literature in his flat.

Roland did not want to talk to me for long. He stressed that no one ever told him why Diana had to be killed. He said he would meet me soon but he then cancelled that arrangement. Guy told me he had gone east again because he felt safer there. I have failed in further attempts to contact him. As my conversation with him was brief, the information I have been given on the method used in this conspiracy is based on what Guy told me and Guy was not part of the conspiracy. He was just the man who laundered the first payment of $500,000 and was hired to launder the second instalment.

Guy's story is sensational but I cannot prove it is true. I remain unsure. Roland might have lied to him and the money was a simple drugs deal or Roland might have told him only part of the truth. But Guy has provided reliable information in two other cases – Grace Kelly and, far more crucial, the death of Madame Marchal. In the Marchal case, his evidence has come under a great deal of scrutiny.

Madame Marchal was a vastly wealthy widow who belonged to the Order of the Solar Temple. In 1991, she was found dead in the garage of her house La Chaumade. Someone – it was presumed to have been her – had scrawled on the walls '*Omar m'a tue*', Omar killed me. She employed a gardener called Omar who had recently come to France from Morocco. Omar Haddad was tried and convicted. But many people did not believe he was guilty and the case became a huge scandal in France, similar in notoriety to the Guildford Four case in Britain.

In January 2002, Guy agreed to take part in a television programme in France about the Omar Haddad case. By then, there were sufficient doubts about Haddad's guilt that he had been released on parole but the authorities refused to pardon him. On the show, Guy explained that he had driven two men and a woman to the village where Madame Marchal lived on the day before the murder was said to have taken place. One of the men was her lover Jacques Tizoti. The other man was Joel Egger whose gun had been used at Salvan; the woman was Dominique Bellaton who had married di Mambro. They had killed people on di Mambro's instructions, Guy knew. Di Mambro was scared Madame Marchal was trying to back out of the Order as she had started to delay her monthly subscription payments to him.

Guy waited outside in the car while the three went into her house. They came out a few minutes later. He had little doubt that these people had killed Madame Marchal and that Omar Haddad had been framed for the murder. Guy told me he had waited ten years to give this evidence because he believed that he could not be charged with a relatively minor offence so long after the fact; he had, after all, only acted as chauffeur for the killers. Before appearing on the show, Guy hired lawyers and went to the police in Nice and told them the same story. That was reported in French papers. They insisted he go with them to the murder site, Madame Marchal's house at La Chaumade where he explained what had happened. Then the police brought him back to Nice and held him for a further two days. Psychiatrists came to interview him and decided he was not a fantasist. He claimed to have an official document, signed by the local colonel of gendarmerie, which said that they had checked his story. Guy said he had been told something like 117 detectives had been put on the case. The police believed his story but they had been in constant communication with Paris and their superiors had decided not to pursue the matter. Guy was released and is now a free man.

Like many of those close to di Mambro, Guy knew a good deal about important people in France and he had some useful contacts with the police. In the case of the Alma Tunnel, Guy's allegations are the only ones I know where someone who claims to have detailed – and first-hand – information of a conspiracy has talked about it. His claims need to be reported. The main reason I remain unsure about the story is the method that Guy described was used to kill Diana. When talking about laundering money Guy is describing something he did. But he was not directly involved in either buying the VX or the plot, so Guy is not in a position to be sure of what method was used since he was not there and has never claimed to be there.

Guy, August 11th 2003

I went back to see Guy when I was writing this book. I wanted to double-check that he was not changing his allegations. Given their serious nature, I wanted to give him every chance to backtrack. If he had made it all up, now was the time to say so.

Guy and the new woman in his life, Carmela, came to meet me at Luxembourg airport. He arrived with two small dogs on a leash and explained they were her dogs. He has mellowed a little and does not stare you so hard in the face. He was very happy because he had just been through a series of medical tests and he had been told he was in fine fettle for a man of fifty-seven. 'I'll live to a hundred,' he said.

We drove back to the flat he shares with Carmela. Except for one thing, his home is a very ordinary flat in a suburban road in a big town in eastern France. The oddity is that every room, apart from the kitchen, is crammed with watercolours and oils. There are three kinds of pictures, Guy explained. First he has a few valuable still lifes which date from the time he worked for di Mambro. Second, Carmela loves painting by numbers and the walls of the hall are full of her pictures. Thirdly, Guy has taken up doing paintings of buildings. 'When I was young,' he said, 'Christine my wife and I dashed off paintings together to sell at markets.' They could produce a passable landscape in fifteen minutes so it was good business. When I went to see him it was furiously hot and he said 'you just can't paint in this weather'.

He asked me if I wanted to have a shower because it was so hot. I said not then, because I was eager to talk. Guy sat me down and said that since I was a psychologist, he wanted to tell me something. He did not usually dream very vividly but he had just had a frightening nightmare. 'He woke me up screaming,' Carmela said. It was a dream about an event that had happened to him when he was ten years old. His parents owned a bar and his father had said to him he could help close up one night. Two men came in. They wanted to be served dinner. 'My father said it's late and then anyway this is a bar, not a restaurant. Then they took out guns and shot at us.' The men missed. Guy mimed how bullets had whizzed past his head and past his father's head. He wondered if I thought the incident had fated him for a life in which violence played a part.

Guy insisted that everything he had told me about Diana was true back in 1997 and as true when we filmed him in 2002. He opened a cupboard and showed me: 'You see I still have the bag.' He meant the bag in which he had picked up the half-million dollars in Divonne les Bains. He then said he had more to say now about this.

Guy asked me if I remembered a place called Aubignan. I did. It is about fifteen minutes' drive from Orange in southern France. Thierry Huguenin had spoken about it to me, as he lived for a number of years in a tiny hamlet nearby called Le Barroux in a house called the Clos de la Renaissance. Di Mambro had bought the property and often came to visit Huguenin. Guy also knew the place well. Two of the dead at Morin Heights came from the nearby town of Sarrians where the Order had another property.

Guy went back to Aubignan on one of his visits to his mother. He met the Mayor of Aubignan who told him he had never been allowed in the house. The mayor then introduced Guy to the man who ran the *pressing* or dry cleaners in the village.

'This man had a curious tale to tell.' Guy claimed the man had been very nervous because one of the dressing gowns he had been asked to clean was made of such luxurious material, not the kind of stuff he usually got in his house. The dressing gown, the cleaner claimed, had belonged to Prince Charles. At the same time, he had also had to do some dry cleaning for di Mambro. This would place the Prince and di Mambro in a tiny village at the same time. All this, he alleged, took place three to four years before Diana died.

Guy then phoned the dry cleaners in Aubignan to arrange for us to visit them together. 'You mustn't rush people,' he said, when he talked to the daughter of the man who owns the cleaners. He said to her that he believed her father would remember him.

I decided to check on Guy's story by going to Aubignan without telling him. It is a very small French provincial town. The main street snakes uphill past two small hotels, a *tabac* and a butcher. I couldn't see any dry cleaners. I was beginning to wonder if I had been entirely wrong to trust Guy. I was beginning to feel all the stress rumbles I described when waiting for Tomlinson when, at the top end of the street, I saw the sign – '*Pressing*'. Just after this dry cleaners the road forks and the right fork goes towards Le Barroux. 'Le Barroux doesn't have a *pressing* of its own,' Guy pointed out, 'because the place is too small.'

Back in London I had checked to see if Prince Charles had had connections with this particular spot in the South of France. There was no great secret to penetrate. There is a well-known photo of the heir to the throne almost naked at a window. It was published in 1994, politely cropped to preserve us seeing the royal equipment. This photograph was taken at Le Barroux and published by *Paris-Match* as well as British papers.

Le Barroux boasts a small medieval castle. It is still being renovated, a process which started in 1929, the guide explained to me. For five euros you can spend fifteen minutes wandering through bleak hall after bleak hall. There is a desolate suit of armour in one corner. The owners keep the electricity off to save money. Some halls are now used to exhibit some rather drab watercolours. From the window of one of the chambers, you can see the large house that used to belong to Baroness de Waldner. She was the mother-in-law of Oliver Hoare, the art dealer Diana had a crush on. (It was Hoare's wife who complained about Diana's calls.) Prince Charles often visited the Baroness at her mansion. He liked to paint watercolours there. The guide at the castle remembered Charles's visits well because of the detectives, staff and servants who accompanied him. The guide had a file of press clippings about them. Charles visited the village in the first week of September from 1991 to 1996 and resumed his visits in 1998 until the death of the Baroness.

Prince Charles was not the only person in this story to visit Le Barroux often. Di Mambro bought Le Clos de la Renaissance in the eighties. It is at the bottom of the village, about three minutes from the castle. Le Clos de la Renaissance had a large hall for ceremonies. There was another house nearby called Le Relais du Silence which also belonged to the Order. Five kilometres away in Aubignan there is a complex belonging to the Order with an underground chamber full of mirrors where apparitions of St Bernard and other saints appeared to the faithful. The head of the municipal police told me he had been amazed by the mirrors and, more cynically, by the way locals stole all the furniture and papers in the house after the tragedy of 1994.

I walked to the highest point of the castle at Le Barroux. I saw how small it is from the top. There are no shops and just one restaurant; the total population is 350. In so small a village, people knew of the comings and goings of these slightly eccentric people especially as di Mambro often turned up in a mustard-coloured Porsche. Guy said di Mambro's car certainly got noticed there.

Spirituality has interested Prince Charles for many years. In the late 1980s Laurens van der Post, whom Charles revered, introduced him to the poet Kathleen Raine who was running an 'academy' called Temenos which published an esoteric spiritual journal. Temenos means the sacred space around a temple. Raine had to stop publishing the journal in 1991 because it was losing too much money. Prince Charles contributed an article to the last issue. Raine decided to concentrate on teaching what she called 'the perennial philosophy'. The perennial philosophy is the study of traditional spiritual, mystical and philosophical truths. Raine was deeply influenced by William Blake and his search for the 'inner light' and also by the Irish poet Yeats, who wrote at length of the Golden Dawn. (Di Mambro called his first sect Golden Way.) 'Here was the mainstream of civilisation from which the culture of the last three centuries had been cut off,' Raine wrote. Raine waxed lyrical about Watkins' Books, London's most famous bookshop devoted to the esoteric arts. In 1996, she wrote: 'Is it possible that our one world is now moving towards a transition?' And that transition would involve heeding 'the perennial philosophy sought by the Renaissance, the inner light of Blake and the Protestant mystics as well as the esoteric teachings of the Kabbalah and the Rosicrucians'.

In 1998, Prince Charles agreed to become the patron of Raine's Temenos Academy and to back the re-launch of its journal, *Temenos Academy Review*. The Prince has contributed a number of articles to it. In one he talks of the fact that 'the soul of each of us [holds] . . . a vital metaphysical spark which makes life worth living' and spoke of the 'spiritual dimensions greater than and beyond the confines of the self'. None of that is sensational but it is interesting that you do not find bishops of the Church of England contributing to *Temenos* because the basic ideas espoused in the journal are eccentrically, and sometimes darkly, mystical. The artwork of the front of the *Temenos Academy Review* has an eight-pointed cross which was used by the Knights Hospitallers and the Order of the Solar Temple itself.

I suggest that Prince Charles's repeated presence at Le Barroux over the years is intriguing. He was certainly interested in some of the spiritual insights di Mambro and Jouret were so skilled at 'selling'. They would certainly have known he was there and a pair that had persuaded Grace Kelly to join their Order would have certainly hoped to interest him in their cult.

The Prince's hostess Baroness de Waldner was, like di Mambro, one of the local personalities of note. She lived part of the year in the village. It seems probable that the Baroness knew some members of the Order who also lived at Le Barroux permanently. All this makes the suggestion that Prince Charles or members of his entourage had some contact with the Order not incredible.

Prince Charles is a man who is under constant surveillance in a world where terrorists attack celebrities. The IRA murdered the uncle he loved, Lord Mountbatten. British intelligence must have known that every year he spent some time in a small French village where houses were owned by members of an esoteric cult many of whose members had died in mysterious circumstances. And it must have worried British intelligence, as the cult had established a somewhat macabre record of bizarre deaths and suicides.

A year after the deaths in the Vercors, another five members of the Solar Temple committed suicide in

Quebec in a beautiful old farmhouse in St Anne de la Perade where di Mambro and Jouret had a centre for alternative medicine. In all, by 1997, seventy-three members of the Solar Temple had died in five different mysterious incidents at different sites – Salvan, Chiery, Vercors, Morin Heights, St Anne de la Perade. The Order was, and I believe still is, a sinister organisation. And one with plenty of experience of 'operations'.

The conspiracy Roland told me about and for which Guy laundered the half a million dollars was a free-lance affair and commissioned by enthusiastic amateurs. The evidence for that has much to do with the history of British intelligence.

13

Political Pressure and the Security Services

In trying to work out what the involvement of British, French, American and other security agencies might be, I have tried to be sceptical and also to keep a sense of history and political reality.

No one has written of the security arrangements that were put in place when Diana spent time with her children on the Al Fayed family estate in St Tropez. Trevor Rees-Jones says nothing about it in his book but is, as his lawyer Christian Curtil affirmed, 'very discreet'. It is hard to believe that Special Branch or British intelligence would relax when Diana took Prince William and Prince Harry to stay with the Al Fayed family and that they would happily rely on the father of the 'oily bed hopper', to guarantee the security of the future king. One of the least-spoken reasons was the risk of kidnapping. The princes were going to the Côte d'Azur and, since the fall of Communism, the Russian Mafia operates in Nice. Just what would Al Fayed's men do if confronted by ex-KGB men who knew William and Harry would fetch, quite literally, a king's ransom?

To ensure security, the royal protection squad would have had to collaborate with the French police and with French intelligence services. Harold of the *Renseignements-Généraux* explained to me that they would have set up a discreet surveillance operation. President Chirac would not have wanted an incident. One fact persuades me that French surveillance continued when Diana returned to see Dodi without her children. It was only when Al Fayed's yacht the *Jonikal* was outside French air space in Sardinia on August 27th that it was buzzed by a helicopter. James Andanson had not rented a helicopter earlier because he knew the French would not have permitted it to fly near to the Al Fayed yacht while Diana was on board.

Diana was used to being under surveillance. Long before her marriage fell apart, there were many well-documented incidents of her mobile phone being listened in to. The intelligence services also knew of her links with certain journalists. It is hard to believe that MI5 and friends of the Palace would not have tried to recruit some journalists to keep them informed about what she was saying and thinking.

I pointed out at the end of Chapter 1 that in the summer of 1997, MI6 were preparing a file on the Al Fayeds to present on September 3rd to the Royal Family. It is not credible that the security services got an attack of ethics and became worried about Diana's right to privacy. MI6 would have wanted to impress Buckingham Palace and its advisers with their up-to-date insights. That meant keeping up surveillance. One also cannot ignore the fact that two of the four passengers in the Mercedes had experience of security services – Henri

Paul and Trevor Rees-Jones. The presence of the police-men at Le Bourget also shows that the French author-ities knew who was landing and provided an escort. Did these officers then forget to report up the chain of command?

But it is not just British intelligence who were inter-ested in what Dodi and Diana were doing that day. Gerald Posner is a veteran American journalist who has written for the *Wall Street Journal* among many others. Posner has always insisted that he does not accept Mohamed Al Fayed's conspiracy theories though he believes they are sincerely held. In 1998 Posner reported that he had listened to 'an innocuous portion of an undated conversation between Diana and Lucia Flecha de Lima'. She was one of Diana's best friends and the wife of the Brazilian ambassador to London. Posner says he was given the recording 'by an active US intelligence asset, who says it was one of several collected by the National Security Agency'. The National Security Agency (NSA) refused to confirm the existence of the tape and insisted that it had never directly targeted Diana. Rather the NSA picked up her conversations as an incidental part of a separate moni-toring operation. Posner did get them to admit that they had thirty-nine classified documents about Diana, totalling 124 pages. It is possible that one of these docu-ments concerning landmines that I quoted in Chapter 1 is among the thirty-nine.

The core of the conspiracy theories is that Diana was targeted because she was a menace to the monarchy and, most particularly, to Prince Charles's hopes of succeeding to the throne. In her *Panorama* interview, she had wondered if he would like or get 'the top job'.

I have no intention of being romantic about the history of British spies, gentlemen all, but it is important to set this in context. In responding to criticisms of Diana for criticising the Tories in her interview of August 27th in *Le Monde*, Robin Cook, then Foreign Secretary, defended her robustly on behalf of Tony Blair's government. The Foreign Secretary, together with the Prime Minister and the Home Secretary, control British intelligence. I find it hard to believe that the intelligence services would sanction the murder of a princess their political masters had just defended. That does not mean it never happened but the circumstances do have to be very particular.

Licensed to kill

In 1956 George Young, the deputy director of MI6 advocated the killing of the Egyptian leader Gamal Abdel-Nasser because Nasser's take-over of the Suez Canal was such a threat to British interests. In the end, we invaded Egypt instead. In September 1960 a senior Foreign Office official, Howard Smith, argued in an official document for the assassination of the young Congolese leader Patrice Lumumba. 'I see only two possible solutions to the [Lumumba] problem. The first is the simple one of ensuring [his] removal from the scene by killing him.' Smith later became head of MI5.

Until 1994, the law controlling British secret services was extremely vague and that led to a number of crises such as the plotting against Harold Wilson by some officers in MI5. In 1994, the Conservative government appointed Stella Rimington as head of MI5, the first woman to hold such a senior security job. It also passed the Intelligence Services Act which made the security services a little more open and accountable to Parliament. One of the act's provisions is to make Ian Fleming's 007s – who were 'licensed to kill' – legal, because it gives MI6 officers immunity from prosecution for crimes committed outside Great Britain.

Intelligence services have also been willing to kill inside the United Kingdom, which is not legal. The Stevens inquiry into how the army and police behaved in Northern Ireland has found evidence of a 'shoot to kill' policy. A number of British agents were involved in the assassination of a number of Catholics after the troubles started.

A recent article in *Asia Today* suggests, however, that the British spy is not what he used to be and that declining standards have forced Whitehall and the Special Intelligence Service to sometimes use foreign intelligence agencies to kill. It has even been suggested that MI6 has been willing to 'sub-contract it to Mossad'. A former British agent quoted by Peter Hillmore and Ed Vulliamy in 'Spies: the beautiful and the damned' (*Observer*, October 12th 1997), said that the assassination in Belgium of the British inventor of the Iraqi 'Supergun', Gerald Bull, is widely believed to have been sub-contracted. *Asia Today* also argues that MI5 has been traditionally able to call on the services of the SAS and the 'Increment', a small special-forces unit dedicated to the most top-secret intelligence operations. The people who carry out these operations are not on the payroll of MI5 or MI6; they are sometimes retired agents, sometimes they are ex-military intelligence with links to mercenary organisations, and sometimes they are linked to organised crime. They are friends of friends who have had some training. It is worth remembering that Richard Tomlinson said there are many people who work at normal jobs and whom MI6 can call on for certain operations. Colonel Bob Denard, the French mercenary who had been fairly frank with me about his dealings with French security services also told me that he had been commissioned by British intelligence to carry out a number of operations in the 1960s and 1970s, for example. They paid well for his skills and, also, for his silence.

But it isn't just a practical question of whether French and British intelligence agencies could cooperate and how. Those who have been killed by intelligence were nearly always very obviously enemies of the state, not someone there was a rather more personal vendetta against. Most were foreigners and nearly all of them were men. The only women we know to have been killed by security services are the IRA woman killed at Gibraltar and, possibly, Hilda Murrell, a peace activist in the 1980s. Diana might have been a thorn in the royal flesh but she was also the mother of the future King and her family was one of the most distinguished in British history. By comparison the four knights who murdered Thomas à Becket knew he was an upstart who had reached high office only because he was good at paperwork.

Furthermore, anyone with experience of relations between French and British security services would have been terrified about asking for help from the French. Richard Tomlinson said that it was extremely difficult to get French and British security agencies to cooperate. He had run one or two combined operations and he had also run one or two operations in France that had been kept concealed from the French. He had always been frightened that the French would find out because there would be hell to pay. The notion that they would collaborate to kill the Princess seems utterly far-fetched.

Buckingham Palace and dirty tricks

Mohamed Al Fayed has conducted a number of his own polls and argues that up to 62 per cent of Britons believe Dodi and Diana died as a result of a conspiracy. He exaggerates, but not that much. On the sixth anniversary of the crash, an NOP poll in the *Sunday Express* claimed 49 per cent of Britons thought there had been a cover-up and 25 per cent that Diana had been murdered. Over 50 per cent of women aged between twenty-five and forty-five believed Diana had been murdered.

I think the public willingness to entertain belief in such conspiracies stems from the fact we no longer trust the Royal Family, with the possible exception of the Queen. Our perception of the royal entourage changed during the 1990s and changed more with the Burrell trial and the Peat inquiry which was set up to investigate how St James's Palace conducted its affairs. The Queen apparently insisted on this as she was dismayed by her son's lavish lifestyle. Sir Michael Peat had been one of her advisers. We have already seen that courtiers at St James's did their best to persuade the world that Diana was clinically insane. The Burrell trial also had a profound effect on public attitudes and on what people imagine the royal entourage – and even the Prince of Wales personally – may permit. The *Daily Mail* claimed in August 2003 that some servants had been paid to be silent and said that this is exactly what Prince Charles had done with his valet Michael Fawcett. Fawcett was first fixed in the public memory as the man who squeezed toothpaste out for the Prince. He, possibly, may also have been appointed to the high position of holder of the royal urine sample bottle. When Sir Michael Peat insisted that Fawcett had to go, he departed with a £500,000 golden goodbye. Hush money, said the *Daily Mail*.

In November 2003, the atmosphere got worse from the royals' point of view. For a number of weeks papers carried rumours of a serious allegation on a tape Diana had made. On that tape Falklands veteran William Smith who worked at St James's Palace alleged he had witnessed a sexual incident with a 'senior member of the Royal Family'. Paul Burrell said Diana called that tape 'the crown jewels' but denies he has it in his possession. The tape has apparently, allegedly, disappeared. One can only hope that it will emerge – just as Dodi's mobile did eventually. Perhaps the inquest will now use its resources to track the tape down.

On Saturday November 2nd 2003, Michael Fawcett applied for an extraordinary injunction against the *Guardian*. It would stop them revealing his name as the person who was suing the *Mail on Sunday* for libel in relation to that incident. Fawcett got his injunction which meant we could not be told he was suing the *Mail on Sunday*, let alone why he was suing them. The judge on duty that Saturday granted the injunction over his mobile phone before the *Guardian* could put their case to him. For a week newspapers reported the surreal story that a paper was going to court to be allowed to name a man who was suing another paper; then the injunction was lifted. The *Guardian* said they would not state what the allegation involving Michael Fawcett might be but they could say it was something to do with St James's Palace. That same day, the royal press office went on the attack. Clearly the allegation was damaging: Sir Michael Peat went on television on behalf of Prince Charles to deny it though it was too dreadful to utter. Nevertheless Sir Michael Peat assured the British public it was 'untrue', 'risible' and that Prince William and Prince Harry knew what was being said against their father and stood solidly by him. By the next day we knew the allegation was of a sexual nature, that it involved Prince Charles. We also knew Sir Michael Peat (before he took the job) had asked a former aide of Prince Charles whether the Prince was bisexual or gay. Some commentators believe Peat's question shows there was real anxiety that the tape Diana made of an interview with William Smith alleged that the Prince of Wales might have been seen by Smith in a compromising situation with one of his male staff.

It was just three weeks after Diana's butler Paul Burrell had released the letters in which Diana had said she was worried she could be killed in a road accident.

Death threats in plummy voices

Anthony Holden, Prince Charles's biographer, has a good sense of the public mood and when I interviewed him for *Diana – The Night She Died* in spring 2003, he talked about how he had been invited to meet Princess Diana and became her occasional lunch guest at Kensington Palace. Holden is used to his role as an expert on royalty.

Holden and I are not close friends but we have known each other a long time. I told him about Guy's allegations. He said then he would reveal on the record something he had never revealed before. 'I am sometimes asked if untoward things happened while I was writing the biography of Charles. I have never talked about this before but my car was broken into six times and my windows smashed.' He didn't live in that rough a part of London, he added.

But it wasn't just the car. 'There had been a burglary at our house . . . the local police noticed something before I did. They'd taken the TV but they had not taken a lot of valuable things.' He noticed when he started looking that the burglars 'had taken a lot of discs and videos and files'. They had not stolen the normal movie videos 'but they had taken all the videos that were marked "Charles and Diana". These might have been nothing but the *Panorama* interview and other broadcasts but for all they knew, these tapes could have been research interviews for my film.'

The local policeman who was in charge asked Holden if he was the writer of the biographies of Charles. When Holden said he was, the policeman made a remarkable claim. 'He said to me it looks to me like a Special Branch job. There's nothing I can do about it, sir.'

But that was not the only disturbing event. 'During that period my wife happened to answer the phone and twice there were deaths threats. Very plummy voices down the end of the phone. I am not alone. Other people I know in the royal entourage . . . other people who have been wronged and who have cut loose from the Prince have had similar experiences,' said Holden.

Holden added that an architectural correspondent had had similar threats made to him when he had been critical of Charles's views. Charles Knevitt had the same architectural agenda as the Prince of Wales but there have been business difficulties between various organisations backed by the Prince and Knevitt. Knevitt laughed a little bitterly when I put to him what Holden had said. Knevitt has also been the victim of five burglaries.

William Smith, who made the allegation of rape at St James's, claims that he was threatened himself. Some papers have pointed out that Smith fought in the Falklands and that it is perhaps undignified to attack his character as St James's Palace has done, claiming he was a deluded soul.

It is hard not to see all these leaks and counter-leaks, attacks and counter-attacks as part of the still-unfinished War of the Waleses. The couple's war involved plenty of mysterious episodes which make sense only if Diana as well as Charles was under constant surveillance, Holden told me. 'Who bugged the phone calls? Who released them to the newspapers? . . . I'm not suggesting the Queen and Prince Philip knew anything about it. I think they take it as a matter of course that their family is kept an eye on for their protection.' Holden added that he was not accusing Prince Charles either. 'But I think there are people who think that is what he would want or the state would want.' To be critical of the heir to the throne 'one would be slightly treasonous'.

With a chuckle, Holden recalled that Paul Burrell, Diana's butler, claimed the Queen had spoken to him of mysterious forces in the country. 'But they are mostly on her side,' he smiled.

Holden doesn't accuse any royals. It's more that people will do things they believe will please those in authority, acts their employers couldn't possibly commission, or even suggest. When I first talked to him, Holden told me he did not believe Diana feared for her life but he thinks it very possible she feared for the life of people close to her given the death of Barry Mannakee and the constant surveillance.

Paul Burrell has now claimed Diana did fear for her life because the letter she wrote in December 1996 said they were planning a road accident to do away with her, as the *Daily Mirror* reported. Holden told me that he thought that letter did not fit the mood of the Princess in 1996 when they talked often. She was much more cheerful then. But Holden added the fears expressed in the letter to Burrell did reflect her mood in 1995 during the divorce negotiations.

Holden's revelations reminded me of Tomlinson's point that matters of state were any matters that affected the head of state, and the question of who was sleeping with her son's estranged wife comes under that heading. That was part of the jigsaw, to use his phrase, as are the allegations Guy made. I believe all this evidence shows there was talk of conspiracies and plans for conspiracies but they were more likely to come from people who felt they were doing what the royal entourage might want than from anyone whose job it was to look after British security interests. Here I have to speculate. Perhaps we are talking about extremist groups prepared to engage in criminal activities because of their mystical or occult view of royalty. But just how do you make contact with a competent killer? The Order of the Solar Temple certainly knew how to do that. Researching this book I kept coming back to the Solar Temple. There is one person in this story who knew of the Solar Temple, had photographed some of its members and had political, underworld and secret-service connections and was extremely used to dealing with courtiers and minor royalty. James Andanson, the paparazzo who said he was not there at the Alma, who had photographed some of those involved with the Order, such as Grace Kelly – and who is now dead.

I am arguing in effect that someone decided something had to be done but this had no intelligence-service approval, no royal approval, no one's blessing. It was a favour to an embattled monarchy. I think this also makes it possible to make some sense of the story Guy told me – and especially why the second $500,000 was not paid.

In the mind

I was always puzzled that the people who had allegedly commissioned Roland to kill Diana had not paid the second $500,000. Guy's view of that is simple. 'Well Roland could hardly go to a lawyer and sue.'

I now want to explore what psychology may have to offer and to return to cognitive dissonance theory. I emphasise that I am now speculating, going beyond the facts I have found out. Psychologists sometimes make up what they call thought experiments where you imagine a situation. This thought experiment is simple. You are someone who imagines they know what might be helpful to the Crown. No one has asked you to foment a conspiracy but, on your initiative, you have decided that the time has finally come to get rid of the person who is causing so much trouble and who has, since her marriage, made the royals a mockery. And who is now making speeches wondering whether Prince Charles will really ever become King. Once that would have been treason.

You have had experience of the military and you have some contacts. You know that in France there have been many unexplained deaths and that it is possible to find people with some experience of carrying out intelligently planned assassinations of important people. You gather the cash needed – which is considerable but, after all, less than the price of a semi-detached house in a modest London suburb. You are put in touch with a man who knows a man who has done this kind of thing before – a man who has worked for a cult you know about because you know about the Order of the Solar Temple and its centre at Le Barroux. You may even have visited. (Roland, as I said before, had worked for the Order, according to Guy, carrying out missions to deal with members who stopped paying, '_pour encourager les autres_'.) Eventually, you meet him in Miami. You can't really check his credentials but you have been told this is not new for him. He talks well. You commission the deed and hand over $40,000 so he can work out a plan.

You are not without certain feelings of guilt. After all, you have paid someone to organise the killing of a woman you know many people love. You do not ask how it will be done, but you stress it must look like an accident.

You are told it can be done and then arrange for $500,000 to be paid. You get a friend of a friend to do it. You don't explain why. A gambling debt perhaps.

When you hear that Diana has died you are pleased, but nothing has prepared you for the reaction of the British people. It is so emotional, so overwhelming, you are frightened. You feel even more guilty. Then, the French authorities first blame the paparazzi and then blame the driver who was 'drunk as a pig', as the headlines say. You begin to wonder if the man you met in Miami, the man who was given $540,000, earned his pay. Maybe he had nothing to do with it, it was just an accident.

You have been careful. The killers don't know who you are or where to find you. Their only way of contacting you is by mobile phone. And this is again where cognitive dissonance may explain what could have happened. You are scared, but if you don't pay the second instalment, you feel you will be less guilty. It will somehow prove — to yourself at least — that you really were not to blame. It was typical of Diana and the ghastly set she had started to mix with that they should have employed a driver who got drunk. So you decide not to turn up for the second meeting. The second payment might also make it easier to track you down. You disconnect your mobile phone. You lie low. Just like the killers.

This is, as I said, a thought experiment — and thought experiments are supposed to make you aware of the psychology and the logic of a situation. I don't want to seem frivolous about a tragedy but there has been so much unfounded speculation about the death of Diana that I think it is worth setting out two syllogisms. The first is straight out of the textbooks.

A   All cats are mortal.
B   Sam is a cat.
C   Therefore, Sam is mortal.

You cannot argue about that. Cats die; Sam is a cat; one day or another, end of cat. But the syllogism which conspiracy theories ask us to believe is of a different nature because it has a hidden assumption. It would go:

A   There was a conspiracy to kill Diana.
B   Diana died.
C   Therefore, the conspiracy to kill Diana succeeded.

To make the loop of logic work in this case, you need a special – and hidden – assumption which would run something like 'all conspiracies to kill princesses succeed'. Many conspiracies fail, of course, but throughout this book I have suggested that France is a good country in which to mount a conspiracy. There have been a series of unexplained and suspicious deaths – often of people linked with rather mysterious societies like Templar Orders or the Société d'Action Civile.

It is now time to try to make sense of the facts.

14

Conspiracy, Cock-Up or Cover-Up

E.M. Forster famously said, 'How do I know what I think till I see what I say.' In this chapter, I try to draw the conclusions and I do so knowing full well I have to speculate at certain points, but let me start where there is no need for speculation. The evidence shows that the French authorities did not carry out a full investigation and wilfully excluded some areas. That was the thesis of *Diana – The Night She Died*. After it was broadcast, Channel 5 got no complaints, no outraged letters, and no accusations from anyone. Conspiracy theories have always seized on anything amiss in the investigation as proof of sinister forces at work.

As I have tried to finalise what I really think by seeing what I say, I remembered something that my history master at school told us. Dr Peter Brooks, who became Dean of Peterhouse at Cambridge, was a man we tended to make fun of in the upper sixth but Brooks had one interesting axiom: 'The truth does not lie in the middle but it lies at both extremes,' he used to say. In this mystery, the two extreme positions have been that either the crash was the result of a conspiracy or that it was an accident. I do not think that either of these theses makes logical or psychological sense in isolation. As this is a complicated investigation, I want to re-state what I believe are well-founded conclusions.

The French police did not cover themselves in glory from the start. They did not use the evidence of a number of important eyewitnesses like Erik Petel who was just behind the Mercedes and would have exonerated the paparazzi at once. Petel was told 'not to make himself known'.

Since the tunnel was re-opened ninety minutes after the wreck of the Mercedes was removed, it is impossible that all the forensic evidence had been gathered, so the official inquiry had to rely on incomplete information.

It is bizarre that it was Al Fayed's detectives who found Andanson's white Fiat Uno rather than the French police, as locating that car was said to be one of the top priorities of the police. The claim that some French police made that Andanson's white Fiat Uno had not been present in the tunnel would be more convincing if they had been the ones to find it. The French vehicle expert Nibodeau accepts the white Fiat was there. The evidence that this white Fiat belonged to James Andanson and that he was in the tunnel seems persuasive.

Andanson's extraordinary suicide makes him the first European to burn himself to death for many years apart from a tiny handful of cases where political protesters have set fire to themselves to make a point. Andanson was not a political extremist of any sort. The evidence of the *Renseignements-Généraux* officer, Harold, as well as the forensic and psychological evidence makes it utterly unlikely Andanson's death was a suicide. And that leads to the question of what Andanson knew or might have known about the events in the Alma Tunnel.

Political pressure from the Élysée led to the disappearance of the speed-camera photograph and to the omission of the fact that cocaine had been found in the car.

The fact that Diana took one hour and forty minutes to reach hospital and that it was only when she finally got to the Salpêtrière that X-rays showed the true extent of her injuries is deeply upsetting. There is no proof of the fantastic notion that secret agents replaced paramedics. She suffered because the ambulance teams followed what they thought proper '*reanimation*' procedure, but they misjudged the situation. *Juge* Stephan went out of his way to exonerate them, however.

It is not possible to work out whether the catalogue of errors afflicting Henri Paul's autopsy were mistakes committed in good faith or something more sinister. The experts commissioned by his family and by Al Fayed concluded that the most likely explanation for the high readings of carbon monoxide in his blood was that at least one sample was taken from another body – and no one could admit that had happened. The official post-mortem pathologist and the toxicologist always denied this, but the simple way to quell doubts – allowing an independent analysis – has never been carried out because the French courts have blocked all attempts the Paul family made to obtain their son's samples. The response of the French legal system to the Paul family requests seems to be extremely harsh.

Juge Stephan seems also to have been unwilling to probe whether Mohamed Al Fayed's Étoile Limousine company might have a case to answer in causing the accident. The technical reasons for not investigating these areas seem perverse.

In Britain, we should not 'whip ourselves into complacency' as William Whitelaw, Margaret Thatcher's deputy, famously said, or glory too much about the failures of the French. British courts have made many flawed decisions over the last fifty years; a list that would include the Bentley case, the Guildford Four, the Birmingham Six and many other injustices.

The evidence suggests, in fact, not one cock-up but a whole series of cock-ups. It also suggests that there were a number of facts covered up or, in Patrick Chauvel's phrase, things where the authorities wanted to 'keep it low'. But having reached this point, I want to make the logically simple point that the fact that there were errors and that these errors were covered up does not, by itself, prove there was a conspiracy. Institutions cover up mistakes for a variety of reasons which range from bureaucratic pride to the need to hide something with implications for national security.

One remedy for all this would have been for the British authorities to insist immediately that it was in the public interest to hold inquests into the deaths of Diana and Dodi before now. It does not seem to me that it is an accident that the British authorities have avoided doing so and that they have, in effect, used every delaying tactic available hoping the story would go away.

Diana was the People's Princess partly because people

identified with her. They loved her both for her good qualities – such as her Aids work, her empathy with people in trouble, her campaign against landmines, her love of her children – and also for being less than perfect. She suffered from eating disorders, she could be vain, she could be a bit of a bitch, especially upstaging Charles after the marriage soured, and she did have a slightly rackety sex life. If she had tried illegal drugs that would hardly make her a monster of depravity given how widespread the recreational use of cannabis and cocaine has become in the United Kingdom. So her faults were faults many of us could identify with and Diana had learned to be open about them. Yet the official attitude in France and in England was that nothing must come out. From the start that compromised the French inquiry.

Most psychologists who study trauma and how it affects families would also suggest that this attitude would damage her children. Research on how bereaved families feel suggests that most of them want 'closure' and that they will not get it till they know the truth. Some of the behaviour which Prince Harry has been criticised for is typical when a teenager loses a parent and feels, but cannot really express, that something is wrong. The truth helps families move on. It means confronting feelings, bitter and uncomfortable feelings you'd rather not feel. But Prince William and Prince Harry are part of a family that seems to believe that to show feelings is to show weakness. It is not *comme il faut*.

But the key question, of course, is whether, in addition to all these errors, there was a conspiracy to murder the Princess of Wales. I believe it is not difficult to show that people were conspiring and I think it is plausible to assume that British intelligence services were worried about that.

Everyone who has ever put the conspiracy thesis forward has always assumed that as Diana died, if there was a conspiracy, it worked. No one seems to have considered the possibility that there was a conspiracy, that the intelligence agencies tried to do something to prevent it working, and that perhaps it did not succeed as planned. Like bureaucracies, conspiracies often don't get it right.

I want now to analyse what a conspiracy might have consisted of. Any conspiracy obviously had nothing to do with the theft of the Mercedes S280 from outside the Taillevent restaurant in April. In April, there was no reason to think that the Mercedes would ever carry Diana. The car was repaired by May and, while it is true that the electronics could have been tinkered with, Diana was still involved with Hasnat Khan. Booby-trapping Ronnie Scott's jazz club would have been a more effective way of getting her than doctoring a Mercedes in Paris.

The decision to use a second Mercedes as a decoy was taken after 11pm on August 30th. Until then the assassins would have expected, unless their spook skills included clairvoyance, that Diana would be travelling in the first Mercedes parked at the front of the Ritz. If Nicholas Davies in *Secrets and Lies* is right, the seat belts on the first Mercedes should also have been tampered with because the decision to use the second car was taken just an hour before the crash. But no one has ever suggested that. Neither Kez Wingfield nor his driver ever found there was anything wrong with the first Mercedes when they drove it to Dodi's flat.

The Mercedes which had been at the front of the Ritz went at 3.30am to pick up Mohamed Al Fayed from Le Bourget airport when he arrived to see his son's body. Al Fayed has always been concerned about his personal security and was hardly likely to leave his seat belt off after his son had just died in a car crash.

And yet what I have found out persuades me that there was some sort of conspiracy. The theory that immensely powerful lights were deployed by a commando unit to force Henri Paul to crash seems too melodramatic and begs the question of why no one saw these commandos. The slightest hitch would have led to a scandal of unimaginable proportions.

The method Guy described to me makes far better sense in terms of timing and opportunity. Once the Order of the Solar Temple freelancer Roland had introduced the transvestite Belinda to Henri Paul, the conspirators had access to someone who was close to Dodi and thus close to Diana. The conspirators then seized the opportunity when they knew Henri Paul would be at the wheel. They had nearly two hours to get Belinda to see Henri Paul and fix the VX bubble-head on him. This part of the story may sound very 'James Bond' but perhaps it shouldn't be dismissed until an inquiry establishes the facts.

It would be far more possible to confirm or dismiss the nerve-agent theory if one could have confidence in the autopsy findings but the literature on VX claims that small doses produce effects on the muscles but do not produce effects that are easy to spot in the brain. In the 1995 paper in the *Lancet*, the Japanese researchers reported that when they did a brain scan on their patient who had been poisoned with VX, they saw nothing untoward. The autopsy on Henri Paul, however, did not even weigh his brain. If there was any analysis of the cortical tissues, they were not reported. Some studies also suggest VX can produce post-mortem signs similar to smoke inhalation. So the VX could explain the inexplicably high carbon monoxide readings. Until the French Ministry of Justice opens the files on the twenty-two other dead bodies in the morgue on the night Diana died we cannot know if the samples really came from Henri Paul but the VX story could at least explain the carbon monoxide.

Two other facts would make sense only if there was a conspiracy. One is the question of why was the Mercedes taking the route it was taking, a route David Crawford described as 'inexplicable'. The other question is the presence of Andanson at the Alma, for which I have a number of sources. Harold's evidence suggests that whatever Andanson was doing, it was not likely to be benign.

I have suggested it is possible that Henri Paul was taking the route through the Alma because Dodi was going to a meeting that he did not wish to advertise. The most direct route to the Passy Kennedy building, where I was told the meeting was to be held, was through the Alma Tunnel. It is also interesting that the Mercedes made no attempt to stay in touch with Kez Wingfield as he drove to Dodi's flat at rue Arsene-Houssaye. That is remarkable if Dodi were nervous; it is also strange because Trevor Rees-Jones and Wingfield knew they were not keeping to the Al Fayed organization's own rules of close protection. It is plausible there was no contact between the cars before the crash because Dodi did not want to advertise where he was going and he was the boss. If he said he didn't want mobiles used, they would not be. If Trevor Rees-Jones ever does remember what happened after they left the Ritz, he might have something to say on this point.

As a psychologist, it seems to me possible that Dodi might have wanted to do something to impress both his father and Diana – a fabulous deal that had nothing to do with drugs. Jean Durieux of *Paris-Match* told us that his witness was a young man who impressed him as reliable. The man claimed that Dodi arranged to meet with three men to discuss buying a nightclub in the Champs-Élysées. It was a good deal because the police had closed the premises and the owners needed cash quickly. Durieux's witness was a friend of one of these men. The meeting was due to take place at the Passy Kennedy building after Dodi and Diana left the Ritz. Durieux met his source a number of times after the crash, but he could never get a meeting with the men Dodi had fixed to see.

James Andanson was at the Alma, as I believe I have proved. His Fiat could not have overtaken the Mercedes but, if this meeting had been fixed, Andanson would have known the route Diana and Dodi would travel and so he could have positioned himself there.

But talk of a conspiracy and even of a lure to get the Mercedes to take the route it did still does not mean that the conspiracy worked.

I want now to look at the analysis of what happened in the seconds before the crash. To do that, we have to leave the world of spooks and secret meetings for the nuts and bolts of engineering. We need to focus on how anti-lock braking systems work and the noise Petel and other witnesses heard before the Mercedes crashed. In Chapter 8 I looked at how ABS systems work, evidence which suggests that Henri Paul braked suddenly before the entrance of the tunnel and that caused the noise Petel described as an 'implosion'. We have also reviewed the evidence that there was a speed camera outside the tunnel and a white Fiat Uno in the tunnel. I have argued that this was Andanson's white Fiat Uno but it need not be to understand the mechanics of the accident.

Far from being out of control of his vehicle, Henri Paul braked outside the tunnel when he realised there was an emergency. What it is impossible to know is whether that emergency was that he saw a white Fiat Uno zigzagging slowly in the tunnel or that he suddenly felt unwell as he started to breathe in VX that had been released or whether it was both. If Trevor Rees-Jones were ever to recover his memory, he might recall which it was. Friends of Rees-Jones have now told ABC Television that he dare not remember anything.

The French vehicle expert Nibodeau accepted that there was a white Fiat in the tunnel and wrote in his report that Henri Paul was suffering from 'information overload'. He blamed it on drink but information overload occurs in sober drivers and pilots. Information overload refers to the fact that the human brain can only process so much information at a time. It has been studied in great detail by psychologists for nearly a hundred years. There were three factors Henri Paul had to deal with as he drove fairly fast down towards the tunnel. The speed-camera flash was one; second, there was a car in front of him in the tunnel moving erratically. But there was also a third factor which would have made it harder for Henri Paul to concentrate. The photographer Patrick Chauvel said that Diana and Dodi were laughing like mad in the back seat.

One factor that exacerbates information overload is where the eyes have to look. Henri Paul not only had three different kinds of stimuli attracting his attention but they were in different perceptual spaces. The Fiat was in front and below; the speed camera in front and above, and Dodi and Diana were laughing behind him. This was a stressful situation. Even if there was no 'assault' from the VX or some other incapacitating agent, and even if Henri Paul had not had a drink all day, this combination would have made it easy for him to make a mistake. If the Fiat had not been there then Henri Paul would just have had to cope with the speed camera and Diana and Dodi laughing behind him. Needless to say the magistrate did not comment on these possibilities in his conclusions because he would have had to admit that the speed camera was working and drawn attention to the failure to find the Fiat. It was easier to blame everything on how drunk Henri Paul was even if the blood with its high alcohol level and inexplicable carbon monoxide readings, was 'the great mystery of the affair' as Stephan put it privately to Francis Gillery.

As I write, I discover precisely what I think. There

was a conspiracy but that conspiracy may not have been totally responsible for killing Diana. Rather it was a combination of factors. At least one of those, the Fiat Uno, belonged to Andanson who had, as Harold put it, 'an intuition' which made him be on the spot when some famous people died. Harold believes Andanson did not pull the trigger, as it were, but he was hired by and helped those who did. I have also shown that Andanson photographed a number of individuals who were in the Order of the Solar Temple.

Furthermore, that combination of factors provides a psychologically sensible explanation for why the conspirators Guy told me about were not paid the second instalment. Those who commissioned the death had asked for it to look like an accident but when everyone said it was just a drink-driving accident, they began to wonder. Did the man they paid $540,000 really do what they had paid him for? Or was Diana's death just luck? Because the conspirators themselves had qualms about what they had asked someone to do, they would almost want to believe it was really an accident – and so they weren't to blame and so the assassins should not get their second instalment.

It is this analysis which makes me suggest that the truth in this case seems to lie at both extremes. There was a conspiracy but the crash was at least partly caused by 'natural' reasons.

As a result of the flaws in the French inquiry, trying to find out the precise truth about the deaths in the Alma Tunnel has been made far more difficult than it should have been. We need the inquest to be relentless and for the authorities on both sides of the Channel to admit what they concealed. We owe the dead the truth. It may be especially hard for Prince Charles to countenance this.

His biographer, Anthony Holden has no doubts that 'in the immediate wake of her death . . . a huge weight had been lifted from his shoulders. But she was not around to snipe at him from the wings and generally discombobulate his life.' He gave me a specific example of how 'William and Harry were Windsorised'. Prince Charles had taken his son hunting. This, Holden pointed out, 'when people are against hunting and [this] shows his father's trait of not caring a toss what people think. She would have known if it was poor public relations.' The latest polls suggest that nearly forty-five per cent of the public do not believe that the monarchy will have its current status after the death of Queen Elizabeth.

It is not surprising that Charles should sincerely believe the best thing for his children and himself is to let the dead sleep in peace. But the dead have a habit of not being quite so docile. Diana was a woman with many qualities and many faults. Like many of us she was not always totally honest with herself, but her life shows that the older she got, the more she tried and she aspired to honesty. Every time one of the trustees of her estate or of the Diana Memorial Fund urges the press not to stir things up and bring back harrowing memories, I am astonished by the psychological naivety. Apart from the fact that Diana was a commoner who became a persistent irritant to the royals, there is something larger here. It has become clear that there are indeed mysterious forces, as the Queen said, at work in her kingdom and even clearer that many people don't want the truth to come out. We, and in that I include the British media I have worked for, owe the dead, and in that I include Dodi and Henri Paul too, the truth. I do not pretend that I have solved the jigsaw entirely; I know many will quarrel with my conclusions, but I think this investigation at least gets us closer to the complicated truth.

Postscript

In January 2004, the Coroner of the Queen's Household, Dr Michael Burgess asked Sir John Stevens, the Commissioner of the Metropolitan Police, to pursue inquiries into the deaths of Princess Diana and Dodi Al Fayed. Sir John went to Paris where he and his team walked through the Alma tunnel and talked to the French investigators. They also talked at some length with Al Fayed and his security team. But Sir John, who made his name in Ulster, investigating allegations that British forces had a shoot-to-kill policy, has kept any findings confidential. Sir John had also started inquiries into the death in 1987 of Barry Mannakee, Diana's bodyguard, who died in a road accident in East London. The Commissioner's press officer Angie Evans told me that the Commissioner had no intention of speaking to the media. 'It would be inappropriate to give any interviews before the inquest,' she said.

But after seven years, we may be inching a little closer to the truth. The most important development has been that the French have been forced to reopen the inquiry into the autopsy on Henri Paul's body. Many of those I interviewed commented on how political the French judicial system is because the French President and Prime Minister control judges far more than in Britain or America. Given that, the decision to reopen the inquiry was almost certainly approved at a senior political level. A second development has been that I have managed to get on-the-record evidence of more oddities relating to the death of the photographer James Andanson – and how it was investigated.

I start on a slightly comic image – Mohamed Al Fayed in a kilt. Al Fayed has a large estate in Scotland and so, assuming the persona of a good Scot, he petitioned the Court of Sessions in Edinburgh. In France, he said, his human rights had been denied as he was entitled to have a proper investigation held into his son's death. The European Convention on Human Rights does guarantee a search for the truth if someone dies in suspicious circumstances. Al Fayed argued that the French had not investigated properly, and that had to be remedied.

The Scottish Court of Appeal threw out Al Fayed's case in April 2004, but he obtained a judicial review of that decision. In August Neil Davidson QC argued, for the Advocate General for Scotland, that Al Fayed had no case. Davidson told the judge, Lord Drummond Young, that it would be wrong to hold an inquiry in Scotland as Al Fayed had also lodged an action against France with the European Court. The two petitions were very similar and, Davidson sniped, they were 'somewhat overambitious'.

Lord Drummond Young listened, said he had 'a lot to think about' and then ruled that it was not for the Scottish courts to pursue the case.

Then events in France took a surprising turn. In his conclusions published in September 1999, *Juge* Stephane argued that the crash was a tragic, but routine, drink-drive accident. The inquiry accepted that the blood samples taken from Henri Paul's body had not been tampered with and it concluded that Paul was not just drunk but also taking tranquillisers. The paparazzi who had followed Diana and Dodi from The Ritz Hotel were too far behind the Mercedes to have caused the crash. *Juge* Stephane hardly deigned to comment on rumours of any conspiracy. There were no important unanswered questions, he insisted.

Henri Paul's parents, however, have always maintained that their son was not an alcoholic. They added that they did not believe the blood samples that contained alcohol came from his body.

Mr and Mrs Paul went to court with the backing of Al Fayed to challenge *Juge* Stephane's 'verdict' that it was a drink-drive accident. The judge, Corinne Goetzmann, rejected their arguments in March 2003. The plaintiffs appealed. In September 2003, the French Court of Appeal queried Goetzmann's judgment and advised she should ask for more information from the team who had conducted Henri Paul's autopsy and analysed the bloods.

Then, on August 13th 2004, the French Court of Appeal made a categorical ruling. The inquiry into the autopsy had to be reopened. The court was especially concerned about the blood samples. Were they from Henri Paul's body? Had they been interfered with or badly stored? It was essential to know. Al Fayed's lawyers argued that Goetzmann should remove herself from the

case and that another judge should take over. So far
however, *Juge* Goetzmann has resisted any attempts to
shift her — and there has been little progress. Nevertheless, John Macnamara, Harrods head of security, told
me the decision of the French Court of Appeal was a
great victory for Al Fayed and the Paul family.

I believe one reason for the French Court of Appeal's
ruling is that the authorities have finally taken note of
information that has been available to them for about
five years. Bizarrely, as we shall see, this information
came from New Zealand.

My own work also progressed because of a contact
which shows the extent to which Diana had become
an international celebrity by the time of her death. My
book was read in Japan by Mr Chiba, the boss of KPE,
a production company linked to one of the major television channels in Tokyo, TV Asahi. Mr Chiba used to
manage Sumo wrestlers but then decided to become a
television producer. He is now the conspiracy king of
Japan with his hit show *It Couldn't Have Happened Like
That*. The show has made a film about the murder of
President Kennedy, and one which claims that it was
not the Titanic that sank but her sister ship. It was all
a clever insurance scam. Mr Chiba told me he wanted
to launch a joint investigation based on my Channel 5
film and on the additional revelations in the book. I
agreed, I've always enjoyed working with Japanese
people in the past.

As a result in late August 2004, I was in Paris with
Mr Chiba's assistant Taka, a nervy young man, and the
large crew he had organised. Mr Chiba first wanted to
verify that it was possible to make a device like the

bubble filled with the nerve gas VX that Guy claimed had been planted on Henri Paul. So Taka had asked an ex-SAS officer, Barry Davies to build such a bubble.

In late August, the whole team is in a suite in the rather grand Hotel Concorde St-Lazare. Barry unveils a small, rather lovely thing that looks like an elongated pearl. Guy had always spoken of the bubble as '*une perlette*'. Barry shows the perlette to the camera and turns it around so we see the wires that protrude from its back and connect to a tiny receiver. You can send a signal to that receiver from a distance. We test the device out in the open. Barry presses a remote control and, milliseconds later, the bubble shatters, just as it would need to in order to release nerve gas.

Barry worries that traces of such a device or its wires would have been found either on Henri Paul's body or in the wreck of the Mercedes. That assumes the site of the crash was properly searched. I have shown, however, that the Alma tunnel was cleaned and re-opened within hours of the crash so that it could not possibly have been searched properly.

After filming Barry, the crew travels from Paris to southern France. We're a weird mix – Taka is anxious because he is under pressure to deliver a show that will pull in a big audience; Douglas Lyon, who fixes shoots for Japanese TV companies in Europe, is also anxious because he has had to set up this shoot very fast. Our party also includes Mr Yomeda, the Japanese director, another producer, two assistants, two translators, a camera-man and a sound recordist. Chiba is not with us because he is doing something mega-secret in Eastern Europe. It's only later I discover precisely what his secret mission is.

Guy and his girlfriend Carmen are with us too. I wanted Guy to come along because he is very adept at getting French people to open up – and we have some sensitive interviews to conduct.

Where James Andanson died

From Paris, we head seven hundred kilometres towards the Mediterranean. On August 22nd, without our Japanese colleagues, Guy and I head for the small village of Les Liquisses in south-west France to make contact with Julian Christian, a local farmer.

Christian lives in a small farmhouse up on a hill. He also owns two huge barns where tractors and harvesters are parked. We didn't ring him in advance because I thought he might refuse to meet us. It's harder to turn someone down if they have come a few hundred miles to ask for help. But no one answers when Guy and I knock at his door. We walk around the back. No joy there either. I now worry I was foolish, I should have set this up in advance. Christian might have gone away on holiday. Mr Yomeda and Taka will be furious if we do not get to interview him. Chiba will probably have some of his Sumo wrestlers demolish me. Already the atmosphere between me and my Japanese 'partners' is not all Zen and light; I don't tell them Guy and I tried – and failed – to contact Christian.

We return the next morning. This time, we are lucky. Christian is in. He is tall, polite, and more relaxed than I expected. He's used to press nosing around. He owns the land where James Andanson's burnt-out car was found. I want him to allow us to film the very spot.

Christian explains he is in the middle of the harvest and he will not let filming interfere with his work. But if we come back after he has finished in the fields, he will help. Christian will also explain what he saw and, then, immediately insists that he did not see much.

At two o'clock we return. Christian has finished with agriculture for the day. He wears a baseball cap. The sun is blazing, heat haze dapples the air. Christian gets in Guy's car and we all drive about a mile out of the village. Christian stops us at a gate leading to fields. From here we have to walk and he leads us up a muddy track. After a few minutes' walk, we see a broken-down old farmstead. Property prices, Christian smiles, have become so crazy he has been offered a small fortune for the farmhouse but he has no intention of selling a metre of his soil. I'm a stubborn peasant, he grins, though he doesn't sound at all like a peasant.

Christian leads us some 500 metres along this muddy track and then turns right. Now we are walking across grass, small boulders and stones. We are going gently uphill too. Two hundred yards up the slope we reach a fringe of trees. The trees conceal a small clearing, which you would never know existed if you were not familiar with the terrain

James Andanson had never been to Les Liquisses before – at least as far as anyone knows.

Christian takes me, Guy and the crew into the clearing. He stops in the middle, points at a patch of grass and says 'that was where the car was'. The grass has grown back quite normally. It was busy and dramatic when he reached the spot in 2000, Christian says. Police, soldiers from the nearby army base and the local fire brigade were examining the burnt hulk of Andanson's car. 'I was told that the army saw a fire and that they came to investigate as it was very close to military land,' he says. He did not get that close to the car and he insists he did not peer inside.

Then he adds something remarkable: 'There were firemen. I heard them . . . who said that there was a hole – it could have been a bullet hole – in the skull of the driver.' We pause to take that in and he confirms he heard it.

The official line has always been that Andanson burned himself to death. Mrs Andanson had been told her husband bought a jerrycan of petrol in the nearest town, Millau. He poured the fuel over himself and the car and then set himself ablaze. No one had ever mentioned the possibility that Andanson had been shot or that he had shot himself.

Christian stresses that he did not see any bullet hole himself. He did not go that close to the body but he is positive the firemen were talking about it. He suggests we go and talk to the local head of the fire brigade.

I hope that my Japanese collaborators will agree but as I say, we have not been getting on too well. I'm a film director and used to running my own shoots. Mr Yomeda, the Japanese director, thinks I am interfering too much and, according to the interpreter, he has twice wanted to hit me. I didn't notice though. To my relief, Yomeda agrees it makes sense to talk to the fire chief. We thank Christian for his help and drive away.

Before I explain what happened then, I should explain exactly where we are – and its significance.

Andanson died very close to a famous Templar site where the French army has long had a base.

P2 – and the Templars

La Cavalerie is high up on the Larzac, an isolated plateau in south-west France. As you drive towards the village, you come to the military camp with rows of grey barrack houses. A tower dominates the surrounding countryside. From its top you must be able to see miles. The military terrain continues for miles. Every field is plastered with Keep Out signs, this is military land. Out of sight there is an airstrip; the camp is used to test explosives and, apparently, small missiles. Curiously there are no soldiers to be seen. It's a ghost base, it seems.

La Cavalerie had been a major base for the Knights Templar in the Middle Ages precisely because it was rather isolated. The place is impressive. You walk along fat ancient walls and there are substantial ruins of an old castle. The streets are narrow, there's a fine old church and a long building that was the old town hall. There is also a museum devoted to the Templars.

I was nervous about what we would find at La Cavalerie. When the minibus carrying the Japanese crew falls far behind us on the road, I take advantage. I persuade Guy to drive fast. I want to get to the village well ahead of the rest of the crew to have time to explore alone. Happily for me, the minibus gets stuck in traffic and the crew want to eat. That gives me plenty of time to recce La Cavalerie with just Guy.

Exploring is one of the pleasures of filming. When

we get to La Cavalerie Guy and I start to wander round the picturesque streets. In one street we spot a suit of armour. The suit — 50% off as we are past the high season — is plonked outside a shop dedicated to the Templars. The shop is small and crammed with stuff — statues of Templars in all sizes, books about medieval history, posters and postcards. The shop even sells flagons of a drink the knights apparently liked.

Behind the curtain at the rear of the shop, a man is cooking mushrooms for his dinner. He comes out to greet us. He is so lean and angular you could cast him as Don Quixote. He introduces himself as Henri de Brolles which he adds is not his real name but 'a *nom de guerre*'. When Guy explains that we are making a film on a sensitive subject, Henri nods. He announces that he was 'in the class of '58'. I don't know what that means, but Guy immediately responds that he was 'in the class of '64'. The class refers to the year when they started their military service. Henri was in a parachute regiment and lets us understand he still has good contacts with the local army base.

When I explain we are here to find out more about the strange death of Andanson, Henri is baffled. 'I've never heard of his death,' he says, 'and I hear about most things round here.' To prove how well-informed he is, Henri explains that a few years ago a party of archaeologists stumbled on a spooky underground cavern. There were nine skulls in this cavern, laid out in a particular pattern. The archaeologists believed this was a Templar sanctuary where secret ceremonies were held.

But the authorities did not want news of the find

to leak out, he says. Within forty-eight hours the police had cordoned the site off so no one could get near the cavern. Henri knew all about that and so he was astonished not to have heard about Andanson's death.

Henri was intrigued when we said there could be a link between Andanson and the death of Diana, and between Diana's killers and the Order of the Solar Temple. And that jogged his memory.

'You should go look at the archives in the museum,' Henri said, 'there is something there you may find interesting.'

The museum is a little municipal building in a pretty square that has been decorated with a fine mosaic. The museum offers visitors maps, more posters, more pennants and yet another suit of armour. The manager is very open, happy to show us the register of visitors.

'What precisely are you looking for?' she asks.

I'm not sure it's a good idea to tell her the truth, but there isn't a library where we can sit and examine the register at leisure. I say what Henri told us. She remembers the entry well and it takes her about two minutes to find the right register.

In mock medieval curvy writing, the entry commends the museum and the way the town celebrates the Templars. A P.S adds that the author is a member of the famous Masonic Lodge P2 which was connected to the Bank Ambrosiana, the Vatican bank. The bank has been linked to various scandals including the death of Robert Calvi who was found hanging below Blackfriars Bridge in London.

Guy takes a photograph of the P2 entry. It is interesting precisely because the Order of the Solar Temple did have some contact with P2, according to Guy. He claims di Mambro laundered money for P2.

We thank the manager of the museum and hurry back to our hotel where the Japanese have finally arrived. We do not explain to them where we have been.

The next morning we return with the crew and film Henri who gives us a potted history of the Templars and how they had used La Cavalerie as a base. After we finish filming, Henri takes Guy and me aside. He has been busy in the last twenty-four hours. He has talked with old parachute regiment colleagues and with contacts at the army base. It is no accident that Andanson was killed so close to the military base, he says. The team who liquidated Andanson could have flown into the base and out again without anyone knowing. He has no evidence of this, he admits, but it makes sense to him.

Henri's speculations are not evidence, of course. But the possibility that Andanson might have been executed seems less far-fetched if he had a bullet in his head and that fact was never disclosed.

We thank Henri and I buy one of his Templar trinkets – a weird statuette of the head of the Sphinx, surrounded by snakes. In its centre a dagger is concealed. Then the crew want lunch.

In the afternoon, we film Julian Christian and the clearing. Then, as he suggested, we go to find the fire chief.

The fireman and the bullet

The fire brigade chief works in a garage between La

Cavalerie and Millau. He is in his sixties and does not want to be named. He is much more reserved than Christian. He was never at the clearing, he says, though it was his job to write a report on the incident and send it to the local fire brigade headquarters. Naturally he does not have a copy of it. Guy is sceptical about this. The report would have been worth selling – and firemen often sell information to the press.

The chief says the man we need to talk to is called Christophe Pelat. He was in charge of the local fire brigade the day Andanson's body was found. Pelat is only a part-time fireman. He also works for a firm of builders and we should find him at their offices. So we drive there. The premises are impressive, a long barn with modern work benches and neat piles of timber. A surly man asks what we want. When we explain, Surly walks us to an elegant glass-fronted office at the end of the barn. 'People to see you,' he tells his boss.

We explain who we are and that we want to talk to Pelat.

'He's at work,' says his boss.

Guy explains we have a very restless Japanese crew in the minibus. They want to stick to their timetable and the timetable did not allow for tracking Pelat down. It would be so helpful if we could talk to him quickly.

'I will see if I can ring him,' says his boss.

Guy and I hover while he telephones. We can't tell whether the conversation is going well or badly from our point of view.

After a time, the boss says we are in luck because Pelat is working in La Cavalerie. If we drive there now, he will talk to us.

'Good news,' I say to the crew, 'he will see us.'

The Japanese film director does not seem thrilled, but Guy and I say we are going to find Pelat anyway. The crew follow.

We stop in a narrow road back in La Cavalerie. To our right there's a building site. Pelat and a colleague are turning a dilapidated little house into a des res for expats who want a bit of the magic of France. I apologise that there are so many of us in the film crew when we want to discuss such sensitive stuff. Surrounded by so many people, Pelat is astonishingly calm. He stays as calm when we have to stop filming because an old man drives a tractor through the shot slowly. The old man parks just where it is wrong for the camera, removes his battered hat and starts scratching his head. We ask Pelat to move because the old man is so distracting.

Pelat has an unsettling story to tell. The day Andanson's car was found the local fire brigade were called to the clearing by the army. When they got there, they found a badly-burnt car and, inside, a badly-burnt body. Pelat insists however, 'it is not right to say Andanson had been burned to nothing. There were bones and there was a skull.'

Pelat is very matter-of-fact. Then he pauses. And he confirm with some authority that there did appear to be a hole in Andanson's skull. Pelat adds that he has no idea how it got there but you could not miss the hole.

The firemen put out what remained of the blaze. Pelat was told it was imperative not to talk to the press. He was also told that the police did not know who the dead person was − and that it would take a few days to find out. So he was surprised, when he went to the gendarmerie the next day, to see Andanson's name was up on a board. It was, Pelat suggests, almost as if the police had known all along whom the deceased was.

The police did not question the firemen in detail about what they had found and what they made of it. Yet the fire and the damage it caused were very unusual. Pelat tells us he has dealt with five or six cases where people had locked themselves in cars in a garage, blocked the exhaust and turned on the engine. This is a 'normal' method of committing suicide. But he had never dealt with a case where a driver burned himself to death as Andanson is supposed to have done. Pelat had never seen anything like it.

The official line was, of course, that Andanson burned himself to death and that there was hardly anything left of his body given the intensity of the fire. Mrs Andanson had been told her husband would have needed to pour two jerrycans of petrol inside the car to produce enough heat. And yet the evidence was her husband had bought only one jerrycan. When we had discussed the case with the French investigating magistrate, *Juge* Marty, she never mentioned any bullet. She had insisted it was obviously a suicide. This interview was filmed.

If Andanson had a bullet hole in his skull, why did his wife never hear about it?

Now very excited, Mr Yomeda badly wants a picture of Andanson's car. I had assumed that the police had taken Andanson's car away for forensic tests and that, like the Mercedes, it was in their custody.

Pelat tells us that is not the case. 'You can of course go to where the car was taken,' he says. The car was towed to a garage in Millau which is owned privately; the police often use it to dump cars. Yomeda is delighted – and I'm astonished.

Millau is not small and we set out on what turns out to be a complicated search for Andanson's wreck. The garage Pelat directs us to deny any knowledge of the vehicle. They did work for the police once but that was years ago. Luckily, however, the garage owner knows where the local police dump wrecks now. We drive all the way round Millau again, looking for a sign which points to a small alleyway near a particular restaurant.

After forty minutes, we find the restaurant and the right alleyway. The place looks like a stereotypical set for the grimy industrial north. The alleyway leads to a courtyard where three old bangers are neatly parked. None have been burned. We walk around the yard and find the entrance to the garage office. It is dark and deserted. Still, we knock.

One of the windows on the first floor opens. A plump lady in a dressing gown leans out and explains her husband, the owner, is not in.

Guy asks if she would come down and speak to us. 'We're not hooligans,' he reassures her, at his most polite. Madame is convinced we are not dangerous, comes down and tells us she remembers the car well. The wreck spent two years in her courtyard. 'Till about six months ago the wreck was here,' she says, 'but it was removed.' She thinks it has been finally broken up for scrap.

We are surprised. There have been many questions about how Andanson died. The wreck is a crucial piece of evidence. Yet it has been left out in the open for two to three years to rust and then it was removed, probably has been demolished.

We ask if perhaps she or her husband took a photo of the wreck.

There are no photos, she thinks.

Guy is sceptical and whispers to me he is sure Madame's husband would have held on to some photos in case someone might want to buy them. The story was in the papers, after all.

Madame does not commit herself. Her husband may know where there may be a photograph or he may not. She has no idea when he will be back to tell us. The best she can do is promise to tell him what we want. Then she goes back to her office.

We've filmed the place and its three neatly-parked wrecks. There is nothing left to do so we drive back to our hotel.

An hour later, the garage owner rings us. He says that he knows the police have photos of the wreck. We should ask them.

'We think it might be easier to get one through you if you perhaps might find one.' We offer to pay him a thousand euros. For his time and trouble. If the elusive picture is found.

He promises to see what he can do but we never hear from him again.

I have told this story at some length because it offers new and interesting information. *Juge* Marty promised she would consider reopening the inquiry into

Andanson's death if we came up with some new information. I write to her explaining what we were told and I ask if she can confirm or deny that Andanson's body had a bullet hole. So far I have not received an answer from her.

Le Barroux again

When I arranged to work with Mr Chiba, we agreed we should also film in Le Barroux. This is the village where Prince Charles spent a number of weeks and where the Order of the Solar Temple had a number of properties. It is 300 kilometres from La Cavalerie to Le Barroux. As we approach the village, the view is dramatic. The castle which the Templars built rises high above the vineyards. Monks are tending the vines. It feels like a scene from another time, another world.

As we drive into Le Barroux, Guy points to a large house with a very long and narrow window of opaque glass, the sort of window you might well find in a church. According to Guy, this house has a prayer room-cum-sanctuary. Guy has been in that house, he tells me, and attended the rituals the Order of the Solar Temple held there.

In my mid twenties, I worked as a director on Thames TV's London news programme. We used to be sent out at eight o'clock in the morning and told to come back with a story by early afternoon when we would edit it to be broadcast that night. I learned that it is always sensible to talk to people you come across in an interesting location.

And here at Le Barroux the next morning, this approach produces something unexpected – witnesses who claim that the Order of the Solar Temple is still in existence and still holding ceremonies.

As we walk to the top of the hill where the castle stands, I see a couple out on their balcony. I explain that we are interested in whether Prince Charles had been here. The lady, Gabrielle, grins broadly. She agrees to be interviewed and says that she saw Charles in Le Barroux on a number of occasions. He was there alone, and with Diana, and with Camilla Parker Bowles, she claims. Gabrielle's uncle was the mayor of the village and everyone was very excited about the royal visitor. The caretaker of the castle says the same.

Guy and I also ring the dry-cleaner in Aubignan a few miles away. The man confirms again that he was sent clothes belonging to both Charles and di Mambro at the same time. The two of them were in Le Barroux the same week, it seems. We record this conversation on tape but the dry-cleaner refuses to be filmed.

Our most interesting evidence concerns the present activities of the Order of the Solar Temple in the village. The official line in France and Switzerland is that the Order has ceased to exist. Here in Le Barroux I get a rather different story from one witness. She is German, a retired professor who used to teach French literature. She asks not to be named. But she claims she is – as are others in the village – aware that meetings and ceremonies are still held in the house with the long window at the bottom of the hill.

By a strange quirk we have been booked into Le Relais du Silence, a hotel on the outskirts of the village.

When the French police investigated the Order after the mass deaths in 1994, they found Le Relais had been owned by members of the Order. The place certainly feels monastic. The rooms are set around a cloister. There are a few Templar crosses carved into the walls. The Relais is affiliated these days to a hotel group which prides itself on providing guests with organic food and the silence in which to meditate.

Guy says he recognises the name of the owner, Andre Pochat, from his time working as di Mambro's driver. Pochat's son is the manager of Le Relais.

It seems, therefore, we have one witness who claims The Order of the Solar Temple is still active in the village. It also seems one of Le Barroux's two hotels is owned by a man who, it has been alleged, was a member of the Order. That is interesting, especially because one of our other interviewees claims that the French and Swiss authorities do not want the truth about the Order of the Solar Temple to be revealed.

I thought it best to put these points to the younger Mr Pochat only after we had checked out of his hotel. So on our last day in Le Barroux, we pay and most of our party pile into the minibus which drives out through the electronic gates of Le Relais. Guy drives his Mercedes outside too. I linger with the cameraman and ask Pochat if he would mind answering a few questions. When I put it to him that his hotel had been used by the Order of the Solar Temple and that ceremonies are still being held in the village, he gets edgy. Yes, he knows about the history of the hotel. Yes, his father bought the place from people involved in the Temple. But that is all. His family knows nothing about sinister spiritual goings-on. He denies that the Order is still operating in the village. That is all stuff from the past – a past they would all prefer to forget. He denies his father ever had anything to do with the Order.

But as I think about these interviews, I feel we have firmed up the link between Le Barroux and the Order of the Solar Temple. That makes Prince Charles's many visits to the village even more intriguing.

After we leave Le Relais, Yomeda, Douglas and the Japanese crew go to Paris where they have more interviews to do. No one tells me the truth – that they may meet up with Mr Chiba or that he had flown to Europe in the hope of buying some VX, the nerve agent Guy alleged was planted on Henri Paul. (I presume that, in the best tradition of the tabloids, he would have made his excuses and left if he had actually found someone willing to sell him nerve gas, but it never came close to happening.) Meanwhile Guy, Kanako and I get into Guy's car to drive the four hours to Geneva. There they will be joined by yet another crew from Japan who will film interviews with people who had been involved with the Solar Temple.

Arrest in Geneva

As we approach Geneva, Guy gets very nervous. He rings his ex-wife because their son is a policeman in Switzerland and Guy wants his help. Guy does not have his son's mobile number and is very brusque with his ex. She rings back to say their son is in a meeting and will ring Guy later.

But by the time we get close to Geneva, Guy's son has not rung back.

Geneva airport is on the Swiss French border. There is a Swiss entrance and a French entrance. Guy heads for the French side and tells me he has no intention of crossing into Switzerland here. The second Japanese crew is waiting in another minibus. As we all shake hands, the Japanese fixer proudly tells us she has booked us into a very smart hotel. But Guy is livid when he discovers that she gave his real name when making the booking. We have compromised his anonymity. That will cause him endless trouble. He walks back to his car and tells me he is completely fed up with the Japanese. I've never seen him so agitated.

I expect he's going to say he wants nothing more to do with the project. But slowly he gets less angry and says it's a good thing he knows some discreet routes into Switzerland. Then he and Carmen drive off.

We meet Guy and Carmen in the evening in a village just by Lausanne. Guy and Carmen have made it into Switzerland. We all eat together, make peace and Guy says he is going to drive back to France. The crew and I go on to interview Mrs Rosemarie Jaton. Her brother Daniel was a member of the Order of the Solar Temple and was killed in 1994. His wife and their two children also died. Mrs Jaton is tall, in her seventies and formidably respectable. It has been a shock for her to discover how the Swiss authorities claimed her brother killed himself when he was shot nine times! She has become immensely sceptical about official inquiries and their interest in finding the truth about the Order.

I get back to our hotel in Geneva round midnight,

exhausted. I fall fast asleep. Next thing I know, the phone rings. The clock on the television tells me it's 01.30.

The hotel operator apologises for disturbing me. There is a woman in the lobby who says she desperately needs to talk to me. She is sobbing and hysterical, he adds.

The woman turns out to be Carmen. 'Guy was arrested . . . the Swiss arrested him at the border. They said they had a warrant for him,' she sniffles. 'I don't know what to do.'

I dress fast and go downstairs. Carmen really is distraught. She has no idea how long the police will hold Guy or why they are doing so. I arrange for Carmen to have a room and promise I will do every-thing I can to help. In fact I have no idea what I can do in this situation.

Back in my room, I fall asleep at once. I often suffer from insomnia but tonight I'm not going to get the chance.

The phone rings again. The clock on the television tells me it is 02.37. Again the hotel desk is apologetic. Now the police want to talk to me.

'We have under arrest here your colleague Guy,' the policeman says. He is worryingly polite.

I ask why the police are holding him. I am not given any answer.

'You may also know, Mr Cohen,' he manages to sound menacing as he speaks my name, 'that we have, with Swiss customs, impounded his car.'

'Yes?'

'But if you want the car back that is possible,' he adds mysteriously.

I am amazed and realise I better play this carefully. I do not own Guy's car. I am not related to Guy.

'We prefer not to have the car in Switzerland,' the policeman adds. He doesn't give me the chance to ask why. 'Could you pick it up by nine tomorrow morning?'

I explain we have an interview to do in Fribourg in the morning. It's a two-hour drive from Geneva. The cop sounds disappointed.

'I could arrange to pick up the car by early afternoon if that helps,' I add. It's better to be accommodating.

'As long as you are there by two,' he says, 'and remember we are doing your friend a favour.'

I now have a very practical problem. I can't drive; I have never had a driving licence and the last time someone tried to teach me to drive I concertinaed her car against a tree. Out here in cuckoo-clock-land I don't know anyone who can drive.

'I will be there,' I say. I even add a thank you.

My only option is to get one of the Japanese crew to drive Guy's car, but my relationship with the Japanese is now more acid and arrogance than milk and honey. Also I cannot expect the Japanese to hurry the interview in Fribourg so that I can retrieve Guy's car. The only member of the crew who is not vital is Taka, the assistant producer. He agrees to help. We get to the Swiss French border just before the cut-off time of 2pm. I expect that we are going to be embroiled in hours of bureaucracy.

I show my passport and explain why I have come.

A plump customs woman nods at me. But she does not give my passport the slightest glance. The passport control officer also doesn't have any interest in checking my papers. I could be the man in the moon.

'Wait here . . .' Customs woman says. Two minutes later, she returns with a colleague.

'Yes, you're Cohen,' he says. Again, no one examines my passport.

'The car's over there.' She produces the keys, gives them to me and points to where Guy's Mercedes is parked.

I nearly say 'is that it? Don't you want to ask me questions?'. But I have enough sense to keep my mouth shut. The train of events is so peculiar. The Swiss seem utterly determined to get rid of Guy's car as fast as possible and with no formalities. I don't argue.

Taka and I drive Guy's car 100 yards into France. Taka spots Carmen waiting for us at the petrol station just over the border. We pick her up. She wants us to park the car round the corner. We get out and open up the boot. It turns out that the police and customs have taken away Guy's notebooks, his files and the computer on which much of his information is stored.

I give Carmen a hug before she drives away. Taka and I take a taxi back to Geneva. I feel desperately guilty about Guy. Working with me has ended up with him inside. I feel even worse when over the next twenty-four hours I hear nothing from him.

I ring Carmen. She does not answer her mobile. I e-mail her and Guy. For forty-eight hours I get absolutely no response.

Then I get a message at the hotel. Guy will be released. A day later, I hear Guy is let out by the Swiss and taken over the border into France. Now he is on his way home.

I can't help wondering why the police have let him go, just like the French police let him go when he went to Nice police station with information about the death of Madame Marchal? Obviously neither the French nor the Swiss authorities want to probe too deeply into Guy's activities. If he was lying about the continued activities of the Solar Temple, I would expect they would want to discredit him; if he had committed an offence, I would expect they would charge him. Neither has happened. The official attitude seems to be 'please don't bother us with stuff we would rather not know'.

But this bizarre set of events is not the only new development I have to report.

Bad blood – reopening the Henry Paul inquiry

Investigative journalists always hope that when they publish, the story triggers someone's memory and that person gets in touch. Many readers who wrote to me were clearly devoted to Diana, but had little new to offer by way of interesting facts. There was, however, one very important exception.

Jim Sprott is an analytical chemist who started work in 1942 and retired in 1983. He built up the largest private analytical laboratory in New Zealand. He appeared as an expert witness in many civil and criminal trials. In 1995 he was awarded the OBE 'for services to forensic science and the community'. He is still active and may well soon be called as a witness in the case of an apparently drunk pilot whose plane crashed. Dr Sprott contacted me after reading my book.

Over the decades Sprott's lab has analysed thousands of samples of body fluids. Nearly always the lab was commissioned by lawyers for the defence. Drivers charged with driving while drunk wanted to challenge the police evidence and hired Sprott as an expert witness. 'There were several occasions when I was able to point out errors and deficiencies in the analytical techniques used by the government analyst, whose laboratory carried out all such analyses for the police,' Sprott said.

Sprott had been curious about the crash in the Alma Tunnel from the start. He wrote to Henri Paul's parents and raised technical issues about the blood samples. I understand his critique was passed on to the French inquiry, but he has never received any official reply. When Sprott learned there would be an inquest in Britain, he wrote to the British coroner (Feb 2004). In Chapter 6 I looked at the criticisms made by the pathologists and toxicologists hired by Al Fayed. Sprott also asks questions from a different scientific base and adds a number of significant points:

'The analysis of blood taken from the body of M. Paul showed that alcohol (ethanol) was present in amount 174mg/100ml (Dr Pepin) and 187mg/100ml blood (Professor Ricordel),' Sprott told me. So much alcohol would 'produce marked effects', but when I found the video of Henri Paul tying his shoelaces nimbly, I argued that a man who was much the worse for wear with alcohol just could not manage that feat, and Sprott agreed.

Sprott calls the alcohol level in the blood an 'anomaly' but one that can be explained. You cannot rely on blood-alcohol analysis as proof of intoxication, when the blood sample comes from the body of a person who died violently. This is especially so when, as was the case with Henri Paul, many organs are ruptured. Many internal organs were ruptured. As Sprott's argument is technical, with his permission I reproduce what he said to the coroner and had said earlier to the French inquiry. Sprott claims:

a) In violent death the bloodstream can become contaminated with stomach contents, including yeasts, and this results in the production of alcohol through the fermentation of blood sugar into alcohol (ethanol), even before the blood sample is taken – it is a rapid process. Thus alcohol can be formed in the blood prior to sampling of the blood.

b) Unless specific preparation of the sample bottle/s has been carried out, with a suitable preservative added to the sample bottle, and the bottle sterilised, fermentation also occurs within the sample bottle, thus generating alcohol. Sodium fluoride is the usual preservative.

c) However, unless such suitably-prepared sample bottles are immediately available, it is common practice for normal blood-sampling vials to be used. These vials usually contain heparin as an anti-coagulant; however this substance has no anti-fungal activity so will not inhibit fermen-tation.

d) As a consequence some or all of the alcohol detected by analysis of *post-mortem* blood can have been formed after death.

The first post-mortem studies to discover this 'anomaly' were of trainee fighter pilots whose planes crashed; clearly these would be violent deaths. Their blood revealed alcohol in the amount of about 180mg ethanol per 100ml blood. But the pilots had not drunk any alcohol before they took off.

Sprott is not just talking theory. He has been involved in a few cases where this phenomenon appeared to have occurred. In all these cases the allegedly drunk driver died. The autopsies typically revealed alcohol in the blood and nearly always in about the same quantity, roughly 160–180mg/100ml blood. This reading 'proves' the driver was incapacitated so the insurers refused to pay out because the 'guilty' driver was over the limit. In one case, though, the estate of the deceased driver took the insurance company to court and won. In another case, the insurers settled out of court because of Sprott's arguments. In both cases, Sprott insisted that the blood alcohol levels were artificial and did not mean the driver had been unable to control the car. The levels did not reveal anything about how much the drivers had imbibed. Rather, the results suggested a poor sampling technique had been used which led to 'fermentation of ethanol (i.e. alcohol) prior to sampling and in the sample bottles'.

Sprott also refers me to a current Australian case. A pilot called Andrew Morris died when his plane crashed. Morris reported mechanical problems soon after the aircraft took off, but the Australian Transport Safety Board seized on the presence of alcohol in his blood to explain the disaster. Morris's blood showed the concentration of alcohol to be 0.081%, which equates 81 milligrams per 100 millilitres of blood. The report to the coroner specifically warned this measure should not be interpreted to mean Morris was drunk. Paragraph 1.13.1 stated:

> '*However, the examining toxicologist stated that, due to the possibility for post-mortem production of alcohol, that result should be interpreted with caution. The nature of the pilot's injuries precluded examination of other body fluids in order to determine the source of the pilot's BAC . . .*' (Blood Alcohol Count)

Sprott believes this phenomenon of alcohol fermenting in the body after death is very relevant to the inquest on Diana and Dodi. If the French are to continue to claim, as they did in their final report of 1999, that the Mercedes crashed because Henri Paul was drunk, they need to prove that the sample bottles in which Henri Paul's blood was kept were properly prepared. The bottles had to contain a suitable preservative. But Sprott does not believe the difference between the two blood readings are significant evidence to the contrary. The readings carried out on duplicate samples, gave the following result:

174mg/100ml blood (Dr Pepin)
187mg/100ml blood (Professor Ricordel).

'These figures are far too disparate (7.5%) to be the result of simple error in analysis. The precision of the analytical method is much better than this,' Sprott said. 'The second result, which was apparently carried out at a later date than the first, showed more alcohol in the blood. It does not require genius to work out the cause. Alcohol was being formed in the second sample, Prof. Ricordel's sample. And that was happening because the bottles in which the blood was stored were defective.'

The proportion of alcohol reported in such cases appears to be fairly constant, about 160–180mg/100ml blood and Sprott has a scientific explanation: 'The source of the alcohol is primarily, if not totally, the sugars in the blood, and the proportion of total sugars in blood is fairly consistent'. He claims that the readily fermentable sugars in blood, if they are fermented, generate a fairly consistent amount of ethanol. And that results in the observed concentration of about 180mg/100ml.

The French authorities should chart minutely the precise circumstances of the sampling of the blood taken from Henri Paul, Sprott suggests. He would like to see details of how long the interval was between death and the sampling of Henri Paul's blood, how the sample bottles were prepared and what preservatives were used and how the samples were stored. I suspect that the French Court of Appeal somehow realised that Sprott had written to the British coroner in February

2004. I surmise they were concerned it would become public that they had been sent Sprott's critique five to six years before. Perhaps I'm being too suspicious in believing this contributed to their decision in August 2004 when they told Judge Goetzmann to get more information from the pathologists and toxicologists who carried out the autopsy.

And here the French authorities have a problem because, astonishingly, they seem to have lost some of the samples and the bottles in which they were held. Sprott is used to framing it in legal language and he told me:

'As matters stand, again based on documents in my possession and my decades of personal experience in the forensic examination of blood for the presence of alcohol, the claim that M. Henri Paul was intoxicated by alcohol prior to his death cannot be sustained'. He adds that this 'was consistent with the evidence of persons who observed M. Paul immediately prior to his driving of the car. In fact the totality of the evidence suggests strongly that he was not intoxicated'.

And that of course leads to many questions I have raised in this book

The continuing saga of Charles

As I write this in January 2005, there is still no news of when the British inquest into the deaths of Princess Diana and Dodi Al Fayed will be reopened. March has been mooted as a possible date, but it has not been confirmed. The inquest will need to consider these new developments as well as the results of Sir John Stevens's inquiries. We also await what will happen when the new French inquiry reports.

I want to return briefly to Prince Charles because the results of the inquest obviously matter to him. In many ways, 2004 was a controversial and unhappy year for him. In November one of his junior staff, Elaine Day, sued Clarence House for unfair dismissal. At her industrial tribunal, she produced a memo the Prince wrote. In it, he complains about child-centred education which encourages the poor, lazy and unqualified to have delusions of grandeur. Without doing any work, without getting any qualifications, some of these upstarts think they could become pop stars. It was a private memo, of course, but it was an unwise outburst. The media pointed out Charles's only qualification for his position is birth. His former public relations adviser, Mark Bolland, wrote that the memo was typical of Charles's self-pitying, self-justifying personality.

I have never claimed that Prince Charles had anything to do with the accident in the Alma Tunnel. I have no evidence for that. But I have claimed it is plausible, given my sources, to think that some of his 'friends' decided it was time to help him by making sure Diana did not remain a thorn in his side. I maintain that, in the light of the new developments I have reported.

Late in 2004, Guy contacted me again. He told me that Roland had been in touch with him. He was extremely worried. Three of his collaborators seemed to have disappeared. He was thinking about meeting me but he could not yet quite agree to that yet. I expect to meet him in the next few months. I suspect we will keep inching closer to the truth.

January 5th 2005

Bibliography

Beriff P (1997) 'Cutting Edge' Baltimore's Paramedics (three part series on Channel 4)

Campbell B (1994) *Diana, Princess of Wales How Sexual Politics Shook the Monarchy*, The Women's Press

Cohen D (1985) *The Development of Laughter*, unpublished Ph.d, University of London

Craig P and Clayton T (2002) *Diana, Story of a Princess*, Simon and Schuster

Gregory M (2000) *Diana, The Last Days*, Virgin Books

Facon R (1997) *Les Mystères de l'Occulte*, Veyrier

Holden A (1993) *The Tarnished Crown*, Random House

Holden A (1997) *Prince Charles at Fifty*, Random House

Huguenin T (1995) *Le 54ieme*, Grassett

Cooke A (2000) Questionnaires in A & E Practice, *Journal of Accident and Emergency Medicine*

Junor P *Charles: Victim or Villain*, Harper Collins

Marhic R (1997) *L' ordre du Temple Solaire*, Horizon Chimerique

Morton A (1992) *Diana – Her True Story*, Michael O'Mara Books

Murphy E (1995) No Role for Prison Officers in Special Hospitals, *British Medical Journal*

Nozaki H, Aikawa N (1995) A Case of VX Poisoning and the Difference From Sarin, *The Lancet*, Sept 9 1995, p346ff

Winek C, Colom WD (1981) Accidental Methylene Chloride Fatality, *Forensic Science International*, 18, 165–168